THE DIVERSITY BARGAIN

THE DIVERSITY BARGAIN

AND OTHER DILEMMAS OF RACE, ADMISSIONS, AND MERITOCRACY AT ELITE UNIVERSITIES

WITHDRAWN

NATASHA K. WARIKOO

The University of Chicago Press   *Chicago and London*

NATASHA K. WARIKOO is associate professor of education at
the Harvard Graduate School of Education. She is the author
of *Balancing Acts: Youth Culture in the Global City*.

The University of Chicago Press, Chicago 60637
The University of Chicago Press, Ltd., London
© 2016 by The University of Chicago
All rights reserved. Published 2016.
Printed in the United States of America

25 24 23 22 21 20 19 18 17 16   1 2 3 4 5

ISBN-13: 978-0-226-40014-3 (cloth)
ISBN-13: 978-0-226-40028-0 (e-book)
DOI: 10.7208/chicago/9780226400280.001.0001

Library of Congress Cataloging-in-Publication Data

Names: Warikoo, Natasha Kumar, 1973– author.
Title: The diversity bargain : and other dilemmas of race, admissions,
and meritocracy at elite universities / Natasha K. Warikoo.
Description: Chicago ; London : The University of Chicago Press, 2016. |
Includes bibliographical references and index.
Identifiers: LCCN 2016007483 | ISBN 9780226400143 (cloth : alk. paper) |
ISBN 9780226400280 (e-book)
Subjects: LCSH: College students—United States—Attitudes. |
Elite (Social sciences)—United States—Attitudes. | College
students—England—Attitudes. | Elite (Social sciences)—
England—Attitudes. | Race—Public opinion. | Minorities—
Public opinion. | Merit (Ethics)—Public opinion. | Cultural
pluralism—Public opinion. | Education, Higher—Social aspects.
Classification: LCC LA229 .W37 2016 | DDC 378.73—dc23
LC record available at http://lccn.loc.gov/2016007483

♾ This paper meets the requirements of ANSI/NISO Z39.48-1992
(Permanence of Paper).

CONTENTS

ACKNOWLEDGMENTS

This book has been in development for many years, and I have had so much help along the way. I feel lucky that so many colleagues, near and far, have indulged my thoughts about race, meritocracy, and inequality to help me fill its pages. I spent an amazing year at the Russell Sage Foundation in 2013–14. I am grateful to Sheldon Danzinger and his staff for providing an intellectual space for that year—not to mention a wonderful place to live and delicious food. I especially thank Aixa Cintrón-Vélez and Jim Wilson for many fruitful conversations about this project. My fellow scholars at RSF provided good cheer and conversation along the way as well. I am especially grateful for feedback on this project from Andy Cherlin, Dalton Conley, Miles Corak, Cybelle Fox, Lee Ann Fujii, Shigeo Hirano, Doug McAdam, Belinda Robnett, Stacey Sinclair, Jane Waldfogel, and Caitlin Zaloom. Cybelle in particular talked with me about probably every word I wrote that year and provided feedback once I got those ideas on paper. The British Academy provided generous support for my research in Britain, as did Harvard's Milton Fund for the United States leg of the research. Harvard's Weatherhead Center for International Affairs contributed additional support in the final stages of this book.

Luckily for me, when I returned to Harvard Graduate School of Education (HGSE), I came back to a wonderful community of scholars and to a dean, Jim Ryan, whose ongoing support of my ideas and development made this book possible. I am so grateful for Jim's support. Other colleagues at HGSE, past and present, have supported this project, including John Diamond, Howard Gardner, Roberto

Gonzales, Paul Harris, Monica Higgins, Nancy Hill, Dan Koretz, Meira Levinson, Dick Light, Jal Mehta, Julie Reuben, Rick Weissbourd, and Hiro Yoshikawa.

Beyond HGSE, Harvard faculty in sociology continue to nurture my development, especially Larry Bobo, Michele Lamont, Mary Waters, and Bill Wilson. Michele and Mary — and Prudence Carter at Berkeley — in particular always seem to have time for me, guiding my professional development way beyond their duties as my advisers so long ago. Also at HGSE, numerous students have worked on this project at every stage. I thank Sherry Deckman, Jay Huguley, and Jenny Jacobs for the skillful interviews they conducted, with gentle probing and care for the students they interviewed. At Oxford, Christina Fuhr did the same. Other students helped with coding and other research tasks, including Utaukwa Allen, Irteza Binte-Farid, Janine de Novais, Raygine DiAquoi, Sebastian Gomez, and Abena MacKall. Christina, Janine, and Sherry also worked with me on papers that were starting points for some of the ideas in this book. Thank you also to Teresa Bergen, Thomas Higinbotham, and Matt Ogborn for transcribing the interviews, and to Kidus Mezgebu, Matt Tallon, and Kevin Walsh for completing administrative tasks.

Outside Harvard, numerous colleagues around the country supported me in this work. My wonderful writing group — Bart Bonikowski, Helen Marrow, and Cinzia Solari — helped me refine my ideas in many ways big and small. Other colleagues — Maia Cucchiara, Brent Harger, David Karen, Annette Lareau, Lisa Smulyan, and Karolyn Tyson — gave feedback on an early draft, for which I am grateful. I especially thank Annette, who bought me dinner and helped me understand the task in front of me as I developed this book. The next day, David bought me breakfast and helped me more clearly articulate my understanding of the relation between meritocracy and race.

I also owe much gratitude to four colleagues who came to Cambridge for a terrifying but incredibly fruitful day with me in which they tore apart and then reconstructed a draft of this manuscript. Thank you to Amy Binder, Steve Brint, Camille Charles, and Ruben Gaztambide-Fernandez for your insights on that cold December day. Ruben deserves special thanks for reading and giving feedback on not one but two versions of the manuscript. In addition to Ruben, an anonymous reviewer for the University of Chicago Press provided helpful feedback. Across the Atlantic, I am particularly grateful for conversations with Anna Zimdars about elite higher education in Britain, and with Nasar Meer and Susanne Wessendorf about British multiculturalism.

I have talked about this research in front of numerous audiences, including at the American Sociological Association, the Graduate Center at CUNY, Columbia University, the Council for European Studies, the Eastern Sociological Society, Ontario Institute for Studies in Education, Russell Sage Foundation, Sarah Lawrence College, University of Pennsylvania, and multiple forums at Harvard. I thank colleagues at these forums for comments that developed this work. In particular, I thank Ellen Berrey, Anthony Chen, Randall Collins, Nancy Foner, Shamus Khan, Joseph Soares, Ajantha Subramanian, Van Tran, Lois Weis, and Richard Zweigenhaft for fruitful exchanges at those and other forums. As should be obvious by now, with all this help the manuscript ought to be flawless. Whatever flaws remain are probably the result of my stubborn neglect of some important insight shared by one of these generous colleagues.

Elizabeth Branch Dyson is simply an extraordinary editor. She supported this project long before a single page was written, and she has patiently guided me as I muddled through my ideas and came to tell the story in these pages, brainstorming with me at every step of the way. Everyone deserves a cheerleader like Elizabeth. Everyone also deserves a critic like David Lobenstine, who helped me see where this manuscript was unclear and pushed me to find my voice throughout it. I also thank Alice Bennett for copyediting and Rachel Kelly and Ruth Goring for shepherding the book through the publishing process.

This project would never have been possible without the participation of students on the Harvard, Brown, and Oxford campuses. I thank each of them for their thoughtful engagement in interviews. I also want to thank administrators at the three universities for helping me recruit students at their particular houses and dorms (unnamable, to protect student identities). Other administrators facilitated this project and generously shared their time to help me understand the Harvard, Brown, and Oxford campuses, including Mary Grace Almandrez, Lisa Coleman, Tom Dingham, William Fitzsimmons, Shane Lloyd, Mike Nicholson, and Leyla Okhai.

Finally, none of this would have been possible without my family. My parents, Shiban and Nanna Warikoo, have provided me with so much throughout my life, and they continue to meet my every request — usually for help looking after my children — with a smile. My husband Ramesh Kumar too often bore the brunt of my stress at critical moments of the writing. And yet his support never wavers and his love seems to envelop me when I need it most. As for my children, they are simply the best. They are fun, interesting, and so very present at every moment. They have helped me on my journey to becoming the person I want to be—patient, generous, forgiving, calm. One day I will get there. Till then, they (and Ramesh, too) are forgiving when I am imperfect. I hope that when it is their turn to apply to college, they will be able to see past the doublespeak about race and meritocracy, appreciate the incredible privileges they have, and commit to doing something that matters for this world. I dedicate this book to them, in pursuit of those goals.

INTRODUCTION

In school I learned two crucial things that shaped my future. First, I learned I was an outsider to my local community. I was raised in an immigrant family in a declining Pennsylvania steel town, where I was the only student of color in my cohort at school. While the culture wars of the 1980s brewed on college campuses, in Johnstown we barely noticed much beyond the covers of *Time* magazine. Instead, our gaze rested on the steel mills that closed one after another, each one adding to the growing number of my classmates' fathers who were unemployed and frustrated. When my older brother went off to New York City to study at Columbia University, I began to hear about racial justice and started to develop a vocabulary for the exclusion I too experienced. Rather than feeling bad about myself when I wasn't invited to classmates' birthday parties, and because I knew no one would even think of asking a brown-skinned girl to prom, I became angry: angry at my community for excluding me; angry at my parents for raising me in a town unsympathetic to my ethnic identity; angry at the world for the racial injustice I now found seemingly everywhere. In 1991 I took these feelings, along with my Run-DMC and Duran Duran cassettes, to Brown University.

The second thing I learned in school was that I was "smart." I went to college thinking of myself as a model student who earned a spot at a top university through my hard work and dedication to school. In high school I often became irritated with peers who lamented not being able to earn top grades like I did. In my mind the equation was simple: I worked hard, so I got good grades and got out of Johnstown. It never occurred to me that my parents' being doctors meant they could send me to private music lessons and residential summer camps where I learned advanced math and computer programming. And I had no idea that our frequent trips to India and other faraway destinations, which I wrote about in my college application essay, surely gave me a leg up in the admissions process. My peers were not even in the game. When I told one classmate I was going to Brown University, she joked that she was going to "Green" and then wondered out loud why her high-achieving classmate was going to a college she hadn't heard of. After all, the farthest other high achievers in my class dared to dream of going was to Penn State or the University of Pittsburgh, both about eighty miles distant, and for most already a world away. Why was it so hard for me to see that my parents' having medical degrees might have helped me get into an elite college? And why couldn't I see that because many of my peers' fathers had lost their jobs in the steel mills they didn't apply to college at all? The answer is simple: I believed in American meritocracy.

I couldn't wait to get to college. I longed to be among peers who shared my interest in addressing racial inequality and my culturally liberal views. What kinds of conversations about race would we have in this racially diverse environment in which most of us identified as liberal? And how would it feel to be surrounded by hardworking high achievers like myself? I couldn't wait to find out.

When we arrived on campus, our beloved President Vartan Gregorian told us as we sat on the college green that we were "the best class ever" to enter the Van Wickle gates at Brown, and that the peers sitting next to us would be our friends and colleagues for decades to come. I took that compliment very seriously, patting myself on the back for my hard work in high school, in contrast to my peers back home. But when classes rolled around I didn't feel so smart: suddenly I wasn't the top student. Just as in high school I didn't understand how my parents helped me achieve, in college I didn't know enough to understand that I was suddenly an average student because many of my peers went to schools where they learned much more than I did about how to think, write, and study, and because many of their parents had gone to Brown and colleges like it, teaching them since birth how to navigate such a place. I clung to my belief in meritocracy even while my sense of my place in it was changing.

My ethnic identity was changing, too. Before college I hadn't developed much pride in my South Asian identity. More than anything else, I just felt embarrassed by my darker skin and my parents' foreign accents. At Brown I learned I was not an outsider after all. Moreover, I came to understand two things about race. First, it matters, and it fundamentally shapes individuals' life experiences in American society, in both positive and negative ways. I learned about the rich diversity of my peers' experiences, whether they were the children of immigrant parents from other parts of the world, African American parents from the South, or white parents from suburban New Jersey. Second, I learned that race-related talk could explode at any moment, leading to accusations of racism and counteraccusations of oversensitivity. At a training session for the Women Peer Counselors program I joined at the beginning of my second year, a white student leader asked us all to choose one of our myriad identities for an activity. I remember thinking it was an odd request but, not having any language to critique the activity, I obliged, though I don't remember what I chose. Other women of color, however, expressed anger at the white woman's insensitivity to the intersectionality of our identities and the impossibility of choosing one or even decoupling our race from our gender. Students on both sides of the conflict stormed out of the room in a rage while I sat bewildered, taking in this new place of racial diversity and racial conflict.

During those years at Brown I learned a lot about race in the United States. Being South Asian meant I was not part of the long-standing aggrieved African American community, but I was also not part of the dominant white community. However, my belief in my own outstanding achievements in high school as well as those of my peers at Brown never wavered. We shared a strong belief that we all deserved this elite education based on our high school achievements. Our knowledge of the policy of affirmative action[1] seemed to bolster that belief—it supported the idea that whatever the negative effects of race in the United States, affirmative action made up for them, so we could feel confident that the admissions process was bringing the best students of all racial backgrounds to campus. Of course, a minority of very vocal students questioned affirmative action, emboldened by Dinesh D'Souza's bestselling *Illiberal Education*, which came out just before we started college.

When I moved to London at age thirty, my identity shifted once again. There British Asians (as Britons with South Asian ancestry call themselves) barely noticed my Indian ancestry—to them I was 100 percent American, with my swallowed *t*'s and overemphasized *r*'s. In Britain accents mean a lot, and soon I could fairly reliably detect people's class backgrounds and guess what part of the city Londoners grew up in from the way their *t*'s came out. At the University of London campus where I taught, as well as during my visits to the Oxford campus, the *t* was always well articulated. I later learned that colleagues with working-class backgrounds had often worked hard after leaving home to develop the upper-class London accent, to fit into the elite university environment. In Britain a person's accent sometimes seemed to signal achievement just as much as the score attained on national exams, even if nearly everyone put faith in the exams to determine students' capability for university-level work.

During my time in London I frequently found myself surprised by the perspectives of friends and colleagues in conversations about ethnic diversity. Friends and friends of friends surprised me with views that, to my Ivy League–educated eyes, appeared racially insensitive. No one seemed to tiptoe around issues of race when they were with me, despite knowing that this was my field of study and that I was a racial minority. Once, when attending a literary festival sponsored by the left-leaning newspaper the *Guardian*, a moderator asked audience members to raise a hand if they felt British newspapers should have printed the offensive depictions of the Muslim prophet Muhammad that had caused violent protest in Denmark a few weeks earlier. To me the answer was a no-brainer: of course the newspapers were right not to publish the offensive images, because that's what multicultural sensibility was all about! And I assumed that if anyone secretly disagreed, this audience would fear the accusation of cultural insensitivity, even racism, too much to raise a hand. Instead, hands shot up all around me. People weren't waiting to see what others were doing: they were angry.

In the United States, when surrounded by colleagues who were working in higher education or who held elite college degrees, I could feel confident that most would express views sympathetic to the needs and concerns of racial minorities, even if we disagreed about particular policies and practices. If those acquaintances did hold negative views about minority groups and supports for them, well, my skin is darker than theirs, so they wouldn't share those views in my presence. But at cocktail receptions in Britain I spent a lot of time staring into my plastic cup while the elite university graduates all around me argued, with no compunction, about whether arranged marriage should be banned, or whether multiculturalism in Britain had "gone too far." The first time this happened I reflexively shrank away from the conversation, as if someone had cursed in church. The second time I wanted to wave my arms at the circle of people around me to remind them that I was standing *right there*. "Don't you know I can hear you?" I kept thinking. The next time, and many times thereafter, I realized they did know that a person of color was standing in their midst, and they didn't care.

What allows for these frank, if uncomfortable, conversations in Britain? And what makes many in the United States express more sympathy for and acceptance of cultural and racial differences? Given my own experiences with encountering diversity-related programs and conversations at Brown, I guessed that college plays an important role in the United States. I was curious about how the admissions process as well as college settings themselves might shape students' perspectives. After all, residential college students are usually at a point in their lives when their ideas are in flux—they have left their home communities and families and are encountering new people and all kinds of new ideas. Also, social scientists have shown us that a generation's political leanings are largely set at this age.[2] So the college experience has important implications for how the leaders of tomorrow might think about diversity and fairness. I knew that college fundamentally shifted the ways I myself thought about race so many years ago. I wondered what colleges today are doing to students' perspectives on race and meritocracy—and, by implication, what they could be doing differently.

Race has been a central topic of campus debates in the United States for decades. According to some accounts, the culture wars that rocked college campuses twenty-five years ago are back. Others say they never left. In recent years the manifestations are many. In the pages of a conservative student newspaper, a Princeton student rejects his peers' exhortations that he (and other white men) "check your privilege." A group of black Harvard students launches an online campaign titled "I, Too, Am Harvard," airing grievances over offensive comments made by their peers. Conservatives lament the so-called liberal indoctrination by faculty and encourage students to host "affirmative action bake sales" in which they charge black and Latino customers less than white customers.[3] Offended peers counter with protests highlighting white privilege.

What makes these questions more pressing, for better and for worse, is affirmative action, the most controversial domain of discussion about race in higher education in the United States. In the 1960s selective US colleges began to systematically recruit and admit more African American students so as to maintain their legitimacy in the public eye in the wake of racial strife.[4] Today, in our supposedly post-racial era, critics of affirmative action say we shouldn't be looking at race as a factor in admissions. They argue that to do so violates the tenets of meritocracy as well as antidiscrimination laws. Critics say further that affirmative action sets minority students up for failure at universities for which they are not sufficiently prepared academically.[5]

Racial justice advocates respond with overwhelming data on racial inequality in the United States. Further, they argue that racial diversity benefits all students through an enriched learning environment. Given its prominence in American public debates, there has been a lot of research on affirmative action. We know that minorities attending selective universities who seem to have benefited from affirmative action (based on their SAT scores and grade point averages) do better as adults and contribute more to society than those who attended lower-ranked institutions without that benefit.[6] And yet black and Latino students are underrepresented on selective college campuses, even after taking into consideration class differences between black and white youth.[7]

The issue of black underrepresentation on elite campuses in Britain, by contrast, was just beginning to surface during my time there. In 2010 a Liberal Party member of Parliament publicly criticized Oxford's admission of just one British Afro-Caribbean student in the previous year (out of thirty-nine applicants, compared with admitting one in four white applicants); soon even Conservative prime minister David Cameron joined the growing chorus of outrage over this statistic.[8] Meanwhile, rather than lamenting the underrepresentation, Oxford University officials defended their admissions practices by claiming no discriminatory intent and hence no responsibility.[9] These debates in Britain and the United States led me to believe that students' opinions about fairness in admissions would reveal their perspectives on race as well. Given that the admissions process results in the underrepresentation of minority groups in both places (in spite of affirmative action in the United States), I wanted to understand how students make sense of those systems and how this meaning making shapes experiences marked by race differences or by racial conflict on campus and beyond.

I had a hunch that admissions was a major domain in which conflicts over race get articulated. For high school students, admission to the most selective colleges is the pinnacle of achievement, a reward for hard work and dedication in high school, the ultimate reward for individual merit. Now that the most selective universities in the United States accept well under 10 percent of those who even dare to apply—and that number declines almost every year—those who *do* get in understandably feel a huge sense of accomplishment and believe they are surrounded on campus by the best of the best. And yet almost half of Ivy League students' families can afford to pay fees that are well above the median household income in the United States. That means that every year those families are paying more than most American households *earn*. Just 14 percent of students attending the top 193 colleges in the United States come from families whose earnings place them in the bottom half of the income distribution. In other words, 87 percent of students at top colleges come from families who are richer than average; 70 percent come from the top 25 percent of household earnings.[10] Among black and Latino students who go to college, seven in ten attend open-access schools, often community colleges, while eight in ten whites in college attend the most selective colleges.[11] And yet the system is seen as meritocratic. This belief in meritocracy blinds students to the vast inequalities in society—by both class and race—and in particular to the way higher education is complicit in reproducing that inequality, in part through admissions systems.[12]

Despite the vast inequality in access to different kinds of colleges and in experiences at those colleges, most Americans, whether poor or rich, whether white or black or Asian, believe in the American dream that anyone can make it to a top college and go on to a comfortable life. Our equal opportunity ideology—a deep belief in the importance and availability of an equal chance for everyone—is strong. Despite so much evidence to the contrary, most Americans still believe that hard work and perseverance can lead to a first-class education, a top job, and a comfortable lifestyle.[13] The American dream rests on the notion of meritocracy—a system in which rewards are based on supposedly fair measures of merit. Indeed, Americans are more likely than people in most other countries to believe that we live in a meritocratic society, and that this is a good thing.[14]

How do admitted students make sense of a system that is wildly unequal in its distribution of rewards—a system that, according to some people, gives black students an unfair advantage and that others say puts black students at a nearly impossible disadvantage? How do members of this supposedly postracial generation think about race in the context of elite higher education, especially college admissions? Last, how do their experiences in college shape those understandings, and what are the implications for race relations on campus? To answer these questions I decided to investigate how students thought about race and merit, paying particular attention to the role of elite higher education in that process of meaning making. I embarked on a project to interview dozens of students, of all ethnic and racial backgrounds, at elite universities. College students are known for their liberal views and for their propensity for social protest, often in the name of liberal causes.[15] Elites are known to hold liberal views on cultural issues like immigrant inclusion and gay marriage.[16] I wanted to investigate our best-case scenario in terms of support for racial inclusion and racial justice among those who will hold power in the future, so I focused on students who had gained admission to top residential universities. White students on Ivy League campuses, I imagined, wouldn't blame affirmative action for denying them admission, since they had been admitted to universities ranked at the very top. I also wanted to understand how elite universities with different kinds of supports for diversity influence students' perspectives on race and merit, so I compared students at Harvard and Brown, US universities that are similar in many ways but differ in their approaches to race and diversity on campus. I made sure to include a significant number of students of color, because I wondered how their perspectives would differ from those of their white peers. How would black and Latino students, many of whom experience racial oppression in American society firsthand but may also be the beneficiaries of affirmative action, speak about these issues? And Asian Americans are outperforming whites in American high schools: What would they think?

Finally, I decided to compare students at Harvard and Brown with students at an elite British university—Oxford—to better understand what is unique to the selective US college experience. The United States and Britain are both multicultural capitalist democracies, and the oldest US universities were modeled after Oxford and Cambridge. But they differ in one crucial domain: race. In Britain there has been no race-based social movement. At Oxford I made sure to include a good number of British-born children of immigrants, to capture the experiences of students who are not part of the dominant group. This project lies at the intersection between conceptions of merit and conceptions of race, all within the world of elite higher education. Merit, as we'll see, is a domain in which concerns about race and diversity get articulated. That is, our conceptions of merit rest on our conceptions of race, inequality, and fairness. Of course, elite universities are not a microcosm of the whole country, but they matter. Everyone pays attention to the likes of Harvard and Oxford, so what happens on those campuses has great symbolic value throughout the country.[17] Events on Ivy League campuses seem to make it to the evening news at least once a month.

I see elite universities as institutional sites for cultivating elite identities and for shaping elite understandings of merit, inequality, and race. In this book I catch young adults at a time of identity development and changing perspectives, after they leave their families but before they enter the labor market. What happens to young adults' understandings of deservingness when they have "won" the most competitive game they've entered so far, the college admissions process? How do they make sense of those who fail to gain admission? Their perspectives will illuminate the way many of our future leaders and decision-makers develop their notions of worthiness, hard work, and "smarts"—that is, their understandings of merit, with implications for how they see themselves, others, and justice. My assumption is that a high proportion of students attending elite universities will go on to become leaders and decision makers in society, so it is important to understand their perspectives and the mechanisms by which they develop their views. Indeed, recent scholarship has shown that elite American firms, especially in consulting, finance, and law, recruit only at the very top universities.[18] In addition, what college a student attends affects the likelihood of actually completing college, with repercussions down the line for income.[19] In Britain a majority or near majority of senior judges, cabinet members, diplomats, and newspaper columnists are graduates of Oxford or Cambridge, compared with less than 1 percent of the British population as a whole.[20] Oxford and Cambridge have also historically been the gateway to the top civil service positions in Britain.[21]

In addition, we need to pay particular attention to this generation's perspectives on merit, inequality, and race if we want to understand how perspectives have shifted in this supposedly postracial era. College is a time when lifelong views are formed on a variety of political issues.[22] The American students in my study were schoolchildren when President Barack Obama was elected; as many understand it, this means we are living in a postracial era. In addition, young adults in the United States today are known for their racial diversity—43 percent are not white.[23] In Britain, young adults hold the lowest levels of racial prejudice.[24] Because elite college students tend to be liberal and to become more liberal on campus,[25] because their parents tend to be well educated,[26] and because they are young, they are the least likely to be racist according to various measures of racism, old and new.[27] If there is a group that will resolve our racial conflicts, it is this one. Investigating conceptions of race and merit among students at elite universities reveals what possibilities the future holds for reducing inequality and for cross-racial understanding in Britain and the United States.

ONE

BELIEFS ABOUT MERITOCRACY AND RACE

By the time of the passage of the landmark Civil Rights Act of 1964 . . . the inherent tension between the emerging meritocratic system and the cause of Negro advancement was already apparent to anyone who was looking closely.[1]

Karen arrived for her interview a few minutes late, lunch in hand. As she spoke she played with her long blonde hair. An athletic recruit, Karen listed a range of merits—socially desirable qualities serving as the basis for reward—that she believed should determine admission to Harvard, "Many people have merits that are different than intellectual—academic merits. I think it's a good thing that those merits are valued [by admissions]." When asked to explain the underrepresentation of black students on campus, Karen pointed out that "if you were to just take everyone based off their SAT scores, then that percentage [of black students on campus] would be even lower than it is now. So, while the percentage is lower than the population as a whole, I view it as a pretty good thing that it is that high, because it's higher than it would be otherwise." In other words, Karen believed that looking beyond SAT scores allowed for more black students on campus, which she supported. On the other hand, she was ambivalent about considering race in admissions:

I don't think because someone checked the black box or the Latino box, that that should be what helps them get in. You know, maybe in their interview you find that since they're Latino they've done all these things that add something different to the cultural fabric of

Harvard. I think it should be something more than just a box you check off. I know people who are, like, a quarter Mexican, who got the Latino Scholars Award, but their entire experience has been a white experience. And I think that we've hopefully gotten to the point where we can consider income more than racial things.

Karen has a particular understanding of what it means to have a "Latino" versus a "white" childhood, and a sense of how the "race" of one's childhood should determine whether one can benefit from affirmative action. Her view is quintessentially American: she values diversity largely for its effect on her and her peers at Harvard. Karen grew up in a New England suburb known for its high-performing public schools. She attended those schools, graduating from a high school that is less than 10 percent black or Latino (and another 6 percent Asian). Karen identified as politically liberal, like most students we interviewed in the United States. She told us she felt "very ignorant about all sorts of races and ethnicities" but was "eager to learn more about them" in college, given Harvard's racial diversity. Karen understood affirmative action as existing to benefit herself through exposure to new perspectives—but only if the beneficiaries did not come from "white" cultural backgrounds.

Contrast Karen to Joseph. Joseph grew up in the north of England and attended an elite boarding school before going to Oxford. Like most Oxford students, Joseph identified politically as liberal. When asked whether Oxford is a meritocracy in its admissions, he said, "Yes. I think its interview process is meritocratic." Joseph explained the underrepresentation of black students on campus as related to unequal access to high-quality education: "You get to Oxford as a result of your education. No matter how naturally brilliant you are, you have to be well educated. And the wealth distribution in society means that white people have more access to the best education." Still, Joseph did not support considering race or ethnicity in admissions, replying with an emphatic no when asked. He saw a different role for Oxford. "Oxford doesn't represent the country. There is only so much that Oxford can do about it, because if the situation in the country at large is such that students aren't sufficiently educated to be at Oxford, then Oxford shouldn't dumb itself down purely to take on the burden of the country." In his mind, considering race or ethnicity would contravene Oxford's very purpose. "I don't think that legitimately they can do that. Oxford has to maintain the highest standards it can. There is so much competition academically from American universities, that if they make allowances of that kind then Oxford would lose prestige as an institution itself."

Ironically, the very universities Joseph believes Oxford is competing with—the very reasons Oxford cannot afford to consider race in admissions—have considered race in admissions for decades. Joseph's remarks show how we take for granted our conceptions of merit. But if we looked outside our national boundaries we would see strikingly different systems. What constitutes merit varies over time and place and is often contested. Even the question of whether merit should involve *who we are* (whether one does or does not possess intelligence or potential, for example) or *what we have accomplished* (such as overcoming adversity or scoring high on a test) is contested. Why do these British and American students have such starkly different perspectives on race, merit, and inequality? I set out to answer this question through the research described in this book.

The term merit has been used for centuries to signify those characteristics that others deem worthy of reward or praise. The notion that individuals should be rewarded for their merit was an ideal of America's founding fathers. In addition to equal rights and government by consent, they hoped for a society in which individual merit, rather than birthright, would determine one's station in life.[2] Merit in this case served as a democratic ideal. Of course, just what constitutes those characteristics to be rewarded has changed over time and has sometimes been contested. For example, during the first half of the twentieth century, elite colleges instituted entrance exams to measure merit—first to determine whether applicants were capable of doing college-level work and later to identify "hidden talent" from around the country.[3] This was an attempt to extend opportunities to anyone who was capable—that is, anyone deemed meritorious as measured by the exam—in the spirit of democracy through equal opportunity. During the same period, Britain instituted grammar schools: state-funded secondary schools that accepted students based on merit as assessed by an exam. These too were an attempt to extend to non-elite youth the opportunities that elite education would provide, in the spirit of democratic inclusion.

Much later, during the second half of the twentieth century, some social scientists were hopeful that a system of social rewards based on merit and achievement rather than inherited status would allow scientists and intellectual leaders to solve the world's most pressing social problems.[4] Further, those leaders and technical experts would be chosen through meritocratic competitions, open to all. Social mobility, rooted in meritocracy, was thought to characterize modern industrial society, even more so than during the early years in America.[5] College admissions were part of this meritocratic system, because mass college education was supposed to propel the country forward. Given that contestations about the definition of merit over the past hundred years have often played out through college admissions, throughout this book I use perspectives on admissions as a means for unpacking conceptions of merit.

While optimists have placed their faith in merit to promote democratic inclusion, critics—and there have been many—claim that merit serves as an ideological tool that allows elites to maintain their position in society and to pass down privileges to their children.[6] Scholars in the tradition of social reproduction have long argued that educational institutions simply reproduce class status. They demonstrate how schools and universities reward upper-class characteristics, such as how one speaks and responds to authority, and label those cultural characteristics as meritorious.[7] Jerome Karabel, in his expansive study of admissions to Harvard, Princeton, and Yale, argues that "the definition of 'merit' is fluid and tends to reflect the values and interests of those in power to impose their particular cultural ideals."[8] For example, he describes how the universities shifted the definition of merit to include "character" during the 1920s, when they wanted to reduce the number of Jewish students admitted. The loosely defined "character" and an espoused desire for "well-rounded" students empowered the universities to ask for letters of recommendation, pictures, and on-campus interviews as part of the application, all designed to promote Protestant applicants over Jews, who were acing the admissions exams. Also, the universities opened admissions to women only when they began to worry that without women on campus elite men would not enroll.[9] More recently, some have argued in both the United States and Britain that elitism under the guise of meritocracy has increased in the recent past.[10] They point out, for example, that as admission has gotten more competitive at the most selective colleges,[11] upper-class families have poured ever more resources into test preparation, extra-curricular activities, and more, increasing overall inequality in oppor-tunities.[12]

In Britain, the grammar school system rested on the notion that some individuals are innately intelligent and that those top students should study in schools that prepare them to attend university, re-gardless of class background. However, in Britain too attempts at expanding opportunity through meritocracy did not turn out to be bias-free. In the early years of grammar schools, just 1 percent of chil-dren with working-class fathers attended grammar schools, compared with 37 percent of children with professional parents; as late as the 1940s, children from professional families were more than six times as likely to attend grammar schools as their working-class peers.[13] The very term meritocracy, in fact, was not coined as an articulation of beliefs in systems of reward for achievement. Rather, British sociolo-gist Michael Young invented it in 1958 as a criticism. He wrote a satiri-cal account of a dystopia, labeled a meritocracy, in which notions of merit were used to reproduce and legitimate class status: "The top of today are breeding the top of tomorrow to a greater extent than at any time in the past. The elite is on the way to becoming hereditary; the principles of heredity and merit are coming together." Young's ac-count warned of the dangers of a system in which elites craft defini-tions of merit to enable them to perpetuate class privilege across gen-erations, with consent from the lower classes based on the perceived legitimacy of the meritocracy. Active in the Labour Party, Young pre-ferred the party to focus on improving life conditions for working-class Britons rather than paying lip service to the potential of class mobility via meritocracy, which he viewed as a false promise. Young's perspective, shared by others in the Labour Party, may explain why little discussion of expanding access to higher education developed in Britain, even during the 1960s expansion of higher education, despite a more generous welfare state and stronger working-class identities than in the United States. Rather than emphasizing mobility through meritocracy, Labour Party members recognized that some proportion of the population will always be working-class; thus, working-class life should have a minimum decent standard of living.[14]

Race, Merit, and College Admissions

The history of intelligence testing in both the United States and Britain is intertwined with the eugenics movement, spearheaded by Francis Galton, which sought to categorize races by levels of intelligence in order to "breed" a better society.[15] Although eugenics was abandoned long ago, the impetus to use testing to sort individuals for social roles and positions, including various types of schooling, the military, and jobs, endures, and the notion that differences in intelligence by race may exist continues to flourish, if as a minority view.[16] As a result, race has been a central part of conversations about merit. From the early 1960s, some selective colleges in the United States, including Brown and Harvard, began recruiting African American students, both from a desire to promote racial justice and as a strategy to avoid accusations of racism and the consequent campus unrest that could unfold.[17] This was also an attempt to maintain the legitimacy of the admissions contest in the face of loud public criticism.[18] Because elite American universities had previously added "character" to their definitions of merit, a holistic approach to admissions to allow for affirmative action was rather easily implemented.[19] Since then race, merit, and college admissions have been inexorably linked.

In 1978 the US Supreme Court ruled that considering race in admissions is permissible only when it serves the goal of providing a diverse environment to enhance the learning of all students on campus.[20] Since then, multiple decisions have upheld this justification for affirmative action, and no others.[21] In *The Enigma of Diversity*, Ellen Berrey traces the shift in university justifications for affirmative action from a moral imperative that expands opportunities during the 1960s and 1970s to this "diversity rationale."[22] Diversity—especially racial diversity—has become a currency for respectable leadership in the United States and a value espoused by institutions of many types.[23] In fact, today racial diversity is one of the many criteria determining college rankings in the United States.[24]

Despite the emphasis on the diversity rationale in court, many public intellectuals, including many legal scholars, have advocated alternative justifications for affirmative action in higher education admissions. For example, some argue that compensation for past discrimination that continues to have adverse effects on minorities, especially African Americans, is an important rationale for affirmative action.[25] Others advocate class-based affirmative action, sometimes as determined by zip code.[26] Lani Guinier goes further, criticizing notions of meritocracy altogether.[27] She argues that universities should consider students' potential contributions to civic life rather than measuring merit through test scores. These voices join more conservative critics who argue against affirmative action,[28] leading to an overall loud chorus of public debate about admission to selective colleges.

Ordinary Americans, too, are very interested in how selective colleges decide admissions. Affirmative action appears on many opinion polls, and in eight states it has faced referenda leading to bans. A recent spate of books written for mainstream audiences has also criticized other aspects of admission to selective colleges, suggesting they privilege already privileged applicants.[29] Nicholas Lemann, in his history of the SAT, demonstrates how the exam reproduced privilege rather than expanding opportunity.[30] Others have called for the end of legacy admission, which privileges whites over all minority groups, and for attenuating or ending athletic recruiting, which mostly privileges whites, given the wide range of sports, such as lacrosse and crew, that most disadvantaged youth never encounter in high school.[31]

There is even more interest in how our most *elite* universities do admissions, and in the affirmative action that happens on those campuses. Elite universities are the very places we uphold as bastions of excellence and meritocracy in the United States. Notions of merit and worthiness at Harvard are watched not only by lower-tier colleges setting their own admissions criteria, but also by ordinary Americans viewing Harvard as the symbol of excellence, opportunity, and meritocracy. Beyond symbolic meaning, considerable evidence suggests that attending an elite college rather than a nonelite one means that a student is more likely to graduate, to earn more, and to hold a position of power.[32] Of course, the 2.8 million full-time students attending private four-year colleges are just 17 percent of college students in the United States; a small subset of those students attend selective colleges.[33] Still, what happens at selective universities, especially the *most* selective ones, has symbolic value in the broader society.

Elite universities need to maintain their legitimacy in the minds of ordinary Americans. If they are to do so, they must take a stand on race in admissions. Do considerations of race go against a meritocratic system by introducing a factor (race) unrelated to merit? Or do they restore the legitimacy of the meritocracy by making up for flawed measures of merit that deflate the "true" capacities of black and Latino applicants and inflate those of white applicants? Should universities consider individual capacity or actual performance, when performance is influenced by resources, as when parents pay for SAT tutoring and extracurricular activities? How does this square with the legal justification of affirmative action as important for contributing to a diverse learning environment?

While ordinary Americans and public intellectuals are divided about the answers to these questions,[34] admissions officers generally are not.[35] Most selective private universities in the United States practice affirmative action, as do selective public universities in states with no ban in effect. Admissions officers' support for affirmative action is bolstered by an extensive body of research on "campus racial climate" that demonstrates the benefits of racial diversity.[36] This body of work generally finds that there are academic and civic benefits to racial diversity on campus, showing that cross-racial interactions are associated with increased self-reported intellectual abilities, increased self-reported ability to get along with other race groups, increased interest in promoting racial understanding, and reduced intergroup prejudice for students of all racial backgrounds.[37] Beyond informal interactions, participation in diversity-related campus workshops and course content, such as courses in African American studies or ethnic studies, is correlated with positive learning outcomes and increased engagement with racial issues.[38]

Whereas private elite US universities have used affirmative action for decades, the practice is not common in Britain. Why? The British case casts the United States circumstances into sharp relief. In Britain no successful social movement propelled race onto the national stage and in turn onto university campuses as the civil rights movement did in the United States.[39] Relatedly, some describe the United States as a race-identified society, compared with Britain, where class identities are foregrounded.[40] Last, in the United States, faith in our system of equal opportunity, resting on meritocracy, is central to our national identity.[41] Starting from the mid-twentieth century, in the United States access to higher education by working-class and minority youth became an important means for promoting equality, especially by the Democratic Party. In 1947 President Truman's Commission on Higher Education issued a report that called for greater and more equitable access to higher education.[42] As a result, in the fifty years after 1940, college enrollment increased by a factor of ten, and the federal government enabled this expansion through dramatic increases in financial aid.[43] This belief in education as a vehicle for social mobility was one important reason affirmative action took hold in the United States as a means to address racial inequality. In contrast, in Britain the Labour Party stressed improvement in working and living conditions for the working class, an emphasis on reducing inequality in *outcomes* rather than in *opportunities*.[44]

Still, over the past half-century British universities have slowly moved toward greater access. From the 1950s to the 1970s Oxford enrolled increasing numbers of working-class and middle-class students.[45] This greater inclusion of nonelite youth boosted Oxford's modernization project, in which social rewards became legitimated through meritocracy rather than through family pedigree. The 1963 Robbins Report of the British government called for the expansion of higher education (though not broader access).

More recently, the British government has used tuition policies to push universities to expand access. Most British universities are government-funded, which allows the government to make decisions about how much, if anything, students pay. The implementation of university tuition fees since 1998, up to £9,000 a year as of 2016, has led to increasing government demands that universities demonstrate "widening participation." That is, since 2006, if a university wants to charge the maximum tuition allowed, the government requires it to develop an agreement with the government's Office for Fair Access to show how it will improve access.[46] Most universities in their agreements plan to take into account "contextual" information—most commonly whether students come from neighborhoods that do not send many young people to college, whether students have been in foster care, and the quality of their secondary schools. Further, universities charging maximum tuition are required to spend a portion of tuition fees on "access"; most of this expenditure is on financial aid and on outreach to encourage disadvantaged youth to apply for admission.[47] So while Oxford's efforts to expand equal opportunity through university admissions are more recent than those at elite American universities, many hopeful signs suggest that Oxford is becoming more inclusive.[48]

Despite these developments, working-class and black British students remain underrepresented on the Oxford campus. For example, while 7 percent of British youth attend private secondary schools, nearly half of Oxford students come from private schools.[49] In addition, the acceptance rate for every minority group at Oxford continues to remain lower than that for white applicants.[50] This difference is not related to achievement levels of applicants: among students with the same achievements, youth who come from privileged families and who are white are more likely to gain admission to elite British universities, and Oxford in particular, than comparable working-class and minority students.[51] So, as with admission to Harvard and Brown, an ostensibly fair and inclusive admissions system produces unequal outcomes.

The Student Perspective

How do winners of merit-based competitive processes make sense of those systems, especially in the face of loud public criticism? In many ways students need to reconcile the obviously unequal outcomes of admissions with justifying the privileges they have as future graduates of elite universities. Andrew Delbanco warns that uncritical belief in meritocracy may lead elites to feel less responsible to society if they believe they *earned* rather than *inherited* their position.[52] Indeed, recent research suggests that elites, young and old, assume they earned their status through hard work, not noticing that those of lesser means also work hard but lack the family networks or wealth that can reward that work with, for example, help in making a down payment on a house or tuition to a private high school or college.[53] Rubén Gaztambide-Fernandez found that white students at an elite boarding school in the United States believed they were admitted because they were unique, well-rounded, and showed initiative, rarely registering the influence of their families' guidance, wealth, or status.[54] Similarly, Shamus Khan found that wealthy white students at the elite St. Paul's boarding school believed their own hard work and strong academic backgrounds had gained them admission to the school.[55] On the other hand, students of color in both Gaztambide-Fernandez's and Khan's studies often did not see themselves as unique in the same ways and sometimes wondered if they gained admission to be part of the "diversity curriculum" for their white peers.[56] Perceptions of group differences can further support students' sense of self-worth. For example, Frank Samson's research shows that when reminded that Asian American students tend to have high GPAs, white adults in California downplay the importance they think GPA should have for college admission, but when reminded that black students tend to have lower GPAs, they increase its importance.[57] Overall this research shows that most people's conceptions of merit rely on criteria that bolster their belief in their own merit and that of their race group.

I wanted to know what happens once students like those in Gaztambide-Fernandez's and Khan's studies go to college. As I reflected on my own college experiences in the United States and on how dramatically my views of race and inequality shifted during that time even while my faith in college as a sorting mechanism never wavered, I guessed that the supports for diversity at most elite US colleges—departments of African American and ethnic studies, minority student centers, orientation workshops on diversity, and much more—might shape students' perspectives toward something different from what Gaztambide-Fernandez and Khan found in their studies at US boarding schools. As I investigated the history of diversity and race on college campuses in the United States, I learned that the African American students recruited through affirmative action during the early 1960s became leaders of student movements demanding a greater presence of minority students, African American studies departments, centers for minority students on campus, freshman orientation events related to race, and much more.[58] By the mid-1980s affirmative action was the norm in US selective college admissions,[59] even if the institutionalizing of affirmative action coincided with "culture wars" on campus, pitting students of the New Left against traditional conservatives.[60] The diversity-related supports on college campuses around the country endure today, and more recently there has been a proliferation of administrative offices in higher education dedicated to diversity or multicultural affairs.[61] As a result, most selective private universities in the United States have important institutions related to diversity. This is different from British universities as well as from American primary and secondary schools. Mica Pollock describes elementary and secondary schools in the United States as "colormute" for their lack of frank and open discussions about race.[62] Discourse around "diversity" also developed in the United States during the 1980s in a range of settings beyond higher education, including in discussions about neighborhood gentrification and in the corporate world.[63] How might this infrastructure shape the perspectives of white and minority students on campus?

Survey researchers tell us that being young adults, being college students, and living away from home with other young adults make college students much more likely than other adults to identify as liberal.[64] And the liberal perspective on college admissions points out the underrepresentation of disadvantaged groups on elite college campuses. Students' liberal identities, along with the diversity-related supports on most residential campuses in the United States and the long history of student protests on college campuses[65] together suggest that students may not accept their universities' admissions policies as sufficiently inclusive of black, Latino, and working class students.

How might perspectives vary across national boundaries? Even while meritocracy is seen as the engine of progress in modern society, relatively little is known about how elites' perspectives on meritocracy differ by country. We also know little about how national traditions embedded in elite universities shape those perspectives. Other research has shown that Americans are more likely than Britons to believe their society rewards merit; furthermore, Americans are more likely to believe that merit—defined as education—*should* determine income.[66] Indeed, Alexis de Tocqueville, writing during the nineteenth century, commented in *Democracy in America* on Americans' strong belief in individualism, in contrast to Europe's greater emphasis on social supports. In addition, the supports for diversity on American college campuses have few counterparts in Britain.

I should point out that the students we spoke with rarely used the word merit. But though it went unsaid, the concept of merit is at the heart of much of their views on admissions. In other words, when describing admissions most students implicitly assume it is a system that distributes rewards based on personal qualities and accomplishments—a meritocracy. Hence I use their perspectives on admissions to understand their perspectives on merit and meritocracy.

Racial Attitudes and Merit

By now it should be clear that in order to unpack how students understand merit and admissions, we need to also unpack how they think about race and its role in society. Recent research on ordinary Americans helped me think about what I might find. On one hand, survey research in both the United States and Britain has documented a sharp decline in overt racial prejudice since the 1970s, toward both African

Americans and the descendants of immigrants.[67] These shifting attitudes on, for example, racial intermarriage and beliefs in racial minorities' biological inferiority have been dramatic. Much debate exists, however, on the existence and nature of continued negative attitudes toward racial minorities and immigrants. The extensive research in the United States on "new prejudice" suggests that while overt attitudes have softened, whites continue to hold racially prejudiced views.[68] These attitudes reveal themselves in myriad ways. Analysis shows, for example, that among white Americans with similar political views, there is a correlation between racial prejudice and views against affirmative action. That is, racial prejudice seems to influence policy preferences on race-related issues like affirmative action, leading some to suggest that views against affirmative action are a cloak for racial prejudice.[69] In addition, whites tend to support policies aimed at increasing *opportunities* without ensuring equitable *outcomes*, even if they support equitable outcomes in principle.[70] For example, during the second half of the twentieth century white Americans' belief in school integration increased dramatically, but support for busing students to promote it remained low.[71] Similarly, Americans tend to support the abstract notion of multiculturalism rather than particular policies such as ethnic representation or support for non-English languages.[72] A different line of work studies "implicit biases"—unconscious preference for whites, as demonstrated, for example, by slow reactions when asked to associate black faces with positive words. Mahzarin Banaji and her associates demonstrate ongoing, rampant implicit bias related to race in the United States.[73] Finally, studies that send out similar job applicants of different races find that employers continue to discriminate. One such study finds, for example, that black graduates of elite colleges have the same likelihood of response to a job query as do white graduates of less selective colleges.[74]

While ordinary Americans' racial attitudes continue to show signs of "new prejudice," there are many reasons to believe that private elite college students' perspectives will be more supportive of policies intended to promote racial equality. College education is associated with greater support for abstract principles of equality, and younger Americans express less racial prejudice.[75] In addition, white students attending the most elite universities have been the winners of a system that some whites see as favoring black and Latino applicants through affirmative action. That is, they probably have not (yet) perceived personal disadvantage due to affirmative action, even if they may soon do so when they look for jobs or even summer internships. Finally, the diversity-related institutions and racial diversity on college campuses seem to be important influences on students, including increased interracial understanding and support for diversity.[76] On the other hand, studies have shown that interracial interactions in the United States can be stressful, especially when conversations turn to topics related to race.[77] Whites worry about being perceived as racist despite their best intentions.[78] Students of color, too, worry about perceptions of race on campus—but their fears lie in white peers' beliefs about their academic abilities and their desire to socialize across racial lines.[79] Cross-group friendships, especially with roommates, seem to mitigate these feelings of anxiety.[80] To figure out where our country is headed in terms of fairness and opportunity, we have to consider how the younger generation thinks about race. Of course, in addition to racial attitudes, universities' admissions policies are the backdrop to how students themselves consider admissions, so next I turn to how admissions decisions are made in the Ivy League and at Oxbridge, as Oxford and Cambridge together are known.

How the Ivy League and Oxbridge Define Merit

Students applying to elite US universities submit at a minimum grade point averages, SAT or ACT scores, letters of recommendation from teachers, and at least one personal essay. Most selective private universities in the United States evaluate students through a holistic look at a variety of qualities, including academic achievements, campus diversity (especially, but not only, racial and geographic diversity), the needs of sports teams (and to a lesser extent other extracurricular groups), whether an applicant's parents attended that college, and whether parents are significant donors.[81] Multiple admissions officers read each application, rating for a variety of qualities like academics and "personal qualities," which encompass leadership, overcoming hardship, and more.[82] Decisions are made by a committee of professional admissions officers. Discussion-based learning, in contrast to Oxford's tutorial system, supports the goal of a diverse student body in the United States because students of different backgrounds are thought to bring unique perspectives to class discussions. There is strong agreement among most admissions officers that racial diversity is an important consideration, and most see affirmative action as part and parcel of building an excellent college.[83]

Thomas Espenshade and his colleagues[84] have attempted to quantify the benefits related to SAT scores for African American, Latino, legacy, and recruited athlete applicants, and also the "penalty" for Asian applicants. They find the largest benefits seem to go to African Americans (equivalent to 230 SAT points compared with whites) and recruited athletes (200 SAT points compared with students not recruited for athletic teams), while Asian applicants seem to pay a "penalty" of 50 SAT points. Of course, this analysis takes it for granted that the SAT is a good measure, while universities contest this claim, citing their holistic evaluations of applicants that consider much more than SAT scores.

What do admissions offices say they are looking for? Brown University's admissions website tells prospective students:

> Our mission demands that we discover how individual applicants would contribute to—and benefit from—the lively academic, social, and extracurricular activity at Brown. . . . [W]e have the humbling luxury of choosing candidates who stand out for special abilities, accomplishments, energy for learning, thoughtfulness, perspective, and many other qualities.[85]

The twin considerations of unique individual characteristics and contribution to a learning community are echoed in the remarks of Harvard dean of admissions William Fitzsimmons:

> While we value objective criteria, we apply a more expansive view of excellence. Test scores and grades offer some indication of students' academic promise and achievement. But we also scrutinize applications for extracurricular distinction and personal qualities. Students' intellectual imagination, strength of character, and their ability to exercise good judgment—these are critical factors in the admissions process. . . . We believe that a diversity of backgrounds, academic interests, extracurricular talents, and career goals among students who live and learn together affects the quality of education in the same manner as a great faculty or material resources.[86]

Here again we see the importance of a diverse cohort that will teach each other, as well as individual excellence and character. It is important to remember that the root of discussions of diversity is racial exclusion and inequality, even while the language of promoting diversity in the student body has spilled over into discussions about women in science and technology,[87] class-based underrepresentation,[88] and sexuality.[89] Indeed, neither of the university quotations above mentions race.

In addition to cherishing diversity, elite universities in the United States pay attention to whether applicants have made the most of opportunities available to them. That is, evaluations of merit are calibrated according to an applicant's opportunities while growing up. Harvard's Dean Fitzsimmons writes, "We are vitally interested in whether or not applicants have taken full advantage of their educational opportunities, whatever they might have been,"[90] and Brown's admissions website tells us, "We know that curricular offerings vary from school to school. Our strongest candidates have taken full advantage of what is available to them in their own schools."[91]

While a complex array of considerations drives admissions, continuity exists from year to year and between campuses, especially related to the percentages of minority groups, athletic recruits, and more.[92] Around the time of this research, 6 to 8 percent of students at Harvard and Brown identified as black, another 6 to 9 percent identified as Latino, and 11 to 16 percent identified as Asian or Asian American.[93] This compares with 34 percent of young adults' in the United States being black or Latino and 4 percent being Asian American.[94] Another 8 to 10 percent were international students.[95] So black and Latino youth are significantly underrepresented on the Harvard and Brown campuses, as is true of most selective colleges.[96] In fact, racial disparities in enrollment appear to be increasing over time, not decreasing.[97] With respect to financial aid, while most private college prices are well over $60,000 a year, 62 percent of Harvard undergraduates received need-based financial aid, as did 46 percent of Brown undergraduates.[98]

British universities have held a relatively stable definition of merit in admissions over time: they strive to admit students with the highest potential to do well in a particular area of study.[99] Whereas elite American universities prize diversity of all kinds, as well as non-academic talents, Oxford emphasizes excellence only in the chosen field of study. For most subjects, Oxford requires students to attain a minimum of three As or A-stars—the highest grades possible—on the national A-level exams.[100] This requirement demonstrates a relatively stable understanding of the minimum academic achievement for study at Oxford, not calibrated to individual circumstances. Signals that Oxford sends to potential applicants from the United States underscore this singular test-based evaluation of merit. Oxford tells American applicants that "the minimum we would usually expect is: SAT Reasoning Test with at least 1,400 in Critical Reading and Mathematics and preferably also 700 or more in Writing. . . . and Grade 5 in 3 or more AP tests in appropriate subjects."[101] The list also includes minimum scores for the ACT test and SAT subject tests. Contrast these published scores with US universities' discussions of test scores, where elite universities like Brown and Harvard rarely state explicit guidelines, even for domestic students. For example, Harvard tells potential applicants:

> We do not have minimum scores or cut-offs; however, the majority of students admitted represent a range of scores from roughly 600 to 800 on each section of the SAT as well as on the SAT Subject Tests. The 25th percentile for admitted students on the SAT is about 2100; the 75th percentile is about 2350.[102]

Notice the higher minimum for Oxford. Brown University is even more vague:

> Are there minimum standardized test requirements or expectations for applicants?
>
> No. While we do receive many applications from students with high test scores, we consider standardized test results in the context of all the other information we have about a candidate. We find that many of our applicants demonstrate strong academic potential in spite of relatively modest test scores.[103]

This public information from Oxford, Harvard, and Brown signals the importance the universities place on standardized tests and the messages they wish to convey to potential applicants about them.

Oxford and Cambridge are the only two British universities that interview a pool of candidates for admission. Over half of applicants to Oxford are invited to an interview on campus.[104] Unlike American college interviews, these interviews are consequential, because admissions decisions are based on them. Interviews are conducted by admissions "tutors," faculty at the university who teach courses and tutorials in the subject a candidate has applied for; these tutors make admissions decisions. Oxford University tells potential candidates that "the interview is designed to assess your academic abilities and, most importantly, your academic potential . . . beyond your written record. The interview allows [admissions tutors] to evaluate your understanding of, and aptitude for your subject, and to give you the opportunity to explain why you are committed to studying it."[105] The admissions website goes on to let candidates know that in interviews tutors are "assessing your ability to learn" as well as searching for evidence of "self-motivation and enthusiasm for your subject." Oxford University's director of undergraduate admissions also emphasizes potential to succeed in one's subject of choice and contrasts Oxford admission requirements to the criteria used at US Ivy League universities. When I interviewed him, he told me,

> We're taking students who really only need be really good at mathematics [for the mathematics degree]. . . . It doesn't really matter whether they've got any social skills or have any interest in liberal arts or humanities or whatever, as long as they're good mathematicians. And that, again, I think is something that sets us very much apart from Harvard, Yale, Princeton. . . . And that means when we're doing admissions we're trying to find ways to identify students who have got the best potential to make the most of a very subject-specific educational experience.

The result is a student body whose UK population (students schooled in Britain, not abroad) about the time of this research was 85 percent white, less than 1 percent black, 6 percent Asian, and 8 percent other (including mixed) or unreported.[106] This compares with a young British population (ages sixteen to twenty-four) that is 82 percent white, 10 percent Asian, and 4 percent black.[107] As at Harvard and Brown, black students are underrepresented on the Oxford campus.

While Oxford admissions' reliance on standardized test scores as an initial screening may suggest a more objective system, recent research has demonstrated race and class disparities in who gets admitted to

Oxford and to other top-tier British universities, owing to disparities not only in testing outcomes, but also in the interview process. Minority youth are just as likely—and sometimes more likely—to apply to elite British universities as their white peers with the same national exam grades.[108] Some admissions tutors at Oxford report that they do calibrate their assessments of students they interview based on the opportunities those students have had.[109] These considerations acknowledge the extensive coaching for the Oxbridge entrance exams and interview that students attending elite private schools receive in school. However, the admissions results suggest that that calibration does not go far enough to compensate for the bias against minority and working-class applicants during the interview stage, which ultimately selects more white British students than their minority peers with the same national exam grades.[110]

Why is admission to US and British elite universities so different? Overall, the universities have played different roles in society, owing to divergent missions. These roles may explain some of the differences in their admissions criteria. Historically, elite universities in the United States have been more "socially embedded"—that is, committed to making contributions to civic and social life—compared with the "socially buffered" model of Oxford and Cambridge as "distant from society and linked to high centers of canonical knowledge."[111] As long ago as 1930 Abraham Flexner contrasted the European university model, dominated by elite research and separation from society, with the American model of universities catering to civic needs such as teacher education, business education, and teaching undergraduates.[112] During the nineteenth century the US government passed two Morrill Acts providing federal land to start state colleges, which at that time focused on vocational research and training. In addition, at the turn of the twentieth century many US universities established professional schools, such as Teachers College at Columbia University, Wharton School of Business at the University of Pennsylvania, and Harvard Business School. During the same period Stanford University was founded, with a mission calling for "service to the children of California."[113] This period marks a point of departure from elite British universities, which maintained their separation from civic life.[114] Oxford's model in particular was to be a center for intellectual development for future leaders from aristocratic families.[115] Although Oxford has slowly become more influenced by civil society since becoming completely publicly funded in 1962, it still remains less so than US universities.[116] Indeed, admissions officers at elite US universities explain their goal as selecting students who will go on to make a strong impact on the world, while Oxford admissions tutors talk about selecting students who will perform best in the tutorial system of teaching.[117] American universities' interest in a civic role may promote attention to opportunities available to applicants and attention to diversity in evaluations of merit, while elite British universities' emphasis on building an elite outside society may explain their attention to subject-specific merit not calibrated to personal circumstances. Of course, the different roles of admissions decision makers—faculty at Oxford and professional admissions officers in the United States—also plays a role. Students who already have strong skills and content knowledge make faculty work in teaching easier, while professional admissions officers often come to that role with goals of promoting inclusion.

Investigating Students' Conceptions
of Merit, Race, and Inequality

To investigate how students make sense of merit, race, and inequality, I decided to talk with a lot of them. I wanted to avoid students who might feel bitter about not gaining entrée to any of their top college choices, which for whites makes affirmative action an easy target. In other words, I wanted to hear from students who had not (yet) experienced a major competitive setback that they could blame on racial preferences, because I wanted to see how winners would make sense of the system as it is, especially when confronted with the inequality it produces. Hence I decided to interview students at top colleges. I wondered, When white students don't feel personally affected by affirmative action, do they support it, or do their group identities as white still shape their views, as researchers have found among ordinary Americans?[118] If they do support affirmative action, what justification do they express, and what does that tell us about their understandings of race?

I started with Harvard, whose name connotes excellence, exclusivity, and achievement to many around the world. At Harvard, I compared white students with racial minorities. White students are the traditional elite in the United States, and on elite campuses they are much more likely than students of color to come from wealthy families and have parents who are graduates of elite colleges.[119] In contrast, black students historically have led protest movements on campus to demand changes such as increased enrollment of black students and inclusion of African American history and culture in the curriculum. Also, black and Latino students have always been underrepresented on elite college campuses in the United States, apart from historically black colleges. Given their underrepresentation and the potential personal and group benefits of affirmative action, we might expect black (and Latino) students to have different views than their white peers. For their part, Asian Americans historically aligned themselves with underrepresented minorities on college campuses, but today they have ended up at the center of criticism of affirmative action. Some claim that affirmative action harms Asian Americans through an Asian quota system,[120] assuming a zero-sum number of seats for minority students in which fewer seats for Asian students means more for blacks and Latinos. In addition, Asian Americans in the United States have experienced greater social mobility than blacks and Latinos, as measured by residential segregation, household income, educational attainment, and even intermarriage.[121] Still, Asian Americans do experience racial discrimination, and anti-Asian sentiment on college campuses is growing.[122] For these reasons, Asian Americans may have unique perspectives, different from both underrepresented minority and white peers. Overall, minority students provided an important contrast to white students in the United States, given the prominence of race on campus, not just related to admissions.

As I considered how the college experience shapes students' perspectives on merit and race, I realized this depends on what the campus is like. Brown University is very similar to Harvard. Both are New England Ivy League universities, with admittance rates well under 10 percent. They also share a history of affirmative action and race-related institutions on campus. However, the universities differ in their approaches to diversity. This made for an ideal comparison, because I could more easily draw conclusions about the influence of those diversity-related differences if other aspects of the colleges were similar. Harvard's programs and policies related to diversity emphasize racial integration and the positive impact on *all* students of life on a racially diverse campus. Brown's programs, in contrast, focus on minority students and emphasize an approach that lays bare the roots of racial inequality in American society. I wondered how these distinct approaches would shape student perspectives. As on the Harvard campus, at Brown students of diverse racial backgrounds were interviewed.

The third comparison I make in this book is between American students and British students. While the United States and Britain share many qualities, especially related to their economic and political systems, elite universities take on different roles in the two societies, as I described earlier. In addition, the civil rights movement shaped social policies and social understandings of race in the United States, and the absence of a similar movement in Britain means that race plays a different role and holds different meanings in British society. The combination of different social roles for elite universities and a lack of a race-based social movement means that British universities have very few diversity-related organizations and programs beyond ethnically defined student groups, and no affirmative action. This made for an intriguing comparison. I do not see these elite universities as microcosms of their respective countries, or even as microcosms of educational institutions or universities overall in the United States and Britain. I recognize, for example, that most K–12 schools in the United States do not have the same supports for diversity, even if multiculturalism has become an important focus for some of them.[123] Rather, I see these elite universities as sites for symbolic meaning making around merit and race. The universities hold symbolic value not only for their students, but also in the wider society. They are especially important for our understanding of meritocracy, because many see admission to those universities as the ultimate demonstration of merit.

In Britain, given that almost all racial minorities are immigrants and their descendants, I compared white, British-born students having British-born parents with British-born students having immigrant parents—the immigrant second generation.[124] Discourse on inclusion and bias in Britain more commonly centers on ethnicity rather than on race, in part because of dramatic differences within race groups in measures of success like educational attainment and household income. For example, British Indian students outperform whites on the national exams at age sixteen, while British Pakistani students are a low-performing group.[125] All the British-born students with British-born parents we interviewed were white, hence I simply call these students white throughout the book.[126] Among the immigrant second generation, we interviewed only students who had at least one parent born outside the European Union. All but one second-generation student identified as nonwhite or "mixed"—these fourteen students had at least one parent from somewhere in Africa, the Middle East, or Asia. Analia, the one child of immigrants who identified as white, had one British-born parent and one parent born in South America. Throughout the book I call these children of immigrants second-generation. Appendix A provides details about every respondent, including racial identity, field of study, and type of high school attended (public, private, or, in Britain, grammar).

I sent doctoral students out in search of undergraduates to interview at Harvard, Oxford, and Brown between 2009 and 2011.[127] We recruited students through e-mail messages to all non–first-year students living in a limited number of residential dorms on each campus. The message explained that the project compared the university experiences of students at elite universities in the United States and Britain, with a focus on their perspectives on a variety of issues, including diversity. At Harvard students were recruited through one residential house. At the end of their first year students at Harvard are randomly assigned to houses of 350 to 500 students.[128] At Brown I recruited students through e-mails to sixteen residential halls (approximately 400 students total); none of these halls were the themed living spaces at Brown, which include fraternities, sororities, Hispanic House-dedicated to Spanish language and Hispanic cultures, and Harambee House-dedicated to African cultures. By recruiting from a limited group of randomly assigned students, I hoped to gain a microcosm of students on each campus. Of course, the word diversity in the recruitment message may have attracted students more sympathetic to diversity and deterred those more critical or ambivalent, making the student perspectives reported in this book more liberal than the average on the campuses. However, because I was interested in perspectives most sympathetic to diversity, just as I decided to interview students at top universities who probably hadn't experienced rejection in college admissions that they could attribute to race, so too I felt that any liberal bias among respondents would demonstrate the liberal perspective on campus. I was not focused on portraying students strongly critical of diversity, given the myriad popular portrayals of those students as well as a recent excellent book by Amy Binder and Kate Wood describing campus conservatives.[129]

At both US universities, residential life assistants, who were gradu-

TABLE 1. Interview Respondents

United States	Harvard	Brown	Total
White	23	23	46
Minority[a]	15	15	30
Asian American	6	7	13
Black	7	5	12
Latino	2	4	6
Total underrepresented minority (black, Latino)	9	8	17
TOTAL	38	38	76

United Kingdom	Oxford		
White, UK-born parents	52		
Second-generation (foreign-born parent[s])	15		
TOTAL	67		

[a] Numbers of subgroups do not add up to fifteen because some students identified with more than one group.

ate students living among the younger students, sent the initial recruiting e-mail to students in their dorms. The recruitment message told students they would be paid $20 for their time. All students who agreed to be interviewed were included in the study, and we tried to recruit others who might initially have been less inclined by sending follow-up messages to potential participants. After being interviewed, students were asked to pass along the interviewer's details to one acquaintance living in the same dorm. White men were slightly underrepresented in the original US sample, so I sent a message specifically asking white men to sign up, a successful strategy for broadening the pool. All together, in the United States seventy-six students participated in interviews for this book, including forty-six white students and thirty students of color. Among the thirty students of color, seventeen were black or Latino and thirteen were Asian American (see table 1).[130]

Compared with their presence on campus, black and Latino students are overrepresented in this sample, because I wanted to make sure I heard from enough of them to get a full picture of their experiences on campus. Even though over 10 percent of students on both campuses come from abroad, I decided to limit the study to American-born students, to understand the American experience of diversity along with how the college experience shaped their perspectives.

At Oxford, students were recruited through e-mails sent to all the students at two of the university's thirty colleges (residential houses where students spend all three years, which typically include 250 to 450 undergraduates each).[131] In an attempt to hear the perspectives of "typical" Oxford students, I targeted colleges that were neither among the oldest, most traditional of Oxford's colleges nor among the newest; the colleges were also not among the top- or lowest-performing in terms of students' grades on universitywide exams. The initial e-mail was sent by a senior professor at one of the colleges and a dean at the other. Both urged students to participate. Like US students, British students were paid (£15) and were asked after the interview to forward our details to one peer living in the same dorm, in the hope that others would sign up to be interviewed. All together, 52 white students and 15 second-generation students were interviewed at Oxford. This is an oversampling of second-generation students, because as at Harvard and Brown I wanted to make sure I had the perspectives of a quorum of nontraditional students. After the initial round of interviews, we specifically recruited more second-generation respondents.

To assess how similar my sample was to the overall student bodies at the universities, I compared students' fields of study, types of high school attended (private or public), and parents' levels of education with published data on the undergraduate populations at Harvard, Brown, and Oxford. I found the percentages between my samples and the university percentages to be similar, bolstering my confidence that I was hearing from a good mix of students on campus (see table 2).

Still, while my recruitment techniques did attempt to capture a diverse range of student perspectives, the sampling is not meant to be a stratified or random sample. My goal was to get a qualitative understanding of how students think about merit, race, and inequality. (To learn more about the particulars of the research, see appendix B; appendix C contains the questions we asked students.) My goal throughout this book has been to paint a sympathetic portrait of all students. As I read and reread the interview transcriptions, I constantly asked myself, "What might lead to this perspective?" Inspired by my colleague Sara Lawrence-Lightfoot's method of looking for goodness in her interviews, I too searched for goodness.[132] This led me to see the confusion many students experienced, the logics through which they made sense of the world, and the dilemmas they faced. I know that the stories I tell will come across to some as too sympathetic to one group and not enough to another. In particular, some may find this book too

TABLE 2. Interview Respondents Compared to Their Campuses[a]

	Harvard Overall	Brown Overall	US Students Interviewed	Oxford Students Overall	Oxford Students Interviewed
Percentage of students with both parents with no BA degree[b]	15	15	14	—	30
Percentage private school graduates[c]	30	29	27	44 (another 18 grammar school graduates)	36 (another 27 grammar school graduates)
Field of Study[d]					
Percentage humanities	20	23	20	36	34
Percentage social sciences	52	44	55	18	27
Percentage hard sciences (including medicine at Oxford)	28	33	24	45	39

[a] As much as possible, I use data from the early 2010s rather than the most recent data, to overlap with the years of this research.

[b] Brown University Office of College Admission 2012; Harvard College Admissions and Financial Aid 2015. I could not find information about the percentage of Oxford students who are first-generation university students. In Britain, school type (private versus state-sponsored) is frequently used as a measure of disadvantage.

[c] Brown University Office of College Admission 2012; Fitzsimmons 2009b; University of Oxford 2015b.

[d] Brown University Office of Institutional Research 2013; Harvard University Office of Institutional Research 2013; Oxford University Academic Administration Division 2015.

sympathetic to whites' lack of reflexivity around race and not critical enough of the ways white students perpetuate white privilege. Others may feel I am too sympathetic to the concerns of minority students and lack sympathy for white students' perspectives. If I make most readers uncomfortable at some point in the book, I will conclude that I have been successful in a sympathetic rendering of student voices of all backgrounds.

Overview of the Book

I discuss the US case in chapters 2 to 5, then bring in the British case in chapters 6 and 7. In chapter 2 I discuss US students' understandings of the role race plays in society. These race frames, as I call them, both influence what happens in higher education and are influenced by such experiences. As we'll see, white students in the United States fre-quently employ a color-blindness frame, and many more whites and also most students of color employ a diversity frame through the col-lege experience. A minority of students in the United States, many of them students of color involved with diversity-related programming on Brown's campus, see race through a power analysis frame. These race frames set the stage for understanding how the universities influ-ence students and how students conceptualize merit.

In chapter 3 I turn to how college experiences influence students' race frames. I highlight differences between students active in diver-sity programming on the Brown campus and others at Brown and at Harvard. I show that embedded in university practices and policies related to diversity are important decisions that shape students' under-standings of diversity on campus as well as in society. I identify two approaches: Brown's power analysis approach, demonstrated most prominently through the work of the Third World Center[133] and the Third World Transition Program, and Harvard's diversity approach, emphasized through Diversity Dialogues and the work of the Harvard Foundation for Intercultural and Race Relations.

In chapter 4 I address US students' understandings of merit in ad-missions, with special attention to considerations of race. Students stress the collective merit of their cohort as well as the need to cali-brate evaluations of merit. I describe the *diversity bargain*, whereby white students in the United States reluctantly agree with affirmative action insofar as it benefits themselves, most commonly through a diverse learning environment. Students who hold the diversity bar-gain believe that minority students admitted under affirmative action should racially integrate rather than participate in ethnic- and race-specific organizations (the *integration imperative*) and that affirmative action should not deprive whites of success in competitive processes. Students of color do not feel obligated by a diversity bargain to inte-grate with their white peers; still, they too extol the benefits of cam-pus diversity.

Chapter 5 details how US students navigate the complex yet sensi-tive racial terrain on campus, given their beliefs about merit and the race frames they hold. Overall, speaking and behaving in ways that help them avoid being accused of racism are high priorities, given that they see not being racist as a moral imperative. However, this desire to be seen as racially enlightened is fraught with confusion and contestation over what constitutes racism. White students fear the accusation "that's racist" in discussions about difference, while students of color also experience frustration and confusion in many campus experiences related to race.

In chapters 6 and 7 I turn to British students. In chapter 6 I analyze British students' race frames and conceptions of merit. They tend to hold a color-blindness frame and to espouse individualist, absolute conceptions of merit. Oxford students do not believe it is Oxford's role to consider the opportunities an applicant has had. Rather, they believe evaluations should be absolute: color-blind and class-blind. Still, like their US counterparts, Oxford students reproduce the admissions policies of their universities in their conceptions of merit, legitimating their own status as winners of the admissions competition. So, even while US and British students express different conceptions of fairness in admissions, both reproduce their universities' definition of merit. Unlike many students of color in the US, second-generation students in Britain expressed perspectives on merit similar to those of their white peers.

Chapter 7 addresses race on Oxford's campus. I found that the boundaries of moral behavior and words pertaining to race and diversity differ between Britain and the United States. So too does the referee—that is, the person who defines the moral boundaries. In Britain, where the diversity frame is absent, white students frequently reject accusations of racism, claiming that minorities are "playing the race card" or lack a sense of humor. Second-generation students at Oxford are also less critical of race-related issues on campus than are students of color in the United States.

Last, in the conclusion I bring together the book's findings on merit, race, and inequality. If elite universities are successful at imprinting their institutional logics on their students' definitions of merit and the worthiness of an elite education, what does this portend for our future leaders' work on inequality and race? Does elite higher education, with its emphasis on diversity in the United States and color-blind reward for merit in Britain, become a vehicle for reducing or for reproducing social inequality?

A Note on Terminology

College and university: In Britain, education toward a bachelor's degree is always called "university" education. "College" in Britain signifies the two years after secondary education, before pursuing a bachelor's degree. Students normally attend college in Britain during ages sixteen to eighteen; it is roughly equivalent to grades eleven and twelve in the United States. Adding further confusion, Oxford and Cambridge's residential houses are called "colleges"; every undergraduate attending the universities belongs to one of the colleges. Hence, when writing about Britain I always refer to "university" education. However, in the United States "university" excludes private liberal arts colleges that award bachelor's degrees only, many of which are considered top colleges in the United States, such as Swarthmore and Amherst. So when writing about bachelor's degree education in the United States I frequently use "college." To avoid confusion, when writing about both together, I use "university." Also, when writing specifically about Brown or Harvard I sometimes use "university," given that both are indeed universities.

American: As a former member of the faculty at the University of London's Institute for the Study of the Americas, where colleagues studied North and South America, I am well aware that "American" signifies origins across the two continents. However, in the United States and elsewhere "American" has come to mean "of the United States." Given the lack of an elegant adjective form of "United States," I use "American" as an imperfect alternative. Hence, throughout this book I use "American" and "of the United States" interchangeably.

AMERICAN STUDENTS

TWO

MAKING SENSE OF RACE

I have a dream that my four little children will one day live in a nation where they will not be judged by the color of their skin but by the content of their character.

MARTIN LUTHER KING JR.

The existence of racial and ethnic diversity in institutions of higher education is vital to [our] efforts to hire and maintain a diverse workforce, and to employ individuals of all backgrounds who have been educated and trained in a diverse environment. . . . Such a workforce is important to [our] continued success in the global marketplace.

BRIEF FOR AMICI CURIAE, 65 Fortune 500
Companies, in Grutter v. Bollinger 539 U.S. 306 (2003)

Many schoolchildren in the United States today learn in class about the extraordinary leadership of Martin Luther King Jr. They learn that King helped many political leaders and ordinary Americans see the injustice of racial segregation, leading to changes in the legal system that ended legal segregation and solved our nation's racial problem. King hoped that in the future black children like his own would be judged not "by the color of their skin but by the content of their character." This vision structures the lesson about race that most children learn before college: that recognition of racial differences inevitably leads to discrimination, so to stop discrimination we should stop paying attention to race. This color-blind vision, as I show later in the book, shapes many students' conceptions of merit, and in particular their perspectives on the role race should play in admissions.

But there is another message about race, especially as American youth enter college, that asks them to pay close attention to race. A group of Fortune 500 companies, quoted above, told the US Supreme Court in a 2006 landmark affirmative action case that racial diversity is essential in college. They argued that a workforce "educated and trained in a diverse environment . . . is important to [our] continued success in the global marketplace." In this framing of the role of race in society, we must pay close attention to race, because it will help us think in new ways and improve our business acumen. This perspective requires diversity in college, aided in part by affirmative action in admissions, to make all students more competitive in a globalized economy. Similarly, a large group of former high-ranking officers and civilian leaders in the US Armed Forces wrote an amicus brief for the same case, arguing that racial diversity is essential to the military's work and its ability to ensure national security.[1]

Each of these understandings of the role race plays in society — race frames, as I call them — has implications for conceptions of merit. They lay the foundation for students' perspectives on whether their universities should consider race in admissions, and for how students explain the underrepresentation of black students on campus. In other words, they are part and parcel of conceptions of merit, and consequently a discussion of students' race frames necessarily precedes my discussion of their views on merit. Under a strict reading of King's words quoted above, one might believe that merit should be judged without attention to race. Indeed, many conservatives have used the "I Have a Dream" speech to suggest that King, like them, was against affirmative action.[2] (King's vision was much more complex, and he did in fact support affirmative action.[3]) On the other hand, the Fortune 500 companies are arguing strongly for affirmative action in admissions.

In this chapter I show how students in the United States conceptualize race, and chapter 3 deals with how college experiences shape those race frames. These chapters set the stage for the discussion of students' conceptions of merit in chapter 4. Race frames shape the way students explain the underrepresentation of black students on campus, and what role, if any, they think their universities should play in changing that underrepresentation.

Race Frames

We don't realize it, but we hold a variety of frames—lenses through which we "observe," "interpret," and respond to social phenomena—and those frames shape how we understand the world and act within it.[4] Frames make certain aspects of the world prominent and obscure others.[5] For example, Mario Small found that seeing a neighborhood through different frames can lead to different levels of civic engagement.[6] Residents of a Boston neighborhood in Small's research who saw the neighborhood as steeped in a strong sense of community and a rich history participated much more than those who thought of it as "the projects." Of course, frames are most often implicit rather than explicit—few of us consider our views and say to ourselves, "Today I'm using a color-blindness frame." But this is precisely why naming these perspectives is so valuable. Even if they are invariably reductive, identifying race frames is a way to make explicit what is often implicit and even unconscious. It allows us to see the conceptions of race we use.

Frames often differ across national boundaries. For example, in Brazil racial identities are fluid and vary according to an individual's level of education, location in the country, age, and skin color.[7] In contrast, in the United States, based on our historical one-drop rule, someone with a small amount of African ancestry may identify as black. Frames in society often shift over time. For example, two generations ago many Americans held biological conceptions of race, but those have waned over time. Beyond meanings shared within a society, we know less about how the frames of *individuals* change over time and how organizational contexts shape those frames.[8] An individual's frames can be influenced by myriad domains of social life, including but not limited to family, schooling, college cultures, national histories related to race, and racial identities. Recent research has shown how the military,[9] the workplace,[10] and schools[11] produce racial meanings for individuals. In most schools, for example, adults avoid talking about race as much as possible, which can lead to a color-blind perspective among students; Mica Pollock argues that this silence reproduces inequality.[12] Universities too play a role in shaping race frames, as we'll see.

But first, in this chapter I take stock of how students on the Harvard and Brown campuses think about the role of race in society and how their college experiences affect those views. Students' race frames both influence what happens in higher education and are influenced by it. Just as with so many aspects of life, each of us as an individual makes sense of race from a vast stew of different and often contradictory ingredients. However, as my interviews demonstrate, some understandings are shared among students on the Harvard and Brown campuses. I ferret out the various race frames that students used in interviews to make sense of race-related experiences and observations. In doing so, I show that individuals can hold multiple, sometimes contradictory, frames. I identify four race frames common in American society — color-blindness, diversity, power analysis, and culture of poverty — and discuss their prevalence among white and minority students at Harvard and Brown. While all four frames are present in the United States and on campus, the regularity of their appearance differs between the two.

"I Barely Notice Race": The Color-Blindness Frame

I start with the frame that assumes race does not and should not play a role in society: *color-blindness*. In the recent past, color-blindness and its twin, postracialism,[13] have garnered much discussion. The color-blindness frame suggests that today race has little social meaning, owing to equal rights legislation, the end of legal segregation, the decline of overtly racist attitudes, and overall growing prosperity for many black Americans. Sometimes a belief that race *should* not matter leads to this color-blindness frame — that is, individuals attempt to make it so by behaving as if it were. This desire for a particular meaning makes color-blindness an *ideology* for those who hope to achieve the demise of the social meaning of race by ignoring it.[14] While color-blindness is most obvious among white Americans, some black conservatives also espouse it, especially as an ideology.[15] For some, color-blindness represents a belief in liberal individualism[16] and a welcome emancipation of all Americans from centuries of racism, culminating in the election of President Barack Obama. President Obama's election confirmed for many that race no longer shapes social life in meaningful ways.

However, many take a more critical view of color-blindness, suggesting that it stems not from a shift away from racism, but rather from a transformation of explicit racism into a more implicit and subtle version that props up continued racial inequality.[17] While white Americans often claim a color-blind attitude to justify their dislike of race-based policies, survey data reveal that whites who disagree with race-based policies to enact equality, such as busing to promote school integration, or affirmative action, are more likely to hold negative feelings toward black Americans than those who agree with the policies. Further, their disagreement seems to originate in negative attitudes toward blacks rather than in beliefs in liberal individualism; scholars have labeled these beliefs "symbolic racism" or "laissez-faire racism," highlighting the changing nature of racism in the United States from overt to more subtle forms.[18]

When students talked about race as being irrelevant, or about their attempts to make it so, I interpreted their race frame as color-blindness. About half of white and Asian American students we interviewed in the United States (twenty-seven students) explicitly employed a color-blindness frame, in contrast to just one student who was black or Latino. Lissa, a white sophomore at Brown, said to her white interviewer, "No one looks at you—like I look at you, [and] I don't think, 'Oh, this is a white person.' . . . That's definitely not the first thing that I see. And I don't think a large amount of the people here see it at all." Similarly, Pat, another white sophomore at Brown, when asked how events on campus have shaped his views on multiculturalism and diversity, said, "A lot of the students here are pretty race blind, . . . in the sense that I attend a lot of events that are filled with people of every color, of every race. . . . And I barely even notice it until I consciously try and think about it. And it's not pointed out."

Lissa and Pat study very different disciplines—Lissa's concentration[19] is commerce while Pat's is media studies—but they share a race frame. For both Lissa and Pat, not seeing race seems to be the morally superior way of "seeing" (or not seeing) it, and both seem pleased to report that they and their peers generally do not notice race. Megan, when asked if racial inequality is a problem, expressed the view that "racial problems" no longer exist in the United States: "I don't really think there is too much of racial problems left in this day and age."

For many white students, beliefs about the end of race-based inequality are compounded by a lack of exposure to racial diversity while growing up. Indeed, coming of age in the United States is frequently a segregated experience, and residential segregation has consequences for the demographics of schools in the United States: 74

percent of black youth and 80 percent of Latino youth attend majority minority schools, while the typical white student attends a school that is 75 percent white.[20] Even within diverse schools, students are often tracked into different classes with varying levels of academic rigor, commonly leading to racial segregation within the school.[21] White students attending elite universities in particular tend to attend high schools that are not racially diverse.[22] White students we interviewed in the United States came from high schools that had, on average, over 80 percent white students, to campuses that were less than half white American.[23] Another way to see this transition for white students: in the neighborhoods these white students lived in before coming to college, the median percentage of black and Latino residents combined was 8 percent; at Brown and Harvard, black and Latino students combined made up 16 percent and 15 percent, respectively, of the student body. Hence the average white student we talked with, when moving from high school to college, moved to an environment with about half as many whites and twice as many blacks and Latinos. These early experiences may make white students more drawn to a color-blind frame.

While most of the previous scholarship analyzes color-blindness among white Americans, I found that nearly half of Asian American students also employed a color-blindness frame. One such student was Shuyi. When I asked whether Harvard should consider race in admissions, Shuyi said, "I think Harvard does a really good job of looking at each student individually and evaluating his or her potential and commitment to excellence based on what background they come from. Whether it should be tied to race and ethnicity per se—I don't think that's the definition of who a person is." Shuyi's experiences with poverty growing up seemed to inculcate strong beliefs about class inequality. Shuyi's parents, immigrants from China, did low-wage work; she was poised to be the first in her family to complete college, graduating soon after our interview. On a full need-based scholarship to Harvard, Shuyi spoke passionately about the generous financial aid Harvard gives to poor, working-class, and middle-class students. Shuyi hoped that powerful Harvard graduates would lobby for changes to reduce class inequality in the United States, especially related to education, so that more children could have the opportunity to consider Harvard as a viable option for college. Perhaps Shuyi's deep understanding of class, rooted in her experiences growing up, led her to a color-blindness approach that favored class over race. When asked about inequality, she said, "People should be paid a living wage. There are a lot of poor white people too. It's not about race. It's about class." Shuyi seemed to understand the problems of class inequality in the United States much more than most of her peers at Harvard. Like some other students who acknowledged class inequality, she perhaps saw attention to class and race as a zero-sum assessment—that is, she prioritized class inequality, given her own class-inflected experiences. In addition, racial exclusion is not part of dominant narratives about Asian Americans in the United States, which may have prevented Shuyi from understanding the role that race, in addition to class, plays in American inequality.

Grace, the daughter of immigrants from South Korea, was a sophomore who planned to concentrate in anthropology. She worried that attention to race could reify perceptions of problems when in fact they don't exist:

> I feel like there is actually one negative thing about having all these cultural societies, these ethnic groups, [which is] that in trying to preserve their own cultural heritage and to promote racial reconciliation it actually brings up more this idea that there is something to be reconciled, that there are problems. . . . It also sometimes just— the heightened awareness maybe makes something out of nothing. So, like problems that weren't necessarily there now are, because of this heightened awareness of cultural diversity.

Among the white and Asian American students employing a color-blindness frame, three acknowledged that racial discrimination in the past continues to have lingering influence. For example, Hannah, a white senior, told us, "The way I see it is just this history of absolutely insane racism that has now sunk minorities into . . . these holes of poverty. So I really see it more as historic." Hannah later explained her perspective on racial inequality: "I don't think that what's keeping minorities down now is so much racism as the fact that they are still at the bottom of the socioeconomic status hierarchy because of centuries of racism." These students, however, insisted on a color-blindness frame, with the belief that middle-class African Americans are not worse off than middle-class whites, and also that poor whites experience the same disadvantages as poor blacks. While this is a hopeful view, research tells us that this understanding is misguided because, for example, poverty affects families over generations, so poor African American families are more likely to have lived in poverty for multiple generations than poor white families, and middle-class African Americans live in neighborhoods with greater poverty surrounding them than do working-class whites.[24]

Overall, the color-blindness frame resonates with a broader movement in the United States to ignore the role that race plays in society, despite considerable evidence to the contrary seen in, to cite a few of numerous examples, racial disparities in areas of education from school discipline to where students attend college.[25] In addition, a growing literature on white racial identities finds that whites often ignore the role race plays in their own position in society, whiteness being the unmarked race.[26] This color-blindness frame, as I show later in the book, shapes some students' beliefs about merit. Sometimes the frame is employed to question attention to a diverse student body, and at others it is used to counter the notion that black and Latino Americans face adversity owing to race.

"The Essence of Harvard Life": College and the Diversity Frame

A second frame—what I call a *diversity* frame—views race as a cultural identity that shapes individuals' worldviews and cultural practices in positive ways. One result of the US civil rights movement was an increased acceptance of ethnic and racial diversity and attention to the positive aspects of non-Western cultures.[27] These shifts in perception led to celebration of cultural differences between race and ethnic groups, sometimes labeled multiculturalism.[28] In contrast to the color-blindness frame, which insists on viewing people as individuals, the diversity frame views people as members of racial and ethnic *groups*, which are assumed to influence their cultural practices, ways of understanding the world, and tastes. I call this frame a diversity frame because it emphasizes the diversity of perspectives, behaviors, and cultural practices that result from racial and ethnic plurality in society. Those who employ a diversity frame commonly emphasize the importance of learning from that diversity.[29] While the diversity frame can be found in various pockets across US society,[30] it is particularly marked on elite college campuses, given the history of race-related campus activism and the subsequent attention to diversity as a crucial part of campus life.

When students recognized group differences by race or ethnicity and talked about diversity in positive ways, I labeled them as holding a diversity frame. Most students employed this frame, including 85 percent of white (thirty-nine of forty-six) and Asian American students (eleven of thirteen) and 76 percent of black and Latino students (thirteen of seventeen). Also, most students had attended at least one diversity-related event on campus (thirty-seven of forty-six white students and all but two students of color). If not confirming the value placed on diversity, the frequent attendance at diversity-related events at least demonstrates the prevalence of and interest in diversity-related programming, even among white students. When asked how diversity affects student life, Jean, a white senior concentrating in social studies, said, "Diversity is at the essence of Harvard life . . . every day here is just about, like, millions of activities by different groups. I think [Harvard] is the place where cultures are always coming together and people are . . . doing things with their own culture but also exposing everyone else at Harvard to it."

Diversity was seen as part of the learning process at both universities. Students believed in the educational value of diversity and frequently brought it up. Thomas, a white sophomore studying biology at Harvard, reported that "diversity is really how you learn here. I mean, you can take as many classes as you want, but your peers are your best teachers." Brandon, an African American sophomore studying commerce, said of the student body at Brown,

> I usually try to hang around with a lot of people from different places, because I want to learn about their experiences and where they come from. . . . If you're open to different kinds of things, they're around for you to try them. You can go and see the Asian type of festival and you can embrace it and you can learn about stuff like that. And if you wanted to go see something else, then you could on the same day. There's a lot of opportunity for you to embrace that diversity and learn from it.

Over 90 percent of students in the United States within all race groups reported that racial diversity on campus had a positive impact on their college experience. In addition, a significant number of students on both campuses specifically took classes in African American studies or ethnic studies, including half of the black students, one in three white students, and two Asian American students.[31]

As I analyzed students' discussions of race, I noticed that many spoke of the diversity frame developing during their college years. White students in particular frequently contrasted the segregated neighborhoods where they came of age, where there was little discussion of race, with their racially diverse colleges, where support for cross-racial conversations was pervasive and the institution prompted an awareness of racial difference. Many specifically described how the shift to a diverse college campus also shifted the way they saw race. Indeed, for many college was the first time they experienced a racially diverse environment. Here is James, a white junior studying international relations at Brown:

> Coming here, I really have a lot more respect for multiculturalism. I mean, as far as diversity goes, like when people said, "Brown has a lot of diversity," I didn't really care about that. I [thought it was] just a college. And since I've been here, I think it's really important. . . . I think that actually experiencing other cultures as opposed to experiencing whatever passes for multiculturalism in like your all-white little preschool or whatever, has actually been influential on me.

During his interview James highlighted his two college summers spent in France as well as his roommates, some white and some Asian, as influencing his view. He also attended a Third World Center workshop at Brown, in which he discussed "notion[s] of whiteness," called White People Talking. This workshop helped inform James's views on what it means to be white in US society and led him to seek more opportunities on campus to engage in similar conversations across different racial groups. Although James grew up in a town that is nearly 90 percent white, he explained his transition as a shift away from the influence of his father, whom he described as conservative on some policy issues.

Kyle, another white junior at Brown, was especially affected by diversity-related experiences on campus. He compared his childhood in a predominantly white suburb with his experiences in college, which have shaped his identity:

[I'm] going through an identity crisis right now. . . . Before I came [to college], I never thought about . . . issues of race and diversity and all the things that that entails. And since coming here, it makes you think more. . . . I mean, I go to all these workshops. And it's stuff I would never have been exposed to.

Presumably the experiences Kyle would have missed stem both from the workshops he has attended and from the diverse peers he has encountered at Brown.

Elizabeth, a white junior at Harvard, spoke more specifically about how diversity-related campus events, combined with her diverse peers, were shaping her views. When asked, "How have events at Harvard shaped your views on multiculturalism and diversity, if at all?" she said,

I think that they have helped me be more open. I've been to a lot of different lectures and discussions. . . . I went to one that was with someone who immigrated from Cuba. One of my block mates is Cuban, which is why I'm emphasizing the Cuban thing, because I've been exposed a lot. It was really interesting. I think it opened my eyes to the immigrant experience and fleeing a country and coming to a new country and starting over.

Aside from campus events, Elizabeth found that social events provided opportunities to imbibe diversity:

I think more so than discussions, I go to the social slash entertainment side of it. Like, going to the Apollo Night talent show, which is run by the Black Students' Association, or like this weekend I'm planning on going to see a bunch of my friends in the Irish step dancers thing.

As these quotations show, many white students' responses make it clear that they develop, or at least enhance, a diversity frame in college, owing to both the compositional diversity of the student body and the diversity culture on campus. Ellen Berrey, in *The Enigma of Diversity*, describes a process by which "diversity" became the language with which race was discussed in the United States, across various social contexts, including corporate firms, neighborhood gentrification, and higher education. In higher education, it is the only rationale for affirmative action that the US Supreme Court has consistently allowed. Students' responses make it clear that Justice Lewis Powell's opinion in the *Bakke* case, in which he declared that "the nation's future depends upon leaders trained through wide exposure to the ideas and mores of students as diverse as this Nation" lives on in the minds of students today.[32]

"Brown's Elitism Is Wrapped in White Supremacy": The Power Analysis Frame

I define a *power analysis* frame as one that views the significance of race in society according to unequal power relations between groups. In particular it emphasizes the ways power operates through racial inequality.[33] This perspective is consistent with a view of race as inherently based in group struggles for power.[34] Those who see race through this frame often come to believe that individuals should actively resist the racial ideologies and injustices they perceive, as part of the broader goal of working toward racial justice and equality. Perhaps because this frame is held by only a small minority of whites, survey researchers have not discussed it. Still, many social scientists, as well as social activists, advocate teaching a power analysis frame, sometimes calling it a "social justice" or "critical race theory" approach.[35] While black and Latino Americans overall are less likely to explain inequality as rooted in structural barriers today than they were the past,[36] I found that black and Latino students on the Brown and Harvard campuses did in fact commonly employ the power analysis frame. Nearly half (eight of seventeen) of black and Latino students we interviewed employed a power analysis frame, compared with just four whites and no Asian Americans.

At Brown, all the students of color expressing this frame had attended the Third World Transition Program (TWTP), an orientation program for students of color that espouses a power analysis frame, most explicitly through workshops on racism, sexism, colonialism, and more, as we'll see in more detail in chapter 3.[37] Imani, a black student, was one of them. She came to Brown from New York City, the daughter of two professionals, one from the United States and one Caribbean. An Africana studies major about to graduate, Imani wore clothes and jewelry of African origin. When asked whether Brown is a meritocracy in admissions, Imani said,

> Absolutely not. I want to laugh at that question so hard. If anyone said yes to this question, that would just hurt so bad. I mean, *buildings* are named after people because people's families paid, like, millions of dollars for them. The university is a corporation, and they're in the business of making money. I know we have need-blind admissions and all, but at the same time, legacy is taken into account. So as long as it's the same US system it's working on that same capitalist structure—trying to get more, get more, get more.

Imani's power analysis frame coexists with her diversity frame, which she drew on when asked how diversity has influenced campus life:

> People are coming from a lot of different places. If you're trying to get to know people other than people like you, you can learn a lot. There's a lot of dialogue. There are discussions, workshops, everything. If you wanted to, probably every day of the week you could go to some sort of event or meeting or something that's addressing the broad concept of diversity in some way. . . . It just creates broader, more truthful education. The more different kinds of people that are within a group or an institution, the more perspectives there are, the less likely it is that you're going to get one-sided stories of history, or biased accounts of the present. Because if different voices are in the conversation, there's someone there to be, like, "No, that's not how it is for me." And then you learn from that. I think diversity challenges us all to think about ourselves and to think about our prejudices and our privileges. And I think all of these things are really important for transforming society so that it's not oppressive the way that it is now.

Imani recognizes the value of diversity in the classroom. However, while most peers expressed value for diversity without acknowledging power differences, Imani alludes to diversity as leading to the inclusion of subordinate voices, or combating a "one-sided story of history or biased accounts." Imani's ultimate goal for the diversity of perspectives in dialogue is the transformation of society. She later argued that Brown's commitment to diversity, alongside its history rooted in white

privilege—and ongoing incidents of racism today—makes it a contradictory place:

> Having an institution that's simultaneously dedicated to diversity
> and also to being an elite Ivy League institution, there's a contradic-
> tion there, because the elitism that Brown represents is wrapped in
> ideas of white supremacy. So if you have a place that is about being
> elite and where we're building the new upper crust of society, and
> when that image of power is a white image, you can't truly be com-
> mitted to diversity. . . . It's a fundamental contradiction to me. So
> when issues come up on campus—like there was this huge thing
> with police brutality in, like, '06, where black males were dispro-
> portionately asked to show their ID cards on campus because BPS
> officers didn't know they belonged here. And, what does the univer-
> sity do in a situation like that? It's, like, "Oh, but we care about di-
> versity. We're so great!"

Imani forcefully claims that the university as an institution rests on
racist assumptions about who belongs. Further, while other students
wanted the university to expand its notion of who can be an elite, she
questions the compatibility of diversity goals and the desire to be exclusive and elite. Imani attended Brown's Third World Transition Program and attributed much of the development of her political awareness to it, though she had also thought deeply about issues of race
well before coming to college. While Imani's view that diversity and
meritocracy are incompatible may be an outlier among her peers, it
reveals the intimate relation between merit and race in the minds of
many students.

Some black and Latino students at Harvard also employed a power
analysis frame, even if theirs tended to be less radical than Imani's.
Sophie, a confident senior studying folklore, who identifies as multiracial—her mother is from the Caribbean and her father is white
American—used a power analysis frame to explain her view on admission to Harvard: "I think they should definitely take into account
that institutional racism and other kinds of–isms are going to prevent
people who are not from the majority from having equal opportunities in life in general, and I think we should try to rectify that." Sophie's
light skin tone meant that others often assume she is white. This sub-
jected her to more overtly racist comments than most of her minority

peers, perhaps pushing her toward a power analysis frame. When asked if she ever experienced racial discrimination, she said, "a lot of discrimination . . . is saying racist shit around me and then assuming that I'm going to laugh along because I'm white. I've had people say pretty hurtful stuff to my face, but again most of it is inadvertently hurtful."

Four white students also employed a power analysis frame.[38] Kyle, quoted above for the strong influence on him of his college experiences with diversity, countered the criticism that affirmative action unfairly advantages students of color by discussing his own life as resulting from racial advantage:

> People say [affirmative action] is an unfair advantage. But basically for twelve years before college I had an unfair advantage. White people have had an unfair advantage their entire life in the United States. So it's not like it puts—it's not even equalizing. I had twelve years of a leg up.

Jeremy stood out among white respondents for his radical criticisms of Harvard, of American society, and of capitalism. For Jeremy, affirmative action is not about poverty, and it need not be:

> I think [affirmative action] can take the focus off the class thing. I think it doesn't solve the class problem, but it's not intended to, so it's not really fair to critique it for that. . . . It is a program to combat racial discrimination and I think it does that. I don't think it's an anti-poverty program, so that's a separate thing.

When asked whether he had witnessed racial discrimination, Jeremy described situations in which he felt someone's actions were racist but could not prove it. He went on to say,

> Really, where I see racism is structural. Racism that matters is like all the schools in Chicago where black children go to school are falling apart. That's racism that matters much more than that guy not holding the door [for my black friends].

Jeremy's power analysis frame makes racially unequal schooling visible as a form of racism to him, unlike other students.

While the views of Jeremy and other students with a power analysis frame may sound controversial, this frame has been a topic of scholarly discussion for decades. For example, the whole field of critical legal studies demonstrates how the US legal system rests on white privilege and the oppression of African Americans.[39] In addition, scholars of social reproduction such as Pierre Bourdieu and Michael Young, the scholar who coined "meritocracy" as a satirical term, have argued that meritocracy serves as a tool to legitimate the reproduction of social class (and, by extension, in the United States, race), in contemporary societies in which the overt reproduction of class is no longer accepted as legitimate.[40]

"When Your Culture Doesn't Emphasize Education": The Culture of Poverty Frame

Five white students (11 percent) and one Asian American student expressed what I call a *culture of poverty* frame, which suggests that minority disadvantage stems from cultural characteristics such as a lack of a strong work ethic or a disregard for marriage. This frame shares with the diversity frame a cultural understanding of racial groups, but it diverges in its negative assessment of nondominant cultures and their impact on life chances. Given the negative assessment, some have labeled this frame "cultural racism."[41] Samuel Huntington employs this frame in his account of Latinos in the United States, *Who Are We*, suggesting that Latino culture challenges the dominant American culture rooted in the Protestant work ethic.[42] Research on the racial attitudes of ordinary Americans shows that the culture of poverty frame is associated with opposition to race-related efforts to reduce racial inequality.[43] Not surprisingly, adherents to the culture of poverty frame also typically argue that affirmative action is wrong, because they see the policy as rewarding minorities for negative cultural characteristics.[44]

Interestingly, all but one of the students espousing a culture of poverty frame also expressed belief in the positive impact of diversity in social life.[45] Orin, a white junior studying social studies, was one such student. When asked to explain racial inequality, she cited "cultural backgrounds." Orin explained her view: "You're taught to do what your parents teach you to do, so with my parents it was always like, you go to school, you do your homework, you work hard. . . . But if your culture doesn't emphasize as much education or something, then [you are] less motivated to go to school." This culture of poverty frame came after Orin's more positive approach to affirmative action, resting on a diversity frame. She told us that the university should "definitely" consider race and ethnicity in admissions, because it "adds as much to the class as a world-class piano player." Just as many students employed the diversity and color-blindness frames in response to different questions, so Orin employs both of these seemingly contradictory frames.

Jeff expressed fear that others would take offense at his culture of poverty perspective. When asked how to explain the underrepresentation of black students on campus, he said, "I feel like someone's going to jump at me and gnaw my neck right now. But I feel like it might have a lot to do with like cultural differences." As we will see in chapter 5, this fear of others' taking offense shapes many students' conversations about race on campus.

Overall, white students expressing a culture of poverty perspective came from towns whose populations averaged 5 percent black. While this is not much different from their peers at Harvard and Brown who did not employ a culture of poverty frame and hence cannot be understood as the *cause*, it does confirm that the frame does not result from sustained contact with black Americans during childhood.[46]

* * *

Frames are lenses through which we filter information and make sense of the world. Students employed the color-blindness, diversity, power analysis, and culture of poverty frames in response to different questions; they were not mutually exclusive.[47] In fact, four students each employed three—the diversity, color-blindness, and culture of poverty frames—in the same interview. And over half of students employed two frames at different moments in our interviews. So, even if the frames seem at odds in terms of their assessment of what different cultures bring to society as well as whether race is significant, students draw on the frames available to them to make sense of particular situations, data, and questions posed, much the way individuals draw more broadly on their "cultural tool kits" to respond in different situations, as Ann Swidler has described.[48]

The interplay between personal experiences in school and in college, and individual orientations and preferences together shape students' race frames, a result of the institutions where they have spent time, the cultures with which they have engaged, and their own dispositions. While I cannot say definitively why students varied in their frames, the influence of the college experience on developing the diversity frame suggests that other experiences in their families, neighborhoods, and primary and secondary schools probably helped shape students' race frames. In the future, their new neighborhoods, friendship circles, and workplaces are also likely to influence their race frames.

We should think of frames as part of a cultural tool kit for making sense of the world and for responding to different situations—in this case, different kinds of interview questions.[50] When individuals enter new social contexts they increase the cultural tools they can draw on to make sense of the world. Hence I argue that while students hold frames they picked up from a variety of domains before college— their schools, their families, the media, and more—many also develop a frame in college (or enhance an existing one). Most commonly, students developed a diversity frame, but some, especially students of color at Brown, developed a power analysis frame. The new frames most frequently added on to existing frames rather than replacing them, even when some frames included incompatible ideas about the significance of race in society and the consequences of cultural practices and power differences related to race. When it comes time to make sense of a race-related situation, students hold up a frame from their cultural tool kits that seems to suit the given situation.

In chapter 6 we will see that British students had less-developed understandings of the role of race in society. Some British students, as I show, seemed to search for a frame to make sense of questions they were asked rather than drawing on an existing frame already in their cultural tool kits to make sense of questions or situations related to race. All but four American students, however, held at least one race frame. It seems it is rare to grow up in the United States without developing ways of thinking about race, even if they are multiple and contradictory.

Brown and Harvard students seemed to hold well-rehearsed ways of making sense of race-related material. In many respects, developing a diversity frame is one way students at elite universities learn to form an elite identity. That is, a taste for and interest in diverse cultural forms is part of elite identities in the contemporary United States. Nearly twenty years ago sociologists Richard Peterson and Roger Kern identified a shift in tastes among American elites: they were moving away from exclusive tastes, for example in abstract art and Western classical music, to what Peterson and Kern labeled "cultural omnivorousness," or a taste for multiple cultural forms.[50] Similarly, in his recent book about the elite boarding school St. Paul's, Shamus Khan describes students as learning to be at ease with a range of cultural forms, from *Beowulf* to *Jaws*, as part of their training to become elites.[51] I found that elite training is about omnivorousness not only in tastes, but also in interpersonal familiarity. That is, learning to be comfortable across racial lines was an essential part of the elite college experience, according to students we interviewed, in part because of the diversity frame. This is in sharp contrast to a past in which, for example, white Anglo-Saxon Protestant Harvard students from wealthy northeastern families lived in different dorms than their working-class peers.[52]

Many have criticized the supposed democratic sensibility of cultural omnivorousness for using open rhetoric while including only particular kinds of taste cultures and excluding others. Elites do this, for example, by incorporating jazz but not rap into what is considered elite music,[53] by valorizing "ethnic" foods that can be obtained only with money for travel,[54] and by privileging English-speaking popular cultures.[55] Similarly, it may be that students enjoy the diversity of their peers at Harvard and Brown because those minority peers have been certified as worthy through admission to an elite university; they may be less inclined to learn, for example, from minorities who dropped out of high school.[56]

I end this chapter with a reminder about the historical link between race frames and evaluations of merit through academic tests such as the SAT, and the link to intelligence testing and desires to rank racial groups. While no students expressed beliefs about biological conceptions of race and achievement, they did link beliefs about the role of race in society to their conceptions of merit, as we will see in chapter 4. So understanding students' race frames and their development is essential to understanding their conceptions of merit. For example, the diversity frame shaped how students justified affirmative action. But first, in the next chapter I dig deeper into how Harvard and Brown shaped student perspectives on race and merit.

THREE

THE UNIVERSITY INFLUENCE

I didn't come to college particularly activist-minded at all, but I'm leaving very much so.

IMANI, black student at Brown

It was just amazing to see different student groups celebrate ethnic heritage and cultural life on stage. There were Chinese fan dances, Irish dancers. There was just the whole spectrum of all these different cultures. And one of the most moving parts of the show for me was the grand finale where different groups danced with each other and blended their different styles. So, like, there was the African dancer dancing with the Chinese fans.

GRACE, Korean American student at Harvard

College campuses are filled with student groups, workshops, performances, and other activities beyond the academic curriculum. Much of that programming in the United States is related to diversity. Elite colleges, in other words, are particular kinds of organizations in which young adults develop their perspectives on merit and race.[1] What influence do these efforts have on students? In this chapter I reveal how diversity-related activities and spaces influence students on the Brown and Harvard campuses. In the previous chapter I described how students developed or enhanced a diversity frame through their college experiences; here I reveal just what happens on campus that leads to those (and other) developments in students' race frames.

Campus diversity work has two major goals as defined by students, administrators, and US society. First, colleges try to build cross-racial understanding and empathy to expand students' worldviews. This goal rests on "contact theory," which states that under certain conditions, greater contact between ethnic and racial groups reduces racial prejudice.[2] As I described in chapter 2, students are explicit that racial diversity is important for their learning during college, employing a diversity frame. Second, some suggest that diversity programming on campus should enable students to understand the roots of racial inequality in society, often with the goal of promoting racial justice and reducing inequality. This perspective, rooted in a power analysis frame, recognizes the absence of teaching about the roots of racial inequality in most secondary schools in the United States, and it often emphasizes the need to promote racial justice in society.[3]

Both of these goals appear, in different places, on most residential campuses. Students with a power analysis frame, for example, may gravitate to an activist group—like Imani, quoted above. Others might attend a multicultural dance performance like Grace. Individual preferences stem from students' own interests, backgrounds, and goals. Still, as I show in this chapter, different colleges have different emphases, with important implications for students' perspectives on race and merit. Aside from students' inclinations, campuses offer a different set of experiences related to diversity, so that the avenues available for engaging diversity are different, with consequences for students' perspectives on diversity. In thinking about students' race frames and their consequent conceptions of merit, material in this chapter makes it clear that what universities are doing matters. We can see, too, the complexity of the goals of addressing race on campus and in admissions. At Harvard, administrators have focused on the goal of building cross-racial connections, while on the Brown campus diversity programming has focused on building an understanding of the complexity of racial inequality in American society and beyond, a story untold in most American primary and secondary schools.

Conversations around race and diversity in college environments are different in many ways than they are in K–12 classrooms, in the workplace, and in other social contexts, because they are more likely to take diversity seriously, to speak freely about difference, and to have spaces in which some share a power analysis frame.[4] In interviews, students on the Brown and Harvard campuses repeatedly brought up the campus diversity centers, orientation events on diversity, and the multicultural Cultural Rhythms performance at Harvard. Those familiar with the Harvard and Brown undergraduate experience may notice that some diversity-related programs and activities do not come up in this chapter. Rather than provide an exhaustive list of activities on campus, which would prevent readers from understanding their significance, I discuss at length only those that came up frequently in student interviews. Students were given a variety of prompts about diversity on campus (see appendix C for a full list of the interview questions), and in this chapter I describe the experiences and institutions that came up most. Students frequently brought up cross-racial interactions in college as important for their learning about race. Student activism around diversity, while reported in campus newspapers, did not come up in the interviews, probably because the small number of student activists weren't captured by my attempts to recruit a broad range of students. Cross-racial interactions and student activism are often the result of programming by the colleges and a campus culture that promotes those activities or at least allows for them, as we will see.

Addressing Diversity on Elite College Campuses

Selective private universities in the United States have much in common, including how they have addressed diversity on campus. Harvard and Brown share a commitment to multiculturalism, celebrating diversity of all kinds. These efforts have historically been prompted by their own students, who since the 1960s have made various demands for greater diversity and supports for minority students, as well as the subsequent desire of the university administrations to be seen as forward-thinking and to avoid racial strife.[5] Black students, many recruited through the first affirmative action efforts in the early 1960s, became leaders of student protest movements that eventually led to African American studies departments, minority student centers, and more.[6] Both Harvard and Brown established programs in African American studies in 1969 in response to student demands.[7] In addition, both universities have created central administrative positions to address diversity. At Brown, President Ruth Simmons created the Office of Institutional Diversity in 2003, and at Harvard the position of chief diversity officer was established in 2009.[8] The percentages of minority students on campus are similar across the campuses and from year to year. These supports for diversity, common to the most selective private colleges in the United States, create a culture that embraces the concept of "diversity" writ large, even while the precise meaning of that value for diversity varies significantly from campus

to campus and between students. As we have seen, the campus infrastructure related to diversity seemed to enhance the presence of the
diversity frame among Brown and Harvard students, white and minority.

While US universities seem quite similar, especially when compared with universities abroad, the national influence does not unfold
in the same way in all universities. Rather, historical circumstances and
the decisions of individual administrations and student leaders medi-
ate national influences on the campus culture of diversity. Organizations sometimes develop in unexpected ways, sometimes in contrast
to the broader culture. In turn, these institutional differences are likely
to shape students' experiences and perspectives.[9] I found two different
approaches to the diversity-related infrastructure on campus: a power
analysis approach, resting on a power analysis frame, which was emphasized on Brown's campus, especially at the Third World Center
(TWC) and during the Third World Transition Program (TWTP),
and a diversity approach, resting on a diversity frame, which was especially emphasized at Harvard through its Diversity Dialogues and the
Harvard Foundation for Intercultural and Race Relations. The power
analysis approach of the TWC and TWTP develops an understanding of privilege, power, and the historical roots of racial oppression
in society among students who participate. Yet many white students
and some minority students feel alienated from that programming
because it creates minority-only or predominantly minority spaces.
For participants this approach highlights how seemingly race-neutral
policies can promote racial inequality. On the other hand, under the
broader diversity frame—present in most activities related to diversity
at Harvard—most students are included and feel satisfied with their
individual experiences with diversity, yet most do not question the
power differences between groups in society and the historical roots
of enduring racial inequality in American society. On both campuses,
varying levels of participation and whether participation is mandatory
or voluntary also have implications for student perspectives.

Of course, institutional influences are not all-encompassing; some
students adopt college messages, while others contest them. Further,
although in this chapter I focus on diversity infrastructure explicitly supported by the universities, the line between the influence of
the universities and the influence of their students is blurry. For example, as we will see, while Brown funds the Third World Transition

Program, an orientation program primarily for incoming students of color, the program is completely student-run, and at times students make decisions against the wishes of the college administrator who oversees it. Still, I emphasize in this chapter how the universities in particular implement diversity-related programs, events, and institutions, to reveal their influence on students' perspectives.

Brown University: Institutional Support for a Power Analysis Frame

Since the mid-twentieth century, Brown has been more willing than other Ivy League universities to accommodate demands for increased opportunity and integration among black students. During the civil rights movement, Brown was a leader among northern elite institutions, establishing a partnership with Tougaloo College in Alabama, a private historically black college with a legacy of activism. The goal of the Brown University–Tougaloo College Partnership was to promote student and faculty exchanges, and the partnership endures today.[10] In the late 1960s, in response to student protests, the university instituted a voluntary orientation program for first-year students of color, now called the Third World Transition Program (TWTP), as well as the Rites and Reasons Theater, which produces works primarily by black playwrights.[11] Soon after, the Minority Peer Counseling (MPC) program established designated counselors with training in issues of racial diversity in all first-year residential halls.[12] Today there are twenty-two MPC counselors who organize TWTP for over two hundred freshmen every year over four days, just before the general freshman orientation for all students.[13] Although TWTP is open to all students, it is attended primarily by American students of color; approximately 40 percent of all entering students of color from the United States, along with a small number of white American students and international students, attend TWTP each year.[14] One part of TWTP's mission is to "introduce new students to the support structures and resources available to them." It also "challenges them to explore systems of oppression that still exist in the United States today."[15] Students participate in workshops on colonialism, racism, heterosexism, and other related topics. The program maintains a particular focus on communities of color, but it also emphasizes coming together across differences as a goal and outcome of TWTP: "Through an examination of the problems

that divide our society, we seek to break down the barriers that separate us in order to build understanding and community."[16] Through its
emphasis on power and inequality, TWTP promotes a power analysis
frame as a means for understanding race in society.

In 1976, Brown's Third World Center (TWC) opened its doors,
in response to student demands for a center to support students of
color.[17] The TWC's current mission statement states that it

> serves as a gathering place for communities of color. Students are
> encouraged to build meaningful relationships across difference, de-
> velop racial and ethnic consciousness, and enact change at Brown
> and beyond. The [TWC] advances the University's mission . . . by
> empowering students of color, cultivating leadership, facilitating
> critical reflection, fostering informed action, and promoting social
> justice.[18]

The TWC prioritizes the needs of students of color, and overall its
goals are about social change. In 2013 Brown's president appointed a
committee to develop a strategic plan for the TWC. Comprising six
undergraduates, seven staff and faculty members, and one alumnus,
the committee affirmed the center's dedication to students of color,
recommending, among other things, that it change its name to the
Brown Center for Students of Color.[19] In addition to accepting the
name change recommendation, the TWC revised its mission in response to the committee's findings. That new mission retains a decidedly power analysis frame, in that it assumes unique needs for students
of color and acknowledges their marginalization. Similarly, the new
name does not emphasize integration, unlike Harvard's diversity center, as I describe below. The TWC's budget is more than $500,000 a
year.[20]

In 1996 Brown instituted a concentration in ethnic studies. Five
years later Ruth Simmons was appointed president of Brown; she was
the first black president of an Ivy League university.[21] In 2003 Simmons created Brown's Steering Committee on Slavery and Justice to
investigate the ways the university had benefited from the slave trade.
As a result of the committee's findings Brown has developed a variety
of initiatives, including a Center for the Study of Slavery and Justice, supports for Providence Public Schools, and a Slavery Memorial
sculpture on the campus green.[22]

These programs—many the first of their kind on Ivy League campuses—still have lasting impact. In terms of student housing, Brown offers a dorm, Harambee House, oriented toward African culture, as well as Spanish House, oriented toward Spanish language and Hispanic culture, and French House, oriented toward French language and culture. Brown's Organization of United African Peoples (also known as the Black Student Union) describes Harambee House as "the African American cultural dorm, [whose purpose is to] serve as an intellectual and artistic principal outlet for African-American students."[23] While Harambee House's official university description is that it exists as "a living center for all those interested in the politics, culture, society, and other aspects of African culture,"[24] the BSU's characterization suggests it serves as a center for African American life on campus. In recent years ten to forty students have chosen to live in Harambee House,[25] and about forty in Spanish House.[26] In addition to the small number of students living in ethnic- and race-themed housing, many more participate in student groups related to ethnic and racial identities. Brown University is home to 437 student organizations, 45 of them "cultural or ethnic" groups.[27] Finally, in terms of academics, between 9 and 22 students have concentrated in Africana studies each year in the recent past, along with 6 to 13 students concentrating in ethnic studies.[28]

"My Worldview Was Rocked" vs. "Discussing the 'White Problem'": Brown's Third World Programming in the Minds of Students

I arrived on the Brown campus in late August, eager to see TWTP in action. When I arrived, the Third World Center's director intercepted me on my way to the building in which TWTP was being held, and where I had lived as a sophomore. Apologizing profusely, she let me know that while student leaders had previously okayed my visit, today there were new concerns. I then noticed a group of about ten students waiting for me. I learned that they were a subset of the upperclassmen who were facilitators of this year's program. We agreed that the director would step away while I chatted with the students. As I sat with them, some shared concerns about my presence affecting the safe space they had worked so hard to establish at TWTP. Others questioned my motivation. We spoke for about twenty minutes. In the end,

I asked if anyone still felt uncomfortable with my presence. One young woman spoke up and was eloquent enough to convince her peers that I should not continue. We agreed that instead of visiting TWTP I would ask for volunteers to have a conversation with me over lunch, away from their planned events.

I was struck by the students' sense of empowerment. That I was a professor at Harvard, and that their director had previously founded multicultural centers at three colleges did not seem to faze them—their questions to me and their responses to the director made clear that they were comfortably in charge. This was the kind of empowerment I was used to seeing in my most privileged students at Harvard—that sense that the world is theirs and that professors and administrators are simply facilitators of their own important goals, not authorities to be pleased. Typically these privileged students are wealthy and white, but in this instance all but one were students of color.

As I walked away, my emotions were mixed. I felt pleased that these students, most of whom have experienced marginalization, whether by class or race or both, had developed a sense of empowerment. I hoped my children would feel so empowered when they grow up. Yet at the same time I was frustrated by their defensiveness and skepticism toward an outsider; to these students, anything that could potentially disrupt the space was suspect, even though I was an alumna of color studying diversity, with liberal credentials to boot.

Later that day I returned to engage in two conversations with a diverse group of eight TWTP participants who were incoming freshmen, and then with two facilitators, upperclassmen who help organize the program. The participants spoke of experiences visiting Brown that had led them to enroll. One student said,

> Coming to TWTP, that's the main reason I came to Brown. Looking at other schools, they had groups for minorities. But it was just a group, and it didn't really seem connected to the community. But as soon as I came to Brown, I suddenly saw all these students of color that were really passionate about learning and broadening their horizons.

Another student spoke of the Third World Weekend, an event for admitted students of color to visit campus in the spring, comparing it with a single event on another Ivy League campus's general admitted students' visiting day. To the student, this separate weekend demon-strated Brown's commitment to students of color and persuaded him to enroll. He said, as if speaking to a representative of the other univer-sity: "Do you know what that says about your university? You don't ap-preciate how much this means to students of color. They need to come and see that they have people to come and talk to." Several students brought up TWTP discussions around homophobia and hetereo-sexism as eye-opening to them. Overall, while TWTP drew many to Brown, the program shifted their thinking as well, and I was witness to this transition during these conversations.

Apart from my visit to TWTP, six of the fifteen students of color we interviewed individually also attended TWTP at the start of their first year. One white student I interviewed also attended TWTP. Of those seven attendees, five praised it enthusiastically.[29] These students re-ported that TWTP gave them a vocabulary to discuss social problems they had intuitively understood in the past. Further, they reported that TWTP led to a diverse group of friends because of the pan-ethnic na-ture of the program. For Nisha, a South Asian junior who was concen-trating in community health and sociology, TWTP presented the first time she had been invited to think critically about social inequality and oppression, an opportunity she found invaluable:

> If you have never been presented with all these ideas of colonial-ism and imperialism, and how they affect you, you're suddenly like, whoa! [laughs]. Here I was just chilling and going to college, and all of a sudden, my worldview is rocked.

Though Nisha did say TWTP can be "overwhelming," she also noted that she "loves" having had the opportunity to engage with these issues. Even students who had spent time before college discussing or otherwise thinking about racial inequality found the program's efforts illuminating. Imani said the experience was "life changing." She ex-plained how talking about "racism, classism, sexism, heterosexism, homophobia, imperialism" at TWTP helped her develop a needed language. Imani said that race had

> always been something I've thought about a lot and that's been really important to me throughout my life. But coming to TWTP . . . gave me a vocabulary to talk about it. . . . It really concretely explained the

difference between interpersonal racism and institutional racism. . . .
It just all started to click and make sense.

Like Imani, many students developed or strengthened a power
analysis frame at TWTP. Indeed, all the students of color at Brown
who expressed a power analysis frame had attended TWTP, and all
but one of the TWTP participants employed a power analysis frame in
some, if not all, of their comments related to race. Imani also felt that
these discussions supported community building: "The other [impor-
tant] piece, I think, was that [TWTP] was led by students and it was
in the context of forming real connections with people. . . . We're not
just talking about these issues, but we're trying to build a community."

Jessica, a Latina social science concentrator, shared Imani's view
on community building: "I went through the Third World Transition
Program . . . so that's where I met most of my friends. And so they're
people from all over . . . all different races, cultures, ethnicities, and
we're all friends."

Similar to most participants' praise for TWTP, many students of
color at Brown expressed praise for the campus Third World Center,
naming it as a support for students of color on campus. Among those
who praised the TWC as a means by which Brown actively supports
students of color and promotes broader understandings of the social
world was Susan, a black junior who had served as a minority peer
counselor (MPC). She said,

> I personally do a lot of work with the Third World Center, and that's
> all about bringing people of diverse backgrounds together. So I think
> multiculturalism and diversity is really stressed at Brown, especially
> in that space. But I mean [Brown] is also a predominantly white
> institution, and sometimes it's surprising how few people of color
> there are in certain places.

Susan's comments suggest a need for understanding the particular,
sometimes challenging, position of students of color at predominantly white institution. Her recognition of the difference in power
and visibility between white and minority students on campus reveals
a power analysis frame.

In contrast to the praise, many nonparticipants criticized TWTP
and the TWC. Overall, eighteen of the forty-six white students (in-

cluding one participant in TWTP) and one-third of students of color (including one attendee) criticized TWTP, and four of the seven white students who brought up the TWC in interviews expressed concerns. There were two consistent criticisms of both: that they create divisions between students of color and white students, because white students are thought to be excluded,[30] and that they inappropriately assume commonality among students of color.[31]

By far the biggest concern was that TWTP and the TWC created racial divisions among students. This criticism had less to do with the topics of the programming—which most nonparticipants may not have known—and more to do with whom the students perceived as the target audience. Many white students viewed TWTP as depriving them of potential friendships with their peers of color. One white sophomore, Jeff, a math concentrator, explained this concern in detail:

> I have a lot of problems with [TWTP] because it assumes that people have more in common . . . with . . . people who have the same skin color as them, and people who have the same background. Brown sends invitations to anyone who checked off a nonwhite box in the right section of the application. So . . . it has a really real effect of creating fault lines across races in the university. . . . It makes it so that all the students who went to [TWTP] got to know each other a week before anyone else came to campus. So when most people come onto campus, like the rest of the Brown student body . . . these people already have a friend group. . . . And those friend groups have persisted even into sophomore year.

Jeff later acknowledged that "everyone is welcome [at TWTP]. But . . . there very rarely are Caucasian people who go to TWTP."[32] Jeff is right in this regard—while TWTP opened up to white students in 2005, less than 10 percent of attendees are white.[33] Here is a key difference in understanding diversity between TWTP participants and nonparticipants. Nonparticipants, especially those who are white, viewed groups of student of color as homogeneous or self-segregating. Minority TWTP participants, however, viewed the situation as precisely the opposite. They saw the pan-minority program as diverse and a means toward building coalitions across racial lines. Yet Jeff and others viewed friendships with students of color as a resource that white students are unfairly deprived of through TWTP.

Sarah, a white student studying sociology, explained in response to a question asking whether campus racial and ethnic organizations are divisive or supportive:[34]

> I think a lot of kids take issue with perceived self-segregation [of the TWC]. They say, "Well I understand why it was created in the '60s and the '70s to promote more acceptance, diversity and solidarity. But now, shouldn't the campus just be open? And if you're creating these programs for only one group of people, isn't that out of necessity creating division?" . . . I think the emphasis should be less on solidarity and creating the separation, but rather . . . sharing one's culture or background.

Like Sarah and Jeff, many white students believed that the structure of the TWC prevented it from benefiting white students, which contravened what I call the *diversity bargain*, in which white students support affirmative action insofar as it benefits themselves. (We'll explore the diversity bargain further in the next chapter.) Because of the emphasis on supporting ethnic and racial identities, the perceived lack of emphasis on cross-racial engagement left white students feeling they had few avenues to engage with students of color on diversity, an important goal for those who held a diversity frame. This left them frustrated.

The criticism of TWTP was not limited to white students. Kelly, an Asian American junior who was concentrating in English and who did not attend TWTP, called TWTP and similar programs "polarizing." She noted that TWTP is

> mostly for people who are nonwhite to come and discuss racial issues. I didn't attend, but I have heard that it's more like discussing "the white problem." . . . I am friends with a lot of people who did the program. . . . Because it starts before school officially starts, it's kind of like building your community of friends and your network—your relationships—before you get to interact with white people, really, at Brown.

In Kelly's view TWTP led to a troublesome separation between students of color and white students at the start of college. Interestingly, her objection seemed to go beyond TWTP. During her interview she complained that Brown "shoves [multiculturalism] in our faces." This points to a tension in diversity planning. When all students are included, some, like Kelly, may resent that mandatory inclusion. But when some are not included, or if their group is a minority of participants (like whites at TWTP), those nonparticipants may resent that separation.

Contributing to the feeling of exclusion is the space allocation of the TWC building. Jenny, who identifies as multiracial (Asian and white), said,

> Upstairs they have a room for every minority. They have a room for African Americans, a room for Hispanics, and a room for Asians. And that doesn't sit well with a lot of people here. [Because] it's like, you have a room that you can only enter if you're part of—Are you serious?[35]

Although Jenny is biracial, this kind of critique came most frequently from white students.[36] Overall, the sentiments critics expressed suggest they are uncomfortable with and opposed to the perceived segregation of the TWC's structure—much like the criticisms of the TWTP orientation program—in spite of their awareness that all students are welcome to attend TWC events and to use the space. Furthermore, they suggest that many white students would prefer that the TWC focus more on intercultural engagement rather than on activities that, as they perceive it, segregate the student body.

The range of student reactions suggests that Kelly's "polarizing" assessment is indeed accurate: most TWTP attendees and students engaged with TWC programming—mostly students of color—reported profound, life-changing experiences, while many nonparticipants, both students of color and white students, viewed the programs as sources of racial division.

Of course, in addition to TWTP and the TWC, other programming on the Brown campus supported intercultural dialogue. Recall from chapter 2 that 85 percent of students employed a diversity frame at some point in the interview; this percentage was similar for students at both Harvard and Brown, and for white and minority students. In other words, the power analysis frame that some students developed at the TWC and at TWTP was compatible with a diversity frame through which they expressed deep appreciation for campus diversity. Still, Harvard's stronger emphasis on intercultural contact seemed to shape students there differently.

Harvard University: A History of Racial Integration

Over the past half-century, Harvard has approached race relations through an integration model, emphasizing actions that would improve race relations and foregrounding the goal of intercultural understanding. The Harvard Foundation for Intercultural and Race Relations — or the Foundation, as it is known on campus — was established in 1981 by the university president five years after the establishment of Brown's Third World Center. Although Harvard minority student protesters had repeatedly demanded a minority-run "Third World" center, the university's administration decided against the Third World name for fear of signaling segregation rather than integration.[37]

Today the Harvard Foundation's mandate is to "improve relations among racial and ethnic groups within the University and to enhance the quality of our common life."[38] Its mission statement notes that it "sponsors annual programs and activities that are designed to promote interracial and intercultural awareness and understanding in the Harvard community, as well as to highlight the cultural contributions of students from all backgrounds."[39] In addition to other activities, the Foundation organizes the race relations tutors program as part of the Office of Residential Life programming. Race relations tutors and proctors are a subset of Harvard's tutors and proctors, who live with undergraduates and advise them on career paths, academics, and a wide range of other issues. The specific role of race relations tutors and proctors is to be first responders to race-related incidents and to offer proactive programming, such as organized discussions related to race and diversity, in each of the dormitories.[40] They attend one two-hour training session in the summer and monthly two-hour sessions at the Harvard Foundation throughout the academic year. The Foundation also puts on a number of small and large events on campus each year that focus primarily on celebrating intercultural communication and understanding, such as Cultural Rhythms, a cultural festival centered on food and performance that attracts thousands of visitors and is one of the largest events on campus each year.[41] The Foundation hires four first-year undergraduate interns each year who stay with the Foundation all four years (for a total of sixteen interns at any given time) and are charged with planning, organizing, and executing programming on diversity and race relations. The interns program is considered a student leadership-development program. Finally, like Brown, Harvard students run more than four hundred student groups, over eighty of which receive funding from the Harvard Foundation and hence are likely to have some link to diversity.[42]

In 1993, under Dean Archie Epps, Harvard established Harvard Discovery, which later became the basis for Community Conversations, in which all first-year students participate in a ninety-minute small-group discussion on diversity during freshman orientation.[43] There is no separate orientation for minority students analogous to Brown's TWTP. Today, Community Conversations are mandatory for all incoming students, facilitated by a variety of faculty members, administrators, and residential advisors. Students are given a set of readings related to "race, class, sexual orientation, and the overlap among these characteristics. Readings are intended to raise awareness of the diversity in society and encourage students to situate themselves within this context."[44] The goal of Community Conversations is to "offer students an opportunity to reflect on the above issues with the ultimate goal of building a more inclusive and cohesive academic community whilst promoting communication about diversity."[45]

Harvard switched its housing policy in 2001 from allowing upperclassmen to rank their dorm preferences to randomized housing assignments. The change was an attempt to combat perceptions of racial segregation between houses on Harvard's campus. In other words, the change was intended to promote more diversity: "Randomization [of housing allocation] is a good example of an institutional policy that supports this core value of diversity," according to Suzy Nelson, then Harvard's dean of student life.[46] For first-year students, Harvard administrators deliberately craft diverse freshmen rooms and units through a complex matching process.[47] Finally, diversity shapes the curriculum. In 2010 ethnic studies was established as a secondary field (a minor) at Harvard; since then, the field name has changed to ethnicity, migration, and rights (EMR). In recent years, more than twenty students a year have graduated with a secondary field in EMR.[48] In addition, in 2015 eleven Harvard students graduated with degrees in African and African American studies, and another twenty-five obtained a secondary degree in the field.[49]

Overall, then, Harvard focuses on supporting racial integration between students of color and white students on campus, placing less emphasis than Brown does on providing minority students with separate spaces to develop racial identities and to consider racial oppression. Hence, despite the many surface similarities, Brown and Harvard have significantly different histories and current policies related to diversity, and these differences continue to affect student experiences and perspectives today.

"Cultural Shows Expose People to What the Real World Is Like": Harvard's Diversity Programming in the Minds of Students

In contrast to my failed attempt to visit TWTP at Brown, at Harvard I simply asked a university administrator for permission to observe undergraduates' first venue for discussions about race, the Community Conversations event during freshman orientation. I then contacted a graduate student facilitator, got her permission, and showed up. After I was introduced by the facilitator and read the script I had prepared to seek permission as required by my university's ethics board, students barely seemed to register my presence, casually assenting to my observing. After an activity in which students placed stickers on identities they felt were most and least privileged, the facilitator opened up the discussion. Students brought up and then discussed the identity choice "language." They debated whether speaking English is a privilege in the world or whether speaking only English is a disadvantage. They also wondered whether "no religion" could be considered an identity. Interestingly, no one brought up race or ethnicity, though race and ethnicity were two of the identity choices. Given the colorblindness frame that many students brought to campus, perhaps this should not be surprising.

A quarter of the Harvard students we interviewed individually—three white students and ten students of color—mentioned their own experiences with Community Conversations, either spontaneously or in response to the question, "Have you attended any diversity-related workshops at Harvard?" Given that the vast majority of students probably attended this mandatory workshop, this low rate of reporting suggests that the conversation did not make a strong impression on many participants. In addition, all white students who mentioned the workshop were dissatisfied, as were two of the ten students of color who brought it up. For example, Eric, a white junior studying biology, complained about his session's facilitator:

> He [told] us this story about how Harvard University police are racist, because he was walking once and he went to go into a building and a police officer asked to see his ID. He made that out to be this horrible thing. . . . And I mean, even so, if that one police officer was racist . . . it doesn't mean all Harvard police are racist. . . . I felt he was definitely very pro-black.

Eric went on to say that his roommates concurred that "[the facilitator] was kind of against white people." Eric and his roommates' discussion after the event shows the importance of expert facilitation in racially fraught conversations in the United States.

Grace, a Korean American sophomore studying social anthropology, remembered the session as "bizarre" and "overdoing it." She said,

> I don't think it really affected me. . . . I just saw how people felt about having to go to this required conversation, and what people were saying about the readings that we had. In general, the attitude was like, "Why do we have to do this? This is really stupid." And other people were like, "These readings are very loaded . . . they're leading us, and it's very obvious." Obviously they want us to think a certain way, and because they want us to think a certain way some people will resent that.

The problem with Community Conversations as Grace identified it is that they are mandatory and thus experienced as an imposition and perhaps even an indoctrination. The responses of Grace and Eric suggest that even well-intentioned diversity efforts can backfire depending on how they are implemented.

Others were ambivalent, such as Joanne, an Asian American sophomore, who said,

> Everyone had to do that thing as freshmen, the Community Conversation thing. . . . We just talked about the different readings that we

had. It wasn't as helpful as I thought it would be. . . . Because when we're forced to talk about diversity, it's not as natural. . . . I didn't leave feeling like, "Oh my gosh, that was such a life-changing experience."

Overall, Community Conversations, a campus initiative meant to "promote communication about diversity,"[50] in part by requiring all incoming students to participate, may not be having the intended effect on students. Requiring all students to participate is meant to enhance interracial dialogue, but a more extended discussion may not be feasible for everyone during an action-packed orientation schedule. Some resented even the ninety-minute period for a discussion of diversity.

Students seemed to appreciate much more the work of the Harvard Foundation for Intercultural and Race Relations. Almost all Harvard students who brought it up praised the work of the Foundation as one way the university supports multiculturalism. When discussing ways diversity has enhanced life on campus, a number of students discussed Cultural Rhythms, one of the largest student-run events at Harvard each year, which is sponsored by the Foundation and run by Foundation student interns. Cultural Rhythms includes a performance showcase where student groups dance, play music, and demonstrate martial arts from various cultural heritages. A final component of the event is to honor a celebrity "artist of the year" who has engaged in humanitarian or philanthropic work. Past artists of the year have included Shakira, Will Smith, and Matt Damon.[51]

One student who praised Cultural Rhythms was Tim, a white sophomore concentrating in linguistics. When asked how diversity has enhanced life at Harvard, Tim replied, "There's some cultural shows and events that people from different backgrounds throw that people, you know, the WASPy culture of yesteryear definitely would not . . . have been exposed to. And I think it's good." He spoke specifically about Cultural Rhythms, which he—and others we interviewed—described as "pretty cool." "I think [Cultural Rhythms is] good. I think it exposes people to what the real world is like." Other students commented that they enjoyed the food festival component. Thomas, one such student, a white sophomore studying biology, said, "Cultural Rhythms was a lot of different ethnic groups' food and that was great, because I love food and it was stuff I'd never had before." These words demonstrate the diversity frame the speakers held.

Whereas one of the criticisms of the TWC and its programming at Brown was its divisiveness, several Harvard students explicitly offered the view that Cultural Rhythms works to bring communities together. To illustrate this point, Genevieve, a white sociology major, said,

> Cultural Rhythms is sponsored by the Harvard Foundation, rather than a specific ethnic group. So I think that's a good example of where the existence of ethnic specific groups really does foster sort of a collective appreciation for diversity. . . . There's a thousand people who come, and you get to see the South African dance team . . . and the Irish step dancers. All the groups get to perform together on one stage. So for me, that's really a beautiful and a powerful picture of the tremendous artistic creativity that every one of these minority groups brings to America.

Interestingly, in this context Genevieve seems to include Irish as a minority group. Comparing white students at Harvard and Brown, white students were more comfortable with engaging with the Harvard Foundation's programming than with the programming of Brown's Third World Center, with its emphasis on social issues like racism. On one hand, this may speak to the transformative potential of the arts for crossing racial and cultural boundaries.[52] At the same time, it is also possible that the arts are a more appealing venue for white students because they are not forced to directly confront social disparities and their own racial privilege. Though many Harvard students noted that they appreciated the glimpse of diversity the Foundation provides through Cultural Rhythms, few mentioned that attending the event significantly affected their views.

Only one Harvard student, Jeremy, a white senior studying history, was critical of the Harvard Foundation or of Cultural Rhythms. When asked whether he sees evidence of multiculturalism on campus, Jeremy said,

> Not really. I see people trying, but a lot of the things they do to try are clearly, to me, very empty gestures. Like, they'll have shows . . . like, Cultural Rhythms, for example. . . . So they have all the different cul-

tural organizations put on their little dances for everyone and, like, "Oh, look how wonderful culture at Harvard is." But . . . it strikes me as empty mannerisms in a place that's actually very homogeneous.

In other parts of his interview, Jeremy expressed views critical of Harvard through a power analysis frame. His words are a reminder that while students share a common campus, they experience and respond to it in different ways, depending in part on their own lives before coming to college as well as on individual preferences and dispositions.

In addition, just as Brown had some programing more in line with a diversity frame, it would be wrong to suggest that Harvard does not have any programs that promote a power analysis frame. For example, Harvard's First-Year Urban Program is a free weeklong program that one hundred freshmen (and forty upperclass leaders) can attend before freshman orientation.[53] The program emphasizes community service and getting to know the local area, promoting dialogue about difference while working on a specific project within the community. The program's website tells potential participants,

> During FUP week you will get to address the politics of race, class, gender, and sexuality and the impact these issues have on communities and our work in them. Your group will talk with the organizers and neighbors of your project to deepen your understanding of what is going on in that specific community. In the evening, [you] will hear from speakers to gain further insight into social justice issues and the Boston and Cambridge communities.[54]

The one student who told us she participated in FUP was Grace, mentioned earlier for her criticism of Community Conversations. Grace employed a diversity frame as well as a color-blindness frame in her interview; however, given that we interviewed only one FUP student, it still may be that the program tends to inculcate a power analysis frame among its participants as TWTP at Brown does. In other words, my best guess is that Grace was an outlier among former FUP participants in her criticisms of the diversity-related discussions, given that most (but not all) Brown students had a positive take on their experiences at TWTP, which promoted similar discussions, albeit in a different format.

In addition, two Harvard students described experiences in classes that shaped their views on race. When asked how events at Harvard have influenced her views on multiculturalism and diversity, Christina, a Latina senior, said,

> Well, none of my classes count as an "event." [But] they definitely helped me articulate my views and helped me learn a lot of things that I hadn't studied before. I'm studying sociology, so I think about these things all the time. So that's shaped my views and just helped me learn more about it.

Later Christina spoke again of her concentration in sociology:

> Sociology is pretty much just like the history of America since 1970. And not in the way that you were taught it in high school. *If* you were taught it in high school, other than "the civil rights movement happened and now everything's fine," which is some bullshit. Before coming to college I would just be like, "The problem is that these people aren't treated right. Latinos are discriminated against, blacks are discriminated against." But now I can be like, "Oh well, you know, the economic structure of, you know, blah blah blah, and like Ronald Reagan, blah blah blah." Because Ronald Reagan has a lot to do with this. So now when I talk about a certain group to someone who may not get it, she'd be like, "Where are blacks coming from? They have the same rights that we do. The Civil Rights Act passed, blah blah blah." I could be like, "Well, you know, schools this, and in the '70s this, and busing this, and sentencing this, and spread to the suburbs this, and immigration law this, and the lies of the Right Wing this." So I've generated this base of knowledge to draw from, which has also enhanced my understanding of how structures— government, corporations, political, all those factors—influence the place of different groups in society.

Christina went on to describe in detail the ways seemingly race-neutral government policies have disenfranchised and excluded African Americans over the past century, bringing up the GI Bill's exclusion of black men, redlining practices that prevented black Americans from obtaining first-time homeowner loans, and racial differences in wealth accumulation.[55]

*   *   *

Although Brown and Harvard share many of their supports for diversity, they have considerable differences. Those differences affect students' understanding of race in several ways. Brown's TWTP and TWC emphasize a deep understanding of the historical roots of racial oppression, in addition to other forms of oppression such as gender and class. This approach especially benefits students of color, many of whom gain a critical perspective on their own socially situated experiences and the unequal institutional structures in the United States today. Participants in TWTP and the TWC reported developing a clearer power analysis frame through their college experiences. On the other hand, this approach's emphasis on racial identities draws attention to differences between minority and white students, and consequently it alienates many white students, who feel excluded from the conversations that go on. The dominant emphases on justice and on solidarity among students of color may inhibit minority-white dialogue and seems to violate the ways many white students, using a diversity frame, expect to deal with racial difference on campus.

Harvard employs a different model, focusing on commonalities across groups in order to build relationships across racial lines, including all students in conversations and celebrations about diversity. This approach resonates with an extensive body of research showing that intergroup contact reduces intergroup prejudice when supported by aspects such as close contact, common goals, and equal status, all present on college campuses.[56] The university thus avoids activities that might draw attention to and reinforce racial separation and instead focuses on building campus unity. This approach provides fewer spaces for students to critically engage questions of inequality, racial discrimination, and power at a deep level.

Some may argue that there is a trade-off between promoting the goal of intergroup understanding and the goal of racial justice. A similar debate exists in K–12 teaching in the United States, between the mainstream multiculturalism that celebrates ethnic and racial differences through, for example, annual International Potlucks, and a more "critical" multiculturalism that teaches children to develop a deeper understanding of race and other forms of difference and oppression in society.[57] I argue that colleges can and must address *both* of these important goals. After our interviews, many white students on both campuses asked for additional readings, while others remarked on how refreshing it was to speak freely about issues of race and ethnicity in a one-on-one, anonymous setting with a stranger. We know, too, from expressions of frustration that students of color crave spaces in which they can talk about experiences with racial exclusion. The "I, Too, Am Harvard" campaign, in which black Harvard students shared experiences with microaggression on campus, is one example of this. These examples lead me to conclude that campuses need both approaches. In this book's conclusion I describe some promising recent models for addressing these two goals together.

What do these twin goals mean for considerations of race in admissions, and more broadly for conceptions of fairness in the minds of students? I turn to this question next.

FOUR

MERIT AND THE DIVERSITY BARGAIN

Just as the spring semester of 2014 was ending, Princeton freshman Tal Fortgang wrote an essay in the *Princeton Tory*: "Why I'll Never Apologize for My White Male Privilege."[1] The story went viral, and *Time* magazine reprinted it a month later. In the essay Fortgang rejected what he saw as the far too common exhortation of his Princeton peers to "check your privilege," which he deemed "a command that teeters between an imposition to actually explore how I got where I am, and a reminder that I ought to feel personally apologetic because white males seem to pull most of the strings in the world." Fortgang claimed that this suffocating vision of race ignores all he has accomplished. In other words, he rejected the emphasis on inequality, power, racism, and sexism and instead advocated for individualism, equal opportunity, and meritocracy. Talking about his classmates who ask him to check his privilege, Fortgang wrote: "I condemn them for casting the equal protection clause, indeed the very idea of a meritocracy, as a myth, and for declaring that we are all governed by invisible forces, that our nation runs on racist and sexist conspiracies." Fortgang went on to point out that his immigrant parents did not have material resources and worked long hours at backbreaking jobs. The piece elicited strong responses from both supporters and critics. Four days after the piece ran in *Time*, it had been shared on Facebook over 29,000 times; by July that count rose to over 40,000.[2] Fortgang soon appeared on *Fox News*. Meanwhile, liberals wrote numerous rebuttals in the *Huffington Post*, *Salon*, the *Guardian*, and many more national outlets, not to mention discussions on the pages of campus newspapers around the country.

Why did this piece, first published in a conservative campus news-paper, gain so much attention? Media analyses aside, Fortgang's views hit on an enduring, unresolved conflict that persists on college campuses across the United States, especially the most elite. He highlights the contradiction between belief in meritocracy and a recognition of inequality—racial and otherwise—in American society. Hence in the minds of Fortgang and others who share his perspective, to charge racial privilege is to reject American meritocracy.

I expected that many students would reject the notion that college admissions was meritocratic, as Fortgang believed they did. As a faculty member at Harvard and a reader of the *Harvard Crimson* and the *Brown Daily Herald*, I see and hear about many instances of student protest, related to diverse issues such as racial microaggressions on campus, university investments in fossil fuels, and more. The ongoing student protests, along with students' identities as liberal and left of center,[3] made me expect the students I interviewed to be critical of their schools' admissions policies. I assumed that disagreeing with the establishment was what residential college students *do*, so the highly charged issue of admissions would surely be on their protest agenda, or at the very least would be something they criticized. I remembered my own freshman year at Brown, when classmates demanding need-blind admissions got arrested for taking over a university building. Today, many critics specifically point out the dearth of poor, working-class, and black and Latino students on Ivy League campuses.[4] Conservative protests from the opposite end of the ideological spectrum criticize practices of affirmative action in elite higher education.[5] Further, I didn't think students' personal interest in protecting the status they had gained through admissions would prevent them from criticism, because I knew that people tend to vote according to their political ideologies rather than their self-interest.[6] I guessed that expressed views, even lower-stakes than voting, would also follow this pattern of emphasizing ideology over self-interest. So I expected students who identified as liberal—the majority of those we interviewed—to criticize the admissions systems of their universities for not being inclusive enough.[7]

Alongside all my assumptions, however, was another possibility: that students would support the admissions practices of their campuses, as Fortgang defends Princeton's meritocracy. After all, they had just won an incredibly competitive contest for which they undoubtedly worked hard in high school. Criticizing that very process would undermine their success and the status they felt they had earned through hard work, as Fortgang explained. Indeed, elite universities are often criticized—and rightly so—as being good at nothing so much as reproducing their own elitism, and that social reproduction begins with the admissions office.[8] It was thus possible that self-interest in maintaining the legitimacy of their hard-earned achievement would dominate students' perspectives. The legitimacy of these institutions, after all, rests on the legitimacy of their systems of reward.

In the end I found something more complex than either simple criticism or blind agreement. Students held complex, nuanced perspectives on admissions and merit. Most believed that evaluations of merit should be calibrated according to an applicant's life circumstances, and further that attention to the collective merit of the college cohort is important in admissions. Further, as we'll see, white students' beliefs about race and meritocracy led to what I call a *diversity bargain*.

"Taking Full Advantage of Opportunities That You've Had": Calibrated Evaluations of Merit

Stephanie, a white junior, gave long, thoughtful answers in her interview. She spoke of the deep influence of her semester spent studying in Jordan, where she learned Arabic. At times Stephanie seemed uncomfortable and conflicted in her interview responses, peppering her sentences with interjections of "I mean . . . ," and "like . . ." (even more than the typical college student). She came to Harvard from the Midwest, having attended a public high school that is over 90 percent white. Her parents are college professors. At Harvard Stephanie studied history. In response to a question asking if Harvard should consider whether a student attended a public or private high school when making admissions decisions, Stephanie said,

> What needs to be considered in your admission is how you've made the most of the opportunities that you've had. . . . And in that sense, like, if you go to a private school that maybe is, like, really rich and a really great education, . . . and you have somebody who went to a public school that maybe didn't have as much money, but they took huge, full advantage of the opportunities that they had there. And, like, they really milked it for all it was worth, and . . . the person from

the private school wasn't like that, [then] the person from the public school should get it.

Students like Stephanie advocated *calibrated* evaluations of merit—that is, viewing applicants' accomplishments in the context of what opportunities they have had.

Stephanie's response and others like hers resonate with the language used by both Harvard's and Brown's admissions offices. Harvard's dean of admissions, William Fitzsimmons, wrote in a *New York Times* blog: "We are vitally interested in whether or not applicants have taken full advantage of their educational opportunities, whatever they might have been. If so, they have a much better chance of maximizing the use of Harvard's resources."[9]

Similarly, in the Frequently Asked Questions on their website, Brown's admissions office tells prospective students:

> We choose to concentrate on how well a student has used the resources available to him or her. We do not start with the assumption that students from a certain school are better candidates than those from another school. . . . We know that curricular offerings vary from school to school. Our strongest candidates have taken full advantage of what is available to them in their own schools.[10]

Stephanie, Dean Fitzsimmons, and the Brown admissions website all use the phrase "take full advantage." Students seem to have internalized the language of their administrators, whether through their own research or as rearticulated by high school counselors and college administrators they've encountered. Nearly half of the white students we interviewed brought up the need for admissions officers to calibrate accomplishments according to what opportunities an applicant had available.

A majority of students of color (seven of thirteen Asian Americans and twelve of seventeen blacks and Latinos) also expressed this belief that evaluations of merit need to be calibrated according to individual opportunities. Dexter, an African American sophomore studying sociology, when asked whether Harvard should consider race or ethnicity in admissions, said, "Definitely. Because this country—everything is not fair. Everything hasn't been fair, so you need to adjust for those things that haven't been done fairly."

Unlike Dexter, some students used their belief in the importance of calibrating evaluations of merit, alongside a color-blindness frame, to criticize affirmative action in favor of calibrating evaluations according to an applicant's class background. For example, when asked whether Harvard should consider race in admissions decisions, Naomi, a white sophomore who listed her major as "diversity," said,

> I don't think it should. It should be based on your parents' education. I think that should be looked upon in terms of, you did really well in school even though your parents, like, didn't go past eighth grade or something. I think that's amazing and it shows great potential, but in terms of race, it shouldn't be a factor.

Naomi's color-blindness frame, along with her belief in calibrating evaluations of merit, led her to stress the importance of calibrating according to parents' education. White students were more likely than students of color to criticize affirmative action in favor of attention to socioeconomic factors such as family income or parents' education, as Naomi did. Alex, a white student from the South whose parents are professionals, studied engineering at Brown. He conceived of disadvantage in terms of family income:

> I think they should consider socioeconomic background and the difficulties that people have. If you're from the same situation or background, you've faced the same problems. Like if a white kid had had the same kind of upbringing with parents of the same income level as a black kid, I don't think [the black kid] should have an advantage over me if we both came from the same background. I know statistically if you're from minority groups you might be more likely to have a [low] socioeconomic background, but I think the socioeconomic background is the key thing, not what your ethnic makeup is.

Alex feels it is important to consider the opportunities individuals have had in their lives, but he does not see race as affecting those opportunities apart from its coincidence with socioeconomic disadvantage. Alex was then asked about class-based considerations. "Definitely. You have to deal with a bunch of things that other people don't have to deal with, which will distract your time and energy from getting the best grades and getting, like, an Eagle Scout or something like that." Hence Alex's beliefs in the importance of calibrating evaluations of merit, along with his color-blindness frame, led him to disagree with affirmative action but to support considering class background. As we'll see, in Britain the lack of belief in calibrating evaluations of merit led students to disagree with considering *either* race or class in admissions. Of course, Naomi's and Alex's comments ignore the different experiences with poverty and disadvantage that black and white Americans experience.

Others, who believed that racial inequality does affect the life circumstances of black and Latino youth, used the same belief in calibrating evaluations of merit to *support* affirmative action. Students of color more frequently expressed support for affirmative action in order to calibrate evaluations of merit, rejecting the color-blindness frame. For example, recall Dexter, who supported affirmative action based on unfair opportunities.

"Diversity Is How You Learn Here": Collective Merit

While many students expressed support for calibrating evaluations of merit, even more supported attention to diversity—broadly defined—in admissions decisions because of its contribution to the *collective merit* of the cohort, a benefit to everyone's learning on campus. Fifty-three of the seventy-six American students stated that the admissions office should consider collective merit. This agreement was similar across racial groups. Many students supported *both* calibrating evaluations of merit and attention to the collective merit of the cohort.[11] Students appreciated the varied backgrounds and talents of their peers and believed that admissions officers should consider these characteristics in admissions decisions. In what follows I discuss the domains in which students thought their peers might contribute to the collective merit of the cohort and hence deserve to be admitted: extracurricular talents, athletic skills, legacy status (financial contributions), and minority racial identities. This belief in collective merit rests in part on the diversity frame, as we will see.

Extracurricular talents and athletics were part of collective merit. Sophie, a Harvard senior studying folklore and mythology, said,

> I know if they just chose people with 1600s [on the SAT], that would be one form of meritocracy, but I don't think it would make for the

kind of merit that they want. So I think some people are good at taking tests, some people are good at composing symphonies, some people are good at sports. And I think they take a lot of very well-rounded people and a few people that are good at very particular things and I think it works out fine. I think everyone that gets in deserves to be here.

Sophie's report that Harvard admissions "works out fine" indicates her belief in the system. She identifies as multiracial and has an Afro-Caribbean mother. Sophie spoke with conviction and precision during her interview, rarely making eye contact as she tried to focus on complex views she wanted to convey. Sophie grew up in a suburb of a small city; her public high school was predominantly white and not poor.[12] Her professional parents hold graduate degrees.

Her experiences at Harvard shaped Sophie's perspective on collective merit. Before she arrived, Sophie was, in her own words, "very antijock." However, now she believes that

> dedication to sports is just like dedication to the arts. Some people are better at a sonata. I wish that they would recruit students because of theater just as much as they do because of football. . . . I don't see a problem with including athletes who may have lower scores, because a lot of times musicians may have lower scores because they were practicing, like, six hours a day.

Sophie seems to understand the athletic recruiting process, whereby athletic coaches at most elite universities can recruit players who meet a GPA and SAT score cutoff, ensuring those top players admission so they can play on the school's team.[13]

Elliot, a white sophomore with broad shoulders and short brown hair, similarly discussed athletic merit and its contribution to the collective merit of the cohort by enriching student life. When asked whether diversity creates any problems for the university or for university life, Elliot replied,

> Before I applied, I didn't like [the fact that] it's really easy for . . . recruited athletes. . . . I've had issues with that. Now that I'm here, I don't have those issues. Because I see, like I love going to the football games. It's fun. It's part of the student life. . . . I used to think

that . . . having athletes who are quote/unquote "less qualified"—I
no longer view them as less qualified. I view them as qualified in a
different way.

Notice that when asked about diversity on campus, Elliot, a religious studies major at Brown, talks about athletics. Even though talk
of diversity in US higher education is rooted historically in the African
American struggle for racial justice, Elliot, like many of his peers, used
the word diversity much more broadly, to signify a cohort with diverse
talents and skills, not just varied racial and ethnic backgrounds.

Despite this expansive notion of diversity, I was still surprised to hear
many students supporting the consideration of legacy status—that is,
privileging the children of alumni in admissions. Given that most parents in the United States do not have a college degree, let alone a degree from the most elite colleges, this practice reinforces race and class
inequality in who gains access to elite colleges. Students expressed support for legacy admissions by again returning to collective merit.[14] That
is, they recognized the financial benefits of alumni donations, which
would contribute to the collective good of the campus, even while
sometimes lamenting the inequality that legacy admissions engender.
Noa, a Harvard undergraduate from New York City who was studying
history, expressed sympathy with the admissions office: "I understand
why the school accepts people because of that. I think that Harvard
relies on a lot of donations, and I think that's one of the ways that that
is fostered." Like Noa, just over half of students in all race groups expressed at least ambivalent support for legacy admissions.

Still, the other half of students criticized legacy admissions.[15] Their
criticism usually acknowledged the university's reasons for giving a
leg up to the children of alumni, even if they disagreed. For example,
Katherine, a Harvard senior studying biology, used the preference
given to legacy applicants to bolster her own sense of self-worth:

> I'm not too big of a fan of the legacy thing. . . . That's the one thing
> that I have a little bit more of a problem with, because I don't see
> how being a legacy contributes to the campus community. I see how,
> like, athletic ability contributes to the community, musical ability,
> you know, being of a certain cultural background. I think those all
> have a lot to bring to the table and can really enhance the community
> and enrich it. I don't really see why your mom having been a Harvard

student brings anything to the table. I mean, it certainly probably brings more money into the coffers. So that might, thereby, enhance the community. Parents are more likely to donate when their child has been . . . But, you know, barring that, I think that my opinions break down when it gets to the legacies. Yeah.

Notice that Katherine, the daughter of doctors, frames her discussion of legacy admissions in the language of contributions to the campus community. That is, she uses the language of collective merit to evaluate whether Harvard should consider family connections in admissions decisions and decides that doesn't contribute in the ways racial diversity, athletic merit, and music skills do.

Overall, student expressions of the importance of collective merit echo what their admissions offices say they look for. Here again is language from Brown University's website on admission:

> Our admission process challenges us to discover how each applicant would contribute to—and benefit from—the lively academic, social, and extracurricular activity here at Brown. We will consider how your unique talents, accomplishments, energy, curiosity, perspective, and identity might weave into the ever-changing tapestry that is Brown University. Throughout our long history of encouraging diversity, we have learned that it is this dynamic mix of individuals that makes for the most fascinating and productive undergraduate community.[16]

Harvard dean of admissions William Fitzsimmons uses very similar language:

> Personal qualities and character provide the foundation upon which each admission rests. Harvard alumni/ae often report that the education they received from fellow classmates was a critically important component of their college experience. The education that takes place between roommates, in dining halls, classrooms, research groups, extracurricular activities, and in Harvard's residential houses depends on selecting students who will reach out to others. . . . The admissions committee therefore takes great care to identify students who will be outstanding "educators," who will inspire fellow classmates and professors.[17]

As with language on calibrating evaluations of merit, students seem to have internalized Harvard's and Brown's language of the importance of maintaining a diverse student body that contributes to the collective merit of a cohort, thus enhancing the college experience. The similarity between the official language of calibration and collective merit between Harvard and Brown is evidence of institutional isomorphism—the tendency for organizations to converge in their practices.[18] As we have seen, Harvard and Brown share a history of race activism on campus, a legal context for affirmative action in the United States, and a history of holistic admissions to justify both exclusion (Jewish quotas) and inclusion (affirmative action). Most students' perspectives echo this holistic perspective on admissions.

Keep in mind that while this emphasis on collective merit may seem civic-minded, ultimately students support it in order to enrich their own individual college experiences. This is not a democratic sensibility; if anything, supporting *calibration* for others less fortunate might be a more democratic inclination. Given that most students attending elite universities are coming from privileged families, calibration to one's opportunities reduces the many advantages privileged students have in the admissions process. Of course that minor discounting, as it is practiced today, still leads to a student body at elite colleges that is incredibly—though not exclusively—privileged.

"Ethnic Diversity Is Beneficial to Everyone": Collective Merit and Affirmative Action

The admissions practice most contested in public debates is affirmative action. Although the language of "diversity" in selective higher education admissions is rooted in racial diversity, race did not always come up in discussions of diversity—for example, recall Elliot's discussion of athletic recruiting when he was asked about diversity on campus. Diversity has become the language through which universities justify affirmative action, due in part to the 1978 US Supreme Court *Bakke* decision, which allowed only this rationale. Indeed, the universities themselves avoid explicit talk of race when highlighting the importance of diversity, as the quotations above show. Nevertheless, many students did support considering race in admissions decisions for applicants' contributions to the collective merit of the student body. This view rests on a diversity frame. That is, when students view racial and ethnic groups as holding distinct cultures to be celebrated and engaged, they believe affirmative action will ensure that they can learn from ethnic and racial diversity on campus. Among white and Asian American students, this justification for affirmative action was more common than justifications based on belief in calibrating evaluations of merit. Black and Latino students expressed similarly high levels of support for both justifications.

When asked whether admissions officers should consider race, Stephanie, a white history major in her third year at Harvard, said yes, because doing so contributes to the cohort's collective merit:

> If you need a diverse community, it's pretty important to make sure that you're admitting a diverse population. So, in that sense, I think that [race] needs to be considered. . . . An ethnically diverse community is beneficial to everyone and is such an integral part of a Harvard education.

Sophie, the multiracial student described earlier, articulated a vision of collective merit, like many of her white peers, talking specifically about religion and ethnicity: "I wouldn't know half of what I do about Muslim people if it weren't for Harvard. Or, you know, to distinguish between Muslims and Arabs, you know?" Just as her white peers might see Sophie's presence on campus as beneficial to them for exposing them to a black perspective, Sophie notes the importance of Muslim peers to her own college experience.

Jenny, a multiracial junior whose mother was born in East Asia, also noted the importance of having racially diverse students on campus to enhance the college experience. When asked whether Brown should consider race or ethnicity when making decisions about who to admit, she said,

> I think they should, because it can't just be a university where students are just of two races. . . . And it's important because a lot of individuals in this university, especially, are concerned about the world. Brown raises its students to be leaders of society. That's what the Ivies are all about. They want to look at our leadership qualities in high school because they know that we're going to be the leaders of tomorrow. It's important that we also come into contact with people from backgrounds other than our own. . . . [If students here] never

come into contact with diversity, they will only ever really base [de-cisions] on a very, very, very superficial level. And they won't under-stand the issues.

Jenny's expression of the need to go beyond "two races" suggests the need for affirmative action, given that Asian Americans and whites are already overrepresented on elite campuses. She couches collec-tive merit in a neoliberal framework of becoming a better worker in the global market. That is, she expresses a form of what Will Kym-licka calls "neoliberal multiculturalism": "the belief that ethnic identi-ties and attachments can be assets to market actors."[19] Jenny's discus-sion of "leaders of tomorrow" and the decisions they will make reflects the way contemporary corporations speak of diversity. In chapter 2 I quoted an amicus brief to the 2006 US Supreme Court affirmative action case in which a group of Fortune 500 companies stated that "a diverse workforce . . . is important to [our] continued success in the global marketplace." Similarly, to Jenny affirmative action in ad-missions to Brown is important because Brown students are likely to become leaders in society, and they can do better work if they under-stand diverse perspectives.

Dexter, quoted earlier for his belief in calibrated evaluations of merit, specifically invoked market benefits when he expressed his be-lief in the importance of collective merit:

> I think race [also] should be taken into consideration for the good of the university [and] for the good of the college experience, because Harvard doesn't need to send some white guy to Wall Street who has never interacted with a black person. He's going to be a business ana-lyst under somebody who is, you know, a black guy from Penn, so he needs to know how to interact with, or to have been around people of different cultures.

Dexter states the benefits to the work a presumably white future business analyst will do. Interestingly, however, he recognizes the im-portance of his (white) peers' understandings of students like himself, an African American, rather than benefits to himself.[20] He was the ex-ception: nearly all other students of color spoke of collective merit for their own benefit rather than for their white peers' benefit. In other words, black and Latino students did not see it as their responsibility to teach their white peers; instead, they too saw themselves as benefiting from campus diversity.

Many students reported that their support for attention to collective merit, especially when thinking about race, increased on arrival to campus, suggesting an institutional influence on conceptions of merit similar to the influence on students' diversity frames. Elliot, quoted earlier for his support for athletic recruiting to create a better campus experience, also expressed support for considering race in admissions decisions, again for its contribution to campus life. When asked whether Brown should consider race or ethnicity in admissions, he said, "I didn't think so before I got here. And I think so now because . . . different groups of people—I had a better experience because they provided me with insight that I otherwise wouldn't have." Elliot was interviewed during his sophomore year. As with athletics, his support for attention to racial diversity increased the longer he was at Brown. Elliot grew up in a town that is 90 percent white and told us his high school was "really segregated," with black and white students maintaining separate social networks. He contrasted this experience to his experience at Brown, where "Looking around campus, you see people from all walks of life—races, sexualities, countries of origin. . . . And like students learn about other [groups], and about themselves, in ways they otherwise wouldn't."

An emphasis on collective merit as the justification for affirmative action led some students to feel satisfied with diversity on campus despite the underrepresentation of black and Latino students. They felt there were already enough black and Latino students to make for a rich educational experience. For example, I asked Sheena, an Indian American student at the end of her first year at Brown, whether it was a problem that 15 percent of Brown's student body was black or Latino, given that 25 percent of the US population was black or Latino. She responded, "On an abstract level it's a problem. But when I'm sitting in class I don't feel it. . . . As part of the Brown community, I'm not sitting here screaming, 'We need more! We need more diversity!' Because I don't feel that we lack it when I'm in it." Similarly, Maggie, a white senior studying biology, felt the admissions office fulfilled its duty to recruit minority students. When asked if Brown should do anything about the underrepresentation of black and Latino students, she said,

I know that there is a lot of emphasis on maintaining a diverse student body [in admissions]. So I don't know if there's anything lacking in that area. I think they're very aware of making sure that Brown
has a representative population. Maybe not exactly reflecting the US
population, but making sure there is a wide range of students on
campus.

Notice that Maggie's belief in attention to collective merit leads
her to emphasize a "wide range of students on campus" when evaluating the success of diversity efforts in the admissions process rather
than, for example, a student body reflecting the racial makeup of
young adults in the country. Proportionate inclusion might signal to
some, especially those with a power analysis frame, that admissions
has truly become racially equal because of its equal outcomes. However, Maggie's concern, and the concern of others like her, relates to
having a quorum of students from all groups so that cross-racial learning can go on.[21]

Overall, then, students emphasized the need for admissions officers to build a diverse cohort of students, and racial diversity was just
one of many types of diversity to consider. When students perceive all
those admitted to have a particular quality that adds to the collective
merit of the cohort in an extremely competitive process, being black
or Latino becomes just another form of diversity. Orin, a white junior
studying social studies, explicitly compared being a racial minority to
being a talented pianist: "[Ethnic diversity] adds as much to the class
as somebody who is a world-class piano player, and . . . it's just a different sort of diversity to add." In other words, according to Orin, all
kinds of diversity, including racial diversity and diversity of talents,
are important for the student body. Orin attended a high school that
is more than 75 percent white and contrasted her high school to Harvard, which is "very multicultural in terms of the amount of foreign
students here and also just American students from all different sorts
of cultures." We might puzzle at first at the range of collective merits Orin lists: one is a characteristic that students are born with, race,
while the other is presumably achieved, world-class piano skills. But
under collective merit that distinction is not relevant, because the
evaluation is about contributions to others, not personal accomplishments. In addition, in many ways world-class piano skill is not solely
a personal accomplishment either—to develop those skills one needs

to be born into a family with the means to pay for piano lessons, and at the very least an electric keyboard if not a nice piano.

The Diversity Bargain

We have seen how students expressed support for affirmative action through beliefs about the importance of the collective merit of their university cohorts, and sometimes through beliefs in the calibration of merit according to racial disadvantage. Below I highlight two consequences of the collective merit basis for affirmative action, which together lead to the expression among white students of what I call a diversity bargain.

First, the potential for feeling victimized by reverse racial discrimination in admissions seemed to lurk beneath the surface of many white students' perspectives. For example, Thomas, a white Harvard student studying biology, said he feels

> personally disadvantaged at times. When you think that they—not lower standards, but that if you're Latino or if you're black you could have a lower GPA and lower test scores and get in and then I could have the same test scores and maybe not get in because there's so many other competitors who may be white that have better test scores, you can feel a bit disadvantaged at times.

Thomas got into Harvard, arguably the most prestigious college in the country. He and other students like him held a reverse discrimination *script* for understanding any personal failure—or even anxiety about the *potential* for failure—in a competitive process.[22] I call it a script because reverse discrimination seemed to be a concept that students held whether or not they had experienced a situation that led them to perceive it. It is the script itself rather than a particular experience of reverse discrimination that seems to be embedded in the minds of these white students. Thomas's words suggest that the reverse discrimination script is already present, even after his recent admission to Harvard.

Thomas's perspective resonates with those of many other whites at Harvard and Brown. In the student survey we conducted, over one-third of white students agreed that "providing extra aid to ethnic and racial minorities in terms of campus admissions is unfair to whites," and another 21 percent were ambivalent (neither agreed nor dis-agreed).[23]

Serena was a white student studying psychology in her junior year at Harvard. When asked if she'd ever experienced discrimination, she too voiced the reverse discrimination script: "If I hadn't gotten into Harvard I would have felt that I'd been discriminated against. If some-one else that I knew and was equally qualified who was an ethnic mi-nority had gotten in above me." The thought that Thomas and Serena *could have* been passed over for a minority student with lower, or even similar, test scores and GPA gives them reason to worry about reverse discrimination.

The responses of students like Thomas and Serena imply that they are primed to see reverse discrimination in the future; this script may emerge quickly when such students are not selected for positions they feel entitled to, such as seats in graduate school, internships, or jobs in elite firms, leading to racial resentment. Donald Kinder and Lynn Sanders define racial resentment as "a contemporary expression of racial discord. . . . [It] features indignation as a central emotional theme, one provoked by the sense that black Americans are getting and taking more than their fair share."[24] Scholars suggest that racial resentment may be rooted in feelings of *group* rather than *individual* threat, which may explain Serena's and Thomas's anxieties despite their admission to Harvard.[25] For example, researchers have shown that whites are less likely to support affirmative action when they are told that whites as a group will lose out.[26]

Some white students did speak of particular internships or jobs for which they felt unfairly bypassed. Craig, a white senior who grew up in what he described as a privileged family, said,

> I've gotten to see affirmative action from, like, the point of the per-
> son who it's being—I don't want to say used against, but kind of,
> like, who's not being favored by it. It makes you a little bitter seeing
> dozens of white or Asian people applying for a job and then your
> African American friend gets it through a minority program that's,
> like, half as competitive.

A biology major, Craig later expressed support for affirmative action, citing a different college with a predominantly white student body where some students were in blackface for Halloween. He advo-

cated a "minimum diversity threshold" to militate against incidents
like that:

> Whitman is a pretty good liberal arts school but just not diverse at
> all, and two people painted themselves black for Halloween. That
> would not happen if you actually had diversity on campus. . . . I think
> the university needs to have some minimum level of diversity.

Hence Craig supports considerations of race so that racial diversity will enrich him and his peers, but he is ambivalent about affirmative action when he feels it does not benefit him—that is, when he
perceives minority peers as having an easier time with competitions
like job and internship applications. Like Craig, many students who
expressed fears of reverse discrimination still supported affirmative
action, but only to the extent that it didn't appear to make them miss
opportunities.

The second consequence of the view that affirmative action is important for its contributions to collective merit is the emphasis on
integration across racial lines, what I call the *integration imperative*.
As we have seen, most students of all races at Harvard and Brown—
like other Americans who hold a diversity frame—believe we have
much to learn from interacting with others with different racial backgrounds. Consequently, white students who believed in the importance of collective merit sometimes expected minority students to
integrate with white peers and were dismayed at perceived racial segregation on campus. These students valued affirmative action for its
contribution to the collective merit of their cohort, much as athletic
recruiting and students' individual talents contribute; but racial diversity can contribute to the collective merit only if minority students engage with their white peers. For example, recall some white students'
criticism of TWTP at Brown for separating students of color from
white students. When asked whether she sees evidence of multiculturalism on campus, Anna, a white student whose high school was less
than 5 percent black or Hispanic and less than 10 percent poor, said,

> Yeah, I think that Harvard is a pretty diverse place. But I think . . . the
> diversity . . . ends up being a lot of different groups . . . that sort of
> self-select and associate . . . within their particular culture. . . . I don't
> know that there is much interaction between the different groups.

Anna, a junior, studied religion at Harvard. When asked to elaborate on her perspective and the self-selection she described, Anna said,

> It really bothers me, because it makes it really difficult to get to know people, because I'm not in any of those—like, I'm not going to join the Black Students Association. And most of the groups that I am in are not [race defined]—because if they had a White Students Association they would probably get in a lot of trouble. . . . I think it's just sort of sad. . . . because the interaction that I have had with people from different backgrounds has been so great for me, and especially coming from a school where there wasn't a lot of that.

Anna laments the lack of greater integration between her minority and white peers. Given the collective merit perspective on affirmative action, interaction with peers of color is a *resource* some white students feel entitled to—or sometimes wrongly deprived of.[27] This integration imperative ignores the important supporting role that black-only spaces have historically provided for students who attend a predominantly white college with privileged peers.[28] Note, too, the parallel Anna draws between a Black Students Association and a White Students Association. This color-blind analysis ignores the different positions of blacks and whites on the Harvard campus.

I call these two consequences of the collective merit justification for affirmative action a *diversity bargain*. Most white students seem to implicitly view affirmative action as a trade-off, which they support as long as it benefits themselves. Under the diversity bargain, underrepresented minority students can be admitted with lower SAT scores or GPAs, as long as those students then contribute to the educational experiences of their peers by not getting rewards "over" white peers and by integrating so that the collective merit of the cohort can enrich everyone's education.[29] To many white students, minority students do not hold up their end of the diversity bargain when they join the Black Students Association or sit together in the cafeteria. More abstractly, students can feel the diversity bargain has not been upheld by institutions when they lose out in a competitive process such as college admission, applying for an internship or job, and more. While my respondents have been highly successful in the ultimate marker of success for an eighteen-year-old—they have been admitted to Ivy League universities with admissions rates well under 10 percent—the future

for most will bring additional competitions for which they may anticipate reverse discrimination. In addition, they will watch carefully to
make sure their minority peers—all of whom they will assume have
benefited from affirmative action—will maintain the integration imperative.

This diversity bargain rests on the diversity frame, which assumes
that those admitted under affirmative action will have different perspectives than white students. Some students made the importance
of this explicit, criticizing the use of race without attention to how
it has shaped a person's life and perspective. If race hasn't shaped an
applicant's perspective, the logic goes, then special admission would
not contribute to the collective merit of the cohort and improve the
learning environment. For these students, race considerations should
not amount simply to "a box to check." Karen, a white Harvard student profiled in chapter 1, expressed this expectation well. It is worth
repeating her explanation:

> I don't think because someone checked the black box or the Latino
> box, that that should be what helps them get in. You know, maybe
> in their interview you find that since they're Latino they've done all
> these things that add something different to the cultural fabric of
> Harvard. . . . I know people who are, like, a quarter Mexican, who
> got the Latino Scholars Award, but their entire experience has been
> a white experience.

Given Karen's view that contributing to the "cultural fabric of Harvard" is what justifies affirmative action, it follows that someone who
is simply "a quarter Mexican" may not have the cultural background
essential to providing an alternative perspective to the mainstream,
white upper-middle-class one so common on campus already. Hence
that person should not benefit from affirmative action, or from a
"Latino Scholars Award," because his admission would not uphold the
diversity bargain by contributing to campus culture.[30]

Along the same lines, Jack, a white junior studying physics and economics, said,

> At my high school there was a black kid who applied to Harvard, and
> I was actually going to be upset if he'd gotten in because he was one
> of the dumbest people I'd ever met. The thought that he could have

gotten in on his mediocre grades but with the fact that he was black outraged me. I think of him specifically when I caution against using race as too much of an indicator, because even though he was black . . . he was the whitest kid most people knew, in the sense that he was living such a clichéd rich, preppy, white kid lifestyle.

Ultimately, Jack got admitted to Harvard. What seems to worry Jack—both during the admissions process and in retrospect—is the potential that a black student who does not demonstrate the cultural identity associated with blackness in the contemporary United States would nevertheless benefit from affirmative action. While at first Jack seems to lament an admissions process that may select a peer with low grades, he later adds that it is "because . . . he was the whitest kid most people knew," suggesting that if this black peer grew up in other circumstances, overlooking his low grades could be justified. Students saw affirmative action benefiting students who do not have a sufficiently "minority" experience as violating some unspoken norm. In different ways, Karen and Jack both disapprove of peers of color benefiting, they claim, from affirmative action despite having had "white" experiences growing up. While they do not elaborate specifically on what they mean by "white" experiences, we can surmise from their comments that they mean growing up with privileges that seem to supersede racial disadvantage and racial difference. Jack, Karen, and others highlighted examples like these to define the boundaries of affirmative action acceptable to them. Those boundaries are shaped by the diversity frame together with the diversity bargain.

If white students implicitly expect a diversity bargain with their black and Latino peers, do students of color enter into that agreement as well? In a nutshell, no. Minority students often object to the expectation that they take on the job of educating whites about matters related to race.[31] Indeed, students of color did not see themselves as being on campus to teach their white peers about life as a minority in the United States, as their white peers positioned them. Instead, they saw themselves also as beneficiaries of campus diversity, pointing to personal gains. For example, recall multiracial Sophie, who cited her new knowledge of what it means to be Muslim and Arab through the diversity of the Harvard campus. Marie, a black student studying sociology, when asked about the influence of diversity on campus life, said,

In my personal experience, it's really cool hearing my roommate talk about Turkey. Or like, my other roommate is very, very Jewish, and I actually don't know anything about the Jewish faith, but then she tells me things like, they don't believe in heaven, and like, whoa! So it's cool. You know all these different things, all these different worlds, all these different ways of living and ideas and food [laugh] that you wouldn't have been exposed to otherwise.

Hence while white students position black and Latino students, the primary beneficiaries of affirmative action, as on campus to enrich whites' educational experiences through a diversity bargain, black and Latino students themselves do not identify with that bargain. Moreover, they too recognize and appreciate other forms of difference they have encountered on campus, many for the first time.

"Last Time I Checked, Racism Was Still Around": Power Analysis Perspectives on Admissions

As I described in chapters 2 and 3, a significant minority of US students, both of color and white, employed a power analysis frame, often influenced by the Third World Center and the Third World Transition Program at Brown. In their views on admissions, these students went beyond the calibration of merit according to one's opportunities and the collective merit of the cohort. They tended to justify their beliefs in affirmative action through a power analysis frame. For example, Sophie, quoted earlier for her focus on collective merit, voiced strong support when asked whether Harvard should consider race in admissions:

I think they should definitely take into account that institutional racism . . . is going to prevent people who are not of the majority from having equal opportunities in life in general, and I think that we should try to rectify that. . . . I know a lot of people don't agree with that anymore, because they think that everything's, like, equalled out now. Even a lot of students here believe that, which is kind of disturbing. . . . Last time I checked, racism, sexism, classism, they were all still around, so I think until we see representations of marginalized people in parts of our country that represent institutional power, we really can't say that we have stopped needing diversity.

Sophie supported the ongoing affirmative action that Harvard currently practices for its contribution to the collective merit of the cohort *as well as* for its potential to disrupt inequality, guided by a power analysis frame. As Sophie's account shows, belief in the importance of collective merit is not incompatible with more justice-oriented rationales, though such a perspective was uncommon among minority and white students alike.

Jessica, a Latina junior at Brown who attended TWTP, explained her support for affirmative action:

> Things aren't really going to change unless we start admitting that certain people have been kept back for a long time. And that means actively and on purpose been kept back. So that means actively and purposefully trying to equalize things.

Imani, another TWTP participant, went further, invoking white privilege:

> I think that as long as we're operating under the idea of this being an individual—I mean, if we're talking about undoing a system that's based on white privilege, some people have to give up in order for others to have, and we have to be committed to that. To me affirmative action is not so much about individuals. It's about working to fix the system over time.

Imani's critique led her to reject the notion that affirmative action is about doling out seats based on individual merit, calling instead for attention to group-based privileges and disadvantages. I expected to hear more of these power analysis critiques from students, as Fortgang also imagined when he penned his criticism. However, this was only a handful of students on both campuses.

* * *

Students we interviewed demonstrated familiarity with, and agreement about, how applicants to their colleges should be evaluated, the kinds of students the college looks for and should look for, and the goals admissions officers should consider. In the domain of admissions and in the definition of merit, it seems that the college years are far from a time of rebellion against institutions; rather, for these students it is a time to reproduce the criteria of evaluation and status that their universities espouse. In fact, some bring their views into line with those of their universities once they get there, even if they disagreed with certain practices before they arrived on campus. While there is a history of social protest and ongoing debates among college students in the United States—activism around the Dream Act to allow undocumented youth attending college to have legal status and divestment in suspect industries, to name a few recent examples—in the realm of admissions, students seem to agree quite strongly with their universities, and when they arrive on campus they come to agree *more* rather than to criticize.

In addition, I found that few recognized the advantages they had in the admissions process, even though most students on elite campuses come from wealthy families.[32] Mary Jackman's research shows that when the legitimacy of status systems is called into question, such as through critiques of admissions to Harvard and Brown, those with high status—like those admitted to elite colleges—insist on the legitimacy of those systems.[33] Perhaps this process led my respondents to strongly support the definition of merit espoused by their universities, despite their liberal identities that otherwise might have criticized the unequal outcomes of admissions. There is a danger to this process: Andrew Delbanco warns that uncritical belief in meritocracy may lead elites to feel less responsible to society if they believe they have *earned* rather than *inherited* their elite position.[34]

I did find soft but significant criticisms of admissions around the edges—most commonly over legacy admissions, athletic recruiting, and affirmative action. Still, most critics assumed the same understanding of merit that supporters expressed—that admissions officers should calibrate evaluations of merit according to individual circumstances, and that contribution to the cohort's collective merit is important. Most disagreements were over what criteria to use for calibration and what it takes to contribute to collective merit. A small group of students did express a more radical perspective on affirmative action, suggesting a restorative justice rationale or a recognition of institutional racism. These students recognized ongoing racial inequality, holding a power analysis frame. This view was more common among black and Latino students, although it was a minority view among them as well.

The overall emphasis on collective merit might at first glance suggest a group-oriented analysis. However, even while these students express the importance of collective merit, ultimately their perspectives are embedded in an individualist frame—collective merit is prized for its impact on the student, not for social justice or for the collective good of society. Indeed, at Harvard and Brown, this desire for diverse peers is a way of becoming elite. Students recognized that it takes affirmative action to make intercultural learning happen. Further, they needed racial diversity and integration to bolster their self-worth and to develop their identities as nonracist elites. Without that diversity, they would not fully embody their eliteness. Students are not espousing, for example, a vision of multiculturalism that emphasizes group identities and the need to support ethnic and racial groups in society as fundamental human rights, as advocates of multiculturalism sometimes do.[35] Nor are many students advocating affirmative action in the service of restorative justice, as advocates of reparations have called for.[36] Rather, their concern about collective merit, a seemingly democratic sensibility, is ultimately focused on personal, individual benefits. Mary Jackman and Michael Muha describe how, in defending the legitimacy of their status, dominant groups privilege individual rights over group rights, much the way respondents emphasized benefits to themselves rather than to underrepresented groups.[37]

In many ways, students attending selective private universities may be our best-case scenario for positive views on affirmative action. Recall that I chose to study two of the country's most selective universities in large part because I wanted to discover perspectives on race and admissions among successful students most poised to not feel threatened by affirmative action. At lower-tier universities, student views on affirmative action are likely to be different, because white students on those campuses may attribute their rejection from the likes of Harvard and Brown to affirmative action. In one sense I was right: most white students supported affirmative action. However, I was wrong in that they did so not with the aim of expanding access to elite colleges, but because they saw benefits for themselves. These benefits accrued, however, only through the integration imperative and a perceived lack of increased competition.

This diversity bargain may be the only justification for affirmative action that will gain traction in the policy and judicial domains, given the propensity for racial justice policies and judicial decisions to hold sway only when white and black interests converge. Over thirty-five years ago Derrick Bell developed a theory of "interest convergence," suggesting that black advancement would gain traction only when middle-class and upper-class whites' interests converged with those of blacks.[38] Bell illustrated this point through a discussion of the 1954 *Brown v. Board of Education* US Supreme Court decision that deemed separate but equal schools "inherently unequal," mandating desegregation. In that case, Bell suggests, whites' interest in demonstrating to the rest of the world that the United States was a democratic nation committed to equality set the stage for the Court's decision. By the 1970s, however, whites' interest in desegregation stagnated, and consequently so did efforts to desegregate American schools. Bell pessimistically concludes that efforts toward racial justice should look for strategies that are, in effect, color-blind to gain the support of influential whites.[39] Perhaps an emphasis on collective merit and the diversity frame, then, is our best hope for maintaining affirmative action in elite colleges; certainly this is the argument that university defendants in affirmative action legal cases have used.

Still, while the diversity bargain makes white students more willing to support affirmative action, it also has dangerous effects and supports a reverse discrimination script that lurks just beneath the surface for white (and potentially for Asian American) students. That is, if affirmative action's purpose is to benefit *me*, then whenever I am not successful in a competitive contest I can easily attribute that setback to affirmative action or reverse discrimination. In addition, the emphasis on collective merit advantages for white students ignores the hardships nontraditional students may face when expected to play a teaching role for their peers.[40]

The focus on personal benefits of affirmative action in contrast to a more compensatory goal also ignores the historical and structural discrimination that continues to affect racial minorities today and suggests that racial inequality and discrimination are no longer significant.[41] Many elite campuses were built by slave labor, as Brown's slavery inquiry revealed.[42] Moreover, the ongoing effects of our racial history mean that black and white youth continue to face unequal life chances. Study after study has demonstrated that, far too often, teachers and the school system itself disadvantage black and Latino students through low expectations, racial segregation, and much more.[43] Researchers have found significant correlations between race and school tracking,[44] school discipline,[45] and even the kinds of houses a realtor will show a client.[46] African Americans in particular have experienced mass incarceration and its debilitating repercussions on individuals and communities.[47] African Americans and Latinos experience job discrimination.[48] Asian Americans are less likely to get promoted at work than their white peers.[49] African American families disproportionately suffer from intergenerational poverty and the neighborhood problems that come with poverty.[50] The list goes on. And yet the justification most students express in support of affirmative action is the one they hear from their colleges: it will benefit me.

FIVE

THE MORAL IMPERATIVES OF DIVERSITY

The first time I heard the phrase "That's racist!" as a researcher was at a high school in Queens, New York, more than ten years ago, while I was working on my previous book. The school was incredibly diverse, with families from all over the world, no majority ethnic group, and very few white students. The claim was made in response to a moment I thought was decidedly *not* racist—a student had described someone by ethnicity—"He is Dominican"[1]—to which a peer responded, "That's racist, yo!" I was perplexed. I had observed many instances of school policies that clearly seemed to affect students differently by race—the sequestering of English-language learners in particular classrooms, the banning of styles, like do-rags, typically worn by black students, and the underrepresentation of teachers of color. In my mind these were situations that could have legitimately been described as racist. But students rarely pointed out these injustices to me, either in our numerous conversations in the hallways or in in-depth interviews. And yet the offhand mention of someone's ethnicity crossed the line. Why?

What lessons did this polyglot bunch of students seem to have learned in school about slavery and segregation? It seems they learned that *naming* race was itself racist—that calling attention to someone's race was behaving in a racist way, because after all it was differentiating people by race that led to the heinous system of racial injustice they learned about in school. And, to be perceived as racist was a moral transgression.

In this chapter I add another dimension to our discussion of race on campus: moral worth. I describe how moral worth on these elite campuses is tied to being seen as not racist. This phenomenon is not limited to elite college campuses, as my high school research experience shows, yet it takes on heightened meaning when students come to college expecting to learn from campus diversity. Students during our interviews spoke in ways that seemed to focus on avoiding the accusation of racism. In other words, their moral identities as "not racist" led to particular ways of speaking (and behaving), on campus. In spite of the heightened sense of importance around conversations related to race—or perhaps because of it—interracial dialogue about ongoing racial inequality and injustice rarely surfaced.

Moral worth is an important aspect of identity for most individuals, even while the definition of what it means to be a moral self varies across national boundaries and between groups.[2] Students we interviewed in the United States implicitly defined being "not racist" as part of their moral identities. Given the history of slavery and racial segregation in the United States, a shared understanding that "racism is immoral" develops at a young age. Children in schools celebrate Martin Luther King Jr. Day by hearing about a time when immoral racism led to the separation of black and white Americans and about King's heroic dismantling of that racism. The shame of our collective history, and the desire to avoid identification with that history, leads whites and people of color alike to identify strongly as "not racist." This imperative is especially salient for whites, because their white identities link them to racism historically, hence their status as "not racist" can more quickly be questioned. Even President George W. Bush, reflecting on rapper Kanye West's accusation that he did not care about black Americans in the wake of Hurricane Katrina, said,

> I was raised to believe that racism was one of the greatest evils in society. . . . I faced a lot of criticism as president. I didn't like hearing people claim I had lied about Iraq's weapons of mass destruction or cut taxes to benefit the rich. But the suggestion that I was a racist because of the response to Katrina represented an all-time low. I told Laura at the time that it was the worst moment of my presidency. I feel the same way today.[3]

Given the basic lessons we learn about race in history classes in the United States, racism often gets limited to legal enslavement, legal segregation, and overtly hostile attitudes toward members of a particular group, letting actions that negatively affect a group, such as inaction in the wake of Hurricane Katrina, prison sentencing laws that disproportionately affect black Americans, racially segregated academic tracks in schools, and more, escape the moral claim of racism. George Bush could thus lay claim to his sense of moral worth to reject West's accusation, despite his slow response when the hurricane hit. This claim is so important to Bush precisely because West's accusation is an accusation of moral failure that is worse, as Bush describes it, than the accusation of moral failure in his tax cuts or lying to the American people.

Many white Americans come to fear that their words or actions will be stamped with the moral judgment "That's racist." Social psychologists have documented the effects of these fears. They find that when whites are prompted to try not to be racist in an interracial interaction, the interaction feels more stressful.[4] In particular, whites are vulnerable to white stereotype threat—a fear that they will live up to the stereotype that whites are racist.[5] The concept of stereotype threat was first developed to explain how some negatively stereotyped groups, such as blacks or women, can underperform when feeling anxious about living up to a stereotype of their group, such as black students taking an IQ test or women taking a math test.[6] Stereotype threat about whites being racist leads some whites to distance themselves from blacks, and this distancing does not appear to be correlated with an individual's level of prejudice.[7] In other words, the mere fear of being perceived as racist can lead whites to shy away from interacting with blacks. This fear stems in part from the diversity frame. Because the diversity frame suggests that race shapes individuals' worldviews and exposure to different worldviews is part of the college experience, students of color are seen as holding authoritative views on race, often with moral weight, such that whites often feel ill-equipped to determine what actions or words are racist. These perceptions are potent because the stakes are high: behaving or speaking in a racist manner is seen as moral failure, akin to the moral failures of slavery and segregation. This leads many white students to feel great angst, because their beliefs in collective merit mean they should engage in cross-race dialogue to enhance their college experiences, even though that dialogue is stressful.[8]

For their part, many minorities, especially blacks, are anxious about how they will be treated by whites. These fears are related to minority "metastereotypes"—that is, stereotypes about what stereotypes whites hold about racial minorities. These metastereotypes can shape interracial interactions. For example, a majority of black Americans in a 1990 survey believed that whites believe blacks prefer to live off welfare, are violent, are lazy, and are unintelligent.[9] The percentage of beliefs about negative stereotypes was higher among blacks with higher incomes. More recently, Kimberly Torres and Camille Charles studied the metastereotypes that black students at the University of Pennsylvania hold about their white peers' beliefs about black students on campus.[10] Many black students believed that white students think black students are not qualified to attend the University of Pennsylvania, are all the same, and do not want to socialize or live with whites. In turn, many white students reported that their white peers in general think black Penn students don't want to integrate with whites and are not qualified to attend Penn.[11] On the other hand, other research has shown that when black students are told that a white student has a diverse group of friends, they anticipate a more pleasant interracial conversation.[12] Overall, these stereotypes and metastereotypes create anxiety in both black and white students on campus. That they create anxiety, of course, does not deny their validity; in fact, black metastereotypes about whites' beliefs about blacks turn out to be fairly accurate assessments of what whites actually think.[13]

It is important to recognize that while both students of color and white students suffer from anxiety about race on campus, those concerns are qualitatively different. That is, white fears of prejudice—real or imagined—cannot have the same material impact on them as racism does on minority students, given the way US society is structured. To see this, it is helpful to distinguish between racism, prejudice, and discrimination. Racial prejudice refers to negative *attitudes* about a racial group, while racial discrimination is *behavior* that discriminates according to race.[14] Going further, racism, according to William Julius Wilson, refers to attitudes or beliefs consistent with the maintenance of racial dominance.[15] According to Wilson's definition, while oppressed groups can hold prejudice against dominant groups or behave in discriminatory ways, they cannot be racist, because their prejudice and discrimination do not uphold the racial hierarchy. Prejudice toward minorities, especially African Americans, on the other hand, is structurally embedded in US institutions and hence can take the form of racism.

That understanding of racism may be respected and widely used in academic circles, but is still far from common in American culture. The diversity and color-blindness frames simply do not allow for this deep understanding of racism, because they do not acknowledge differences in power between racial groups. Without a power analysis frame, white college students cannot see the difference between their own and their minority peers' anxieties over race on campus. Dominant discourses about minority sensitivity, such as Fortgang's claim that peers frequently ask him to "check [his] privilege," support this rejection of the difference between structurally embedded racism and interpersonal prejudice.

"If You Say Something, Maybe You're Contributing to Racism": White Students' Experiences with Race

Discussions of race taught most white students to tread lightly when speaking about race, if only in the company of racial minorities.[16] According to students we interviewed, the accusation of racism weighed heavily on them, and many were stung by various experiences in school and beyond. When asked to recall a negative experience with race, many white students cited accusations of racism. For example, Stephanie, a white junior from the Midwest studying history, said,

> This was in middle school. There was a black student and I think she always thought that I was a racist, and it made me feel really bad. But I didn't really get along with her for other reasons. It was just a personality thing. But I just remember thinking that she thought that I didn't like her because she was black. It made me feel really bad, and then I felt like I should be nicer to her so she wouldn't think that. . . . So sometimes it's very hard if you are a white student, especially with blacks, because of the history in this country. . . . I feel like if you're a minority you have to be very careful not to just think that if somebody doesn't like you, that it's because they're racist, because it could be, but it also could not be.

Stephanie's discomfort with the potential accusation of racism, and the realization that her attitudes and behaviors toward a black student could be construed as racist, were common. In spite of the ambiguous situation ("I *think* she always thought I was racist"; my italics), the experience has stayed with Stephanie for ten years, which suggests it carried great meaning. She tells us twice that the situation made her "feel really bad." On the other hand, Stephanie rejects her peer's potential accusation. In the end, she places responsibility squarely with minority students for misinterpreting white peers' intentions. Expecting peers of color to "be very careful" before thinking someone is racist resonates with the diversity bargain's expectation that students of color educate white peers about diversity.

The confusion Stephanie experienced happens frequently in the United States, given the anxieties about crossing the moral boundary of racism. Many situations *are* racist, others are not, and still others are debatable or ambiguous. But the phrase puts whites on the defensive, needing to protect their moral self-worth by quickly rejecting the claim, which in turn can upset people of color even more because of whites' seeming indifference to, or denial of, the ways race influences interactions.

An instance in which Kyle, a white junior at Brown studying neuroscience, kept revisiting an interaction on campus shows his deep concern over the accusation of racism. Asked to describe a negative experience he's had with someone of a different race, Kyle said:

> I was hanging out with someone and I don't know, I said something, and he took it as white privilege or what have you, and made a joke. And the entire night was awkward as anything from that point on, because the entire night, in my mind, I was going over it. And so I was thinking, "Was that a messed up thing to say?" Maybe it was. How did — like trying to think about how what I said was messed up. I'm still going over it in my mind.

Using the diversity frame, Kyle recognizes that this peer may have a perspective entirely different from his. White students sometimes expressed a lack of confidence in speaking about race or in making sense of racially charged situations, given their identification with a group that oppressed African Americans for so long (and, some argue, continues to do so). Determining whether an action or speech was racist was often left to students of color because white students could not always rely on their own moral compass to evaluate whether doing or saying something would be deemed racist. Of course, I cannot know definitively whether whites merely fear public shaming from minority peers or if they truly accept their assessments. Regardless, the dynamic shapes cross-racial interactions on campus in important ways, and in Kyle's case it seems the accusation forced him to repeatedly reconsider the words he spoke that night.[17]

In response to the same question about a negative interracial experience, Eric states that the incident he recalls was not racial. Eric and his family were seeking help at the airport:

> I mean, I've had bad experiences with white people. . . . [This was] nothing specific to them being black or Hispanic. . . . We got to the airport, like, four hours ahead of time and the people there were all black that were working—they just happened to be—and none of them were of any help whatsoever. They were just rude and really not helpful at all. . . . It was ridiculous, because they were just so unhelpful. They just happened to all be black.

Eric, a junior biology major at Harvard, certainly remembers that the airport workers his family dealt with were black, yet he emphasizes his belief that their behaviors were not race-related. In his response Eric seemed to be anticipating a possible reaction—that his interviewer would think his description of the incident was racist. The memory of the individuals' race, juxtaposed with Eric's color-blind beliefs, leads to consternation over the possibility that he will be seen as racist. Eric's color-blindness frame also seems to prevent him from understanding how labor market dynamics along with sociocultural history together produce situations in which all workers in a particular context are of one race, unlikely a mere coincidence.

Even if they learned little about the details of African American history in school, white students understood that whites were responsible for oppressing blacks in the past. For some students this awareness led to feelings of guilt over their white racial identities. When asked how their identity shapes their views on race and ethnicity, some white students used the word guilt or self-conscious. This kind of response was more common at Brown (six of twenty-three whites) than at Harvard (two of twenty-three whites), perhaps owing to the differences, and relative influence, of diversity-related workshops and events on the two campuses. Meredith, a sophomore at Brown planning to major in education, worried that she represents the negative image of the United States. When asked how her racial identity shapes her views on race and ethnicity, she said,

I almost feel like—this is a weird thing to say—but it's made me
hypersensitive to multiculturalism, because I've sort of felt this guilt
complex for being white Caucasian. That is, in my mind, this Aber-
crombie image of American culture with this white, blonde hair,
blue eyes, like classic American girl. And since I don't believe that
that is the American identity, because there are so many cultures
that play into it, I start to feel guilty that I am this hated, incorrect
image of what it means to be American. So I think that over the years
I've definitely been hypersensitive to really appreciating and at least
just wanting to learn more about and recognize all the other cultures
that play into the American identity that aren't what I look like.

Meredith, a first-generation college student at Brown, identifies an
alternative cultural representation of the United States, one that sees
a blonde, blue-eyed young woman as the representation of racial oppression. She concludes by invoking the diversity frame, expressing
her desire to "learn more about and recognize other cultures."

Pat, a white sophomore studying media studies at Brown was active
in the arts. He too felt guilt over his white racial identity:

It makes me feel a lot of guilt. It makes me feel like I need to compensate for it. . . . Being white in America is very bizarre in this day and
age, to be totally honest. . . . And it's a very difficult thing to know
how to approach your daily life with that in mind. . . . I think that the
hard thing about being white is that you sort of have to trick your
brain into forgetting that you're white. . . . Because we're still the
dominant culture in the sense that we're the wealthiest. And we're
the ones who have, over the course of history, imposed all of these
restrictions and prejudices on other people. So it's really up to us to
enact a change. We're the ones who are going to have to go, "Hey,
I know I am actually color-blind." . . . That's hard, because no one
wants to talk about it, and no one tells you how to do it. You have to
figure that out on your own.

While Meredith responded to her guilt by attempting to learn from
other cultures, a benefit of diversity on campus, Pat took a color-blind
approach. He suggested the need to "trick" his brain into forgetting his
racial identity, because of the stigma attached.

As we have seen, for many white students dealing with the cultural meanings of race and racism in the contemporary United States was fraught with guilt, mixed emotions, and misunderstandings. In addition to a moral imperative to not be racist, to be an elite in the United States means to be familiar with a range of cultural repertoires and to be decidedly antiracist.[18] Disapproving of racial jokes was one way white students could signal their moral standing with respect to racism. That is, standing up to racism embedded in racial jokes could bolster one's sense of self-worth, and not standing up to them could damage it. For example, James, a white junior at Brown studying international relations, almost shamefully admitted that he didn't intervene when he heard racial jokes, although he should have: "What you're told to do is to speak up. And I'm just much more interested in observing people than I am in judging them. . . . So I think when my friend told a racist joke or a joke I found offensive, I would have probably just smiled and nodded." James hints at a moral transgression in his inaction, blaming his complacency on his personality. He makes clear that the "right" thing to do—"what we're told to do"—is to speak up.

Hannah, a white senior majoring in comparative literature at Brown, reported wondering, "Since when is this allowed?" after hearing a white comedian in New York make jokes about black sexuality. Experiences like Hannah's provided students with a sense of moral superiority in contrasting others' offensive joking to their own sense of identity as not racist. In many ways students resembled comedians dancing close to the "hurtline"—the boundary between jokes that are funny and jokes that are offensive.[19] The heightened feelings about race and racism led many to move cautiously and stay well clear of the line for fear of accidentally crossing it.

Note that both James and Hannah are talking about incidents they experienced at home rather than in college. Indeed, most reports of racial jokes in the United States were from experiences in high school. The diversity culture of their elite campuses may prevent racial jokes for fear of offending peers in a campus culture that perceives racism as morally reprehensible, even more so than the cultures of their high schools.[20] These students lived in a social milieu—two of the country's most elite college campuses—in which race-related talk easily falls on the wrong side of the hurtline; moreover, many white students have a hard time identifying the location of the boundary, having experi-

enced or witnessed situations in which someone was criticized for un-
knowingly expressing racially offensive ideas, beliefs, or even words.
Also, the diversity culture of their college campuses signals to them
and their peers that diversity matters—after all, collective merit is a
key ingredient in admissions—and students seem to internalize that
message. To take advantage of the benefits of that diversity provided
by the admissions process, students need to avoid offending their
peers, who might disengage in response to offensive words or behaviors. They do this by trying to steer clear of racial jokes and by using
language they understand to be inoffensive.

Sometimes, however, these heightened emotions around race led
to racial resentment toward minorities, especially African Americans,
just as perceptions of reverse discrimination could do. Pat, the student
who wanted to "trick" his brain into color-blindness, went on to say,

> There is an element of self-righteousness to a lot of African Ameri-
> cans. And if anything, that's only increased in the Obama age. There's
> a certain element of "The president is black now," so it gives some of
> them maybe an excuse toward sort of a counterracism, where it's a
> little easier to get away with discrimination against whites.

A student who grappled with his feelings about race and racial
interactions both in high school and in college, Pat expresses resentment toward black peers for what he perceives to be slippery use of
the accusation of racism, such as the black student in his high school.
Given the moral weight of that accusation, Pat employs his color-
blindness frame to defend his moral self-worth.

Hannah, the student quoted above discussing a racist comedian,
was asked if she'd ever experienced racial discrimination. She said,

> I've definitely encountered people who I thought were aggressive
> with me because I'm white. . . . I have a somewhat confrontational
> personality, and I feel like it always becomes a race issue. You can't
> get into an argument with a black person in a subway without them
> calling you racist. It always turns into a race issue. It's like, "No,
> you're just rude, and I'd be fighting with you no matter what you
> looked like!" . . . Just the attitude that you get sometimes from, hon-
> estly, black women. And once from a black man at Port Authority. I

was at the bus station in New York. I was in a hurry. And he was just talking and talking and talking and talking to the ticket woman. And my bus for Providence was about to leave in three minutes. And I just said, "Excuse me." And he just flipped out at me. And sometimes you encounter anger that's just—in my eyes, at least—directed at me because I'm white. He sees me like it's an act of white supremacy that I'm telling him to get the fuck out of the way at the ticket station. At Port Authority I've had several racial incidents.

Hannah perceives anger toward her, when coming from blacks at Port Authority and the subway, as racialized, which she challenges. In her interview Hannah spoke of a process of moving past her father's views, which she described as racist. Later, after her interview, she asked us what she could read to help her understand the issues. Her struggle to move past the racism in the United States and in her own family, combined with experiences in which she believed minorities unfairly saw her as racist, led to a complex stance that she brought with her to Brown. Considering that Hannah attended a private high school known for its very liberal politics, her father likely identifies as liberal, so his racism may be more subtle than the old-fashioned racism of the past. Still, she feels resentment toward the people who accuse her of racism, an accusation she sees as unjustified and one that may cut away at her sense of moral self-worth, eliciting strong emotions.

Thomas, a white sophomore at Harvard, told us that being a white male has its challenges related to diversity on campus:

> I think it's hard being a white male at times, because you feel like if you do say anything, then maybe you're contributing to the racism or something. Like, you're in no position to really have an opinion on a lot of these race issues, because you're the majority and so you're looked at as, like, the oppressor. And you're looked at as the one who's had all these opportunities. So to say anything about it is kind of hypocritical, in a sense.

Thomas voices a sentiment often expressed by critics of liberal colleges—that the "politically correct" culture on campus stifles dialogue, and especially the voices of white men. This racial resentment seems to lurk just beneath the surface for many white students, who despite their liberal identities may ultimately be ambivalent about diversity.

"My White Teacher Said 'You Don't Look Smart'": Students of Color and Experiences with Race and Racism

In spite of the precipitous decline in overt racial prejudice over the past fifty years, many more subtle causes of racial inequality endure. Aside from structural exclusion and socioeconomic and educational inequality, there are also the day-to-day experiences with race in the United States. Elijah Anderson, in a book about cosmopolitan spaces of Philadelphia, writes of the "N-moment":

> There comes a time in the life of every African American in which he or she is powerfully reminded of his or her putative place as a black person. . . . At the time it occurs, however, the awareness of this act of acute insult and discrimination is shocking; the victim is taken by surprise, caught off guard. . . . Emotions flood over the victim as this middle-class, cosmopolitan-oriented black person is humiliated and shown that he or she is, before anything else, a racially circumscribed black person after all.[21]

Many students of color we interviewed described such moments. These were incidents in which teachers held low expectations, boyfriends or girlfriends dumped them in deference to their prejudiced parents, and more. Those experiences often shaped students' identities and, just as much, their self-confidence. For example, Imani said,

> I had a teacher in seventh grade who was giving out report cards — a white teacher — and when he got to my report card and saw that I had really good grades he was like, "Oh, this is yours? I had no idea you were smart. You don't look smart." . . . He was my homeroom teacher, so he didn't have me in any classes. He just saw me every morning. He was like, "Look at all the other kids who are at the top of the class. You don't quite fit into that. I was kind of surprised." That had a big effect on how I saw myself and my self-esteem in school. I felt like, "Oh wow, if he thinks I don't look smart, does every other student think I don't look smart when I first get into a class?" And

it made me a lot more quiet in school. I felt like I always had something to prove, and I really took that into myself, and would be really
quiet, just do my work.

Imani grew up in a household with two professional parents, in a
middle-class urban neighborhood. About one-third of her high school
peers were white. Despite this diverse setting, or perhaps because in
diverse schools the separating of white and Asian American students
into high tracks and black and Latino students into low tracks makes
achievement even more racialized,[22] Imani's teacher labeled her
achievement surprising. Although her high school was diverse, Imani
told us that speaking of race was taboo there:

> I went to a high school where we weren't even allowed to talk about
> race or ethnicity. We couldn't have—there were no cultural groups
> at school that you could be a part of. It was pretty much seen as an-
> tagonistic. Even though I had been around a lot of different types
> of people, it wasn't really something that was on the table for dis-
> cussion. . . . Brown put it on the table for discussion, so I learned
> more about all those different groups, including groups that I'm a
> part of, just because it was something that was encouraged to be
> spoken about outwardly.

Imani also described her experiences in the Third World Transition Program at Brown as "life-changing" and the start of her work
in diversity, "From that point on I became a leader of that program,
and I do a lot of workshop programming on all these issues." A senior
Africana studies major, Imani attributes her political awakening to
Brown. "I didn't come to college particularly activist-minded at all,
but I'm leaving very much so." Given Imani's disturbing experience
with racism as a child, the diversity-related programming may have
spoken to her experiences at a deeper level, providing language for
making sense of those experiences—and probably others like them—
in empowering ways. She further spoke of experiences on campus as
influencing her to figure out "how I want to live my life after Brown
and the kind of work I do." In her senior year, Imani was leaving Brown
with a power analysis frame.

Many students of color described the lack of agency they felt when facing discrimination. Dexter, an African American sophomore at Harvard who grew up in the South, described his feelings when a girl's parents prevented her from dating him in high school:

> Her parents flat out said I couldn't date her. . . . It was solely because of my race. Her parents knew who I was. . . . It was known that I wasn't a person who is out to cause any trouble or anything like that. It was a very hurtful situation. It was something that just bothered me. . . . The thing that bothered me so much about it was I didn't even get—I had this idea in my head that if I could just get them to talk to me, if they would just talk to me one time, then they'd understand. But they wouldn't even do that.

Dexter was a sociology major. In a different part of his interview he reported that his Harvard experiences provided him with a language and context to make sense of the racialized experiences of his childhood, just as Imani's Brown experiences did for her.

While accusations of racism injured white students' sense of moral self-worth, for students of color such as Imani and Dexter, the impact of racism seemed much more profound, affecting the way they saw themselves, their confidence, and their feelings of self-efficacy. Being *accused* of racism and *suffering* from racism are qualitatively different. White students' experiences with prejudice most often led to frustration and the perception that the racism they had been taught was so terrible was now being inflicted on them. Because they didn't experience—and often never heard about—the N—moments of their minority peers, they didn't understand the gravity of those experiences for students of color. The color-blindness frame, then, seems to blind white students to the qualitative difference between a charged encounter at a bus terminal and a teacher's saying he didn't expect you to do well in school. This difference was all too clear to their minority peers.

Students of color described myriad experiences on campus in which they concluded that race was at play. For example, Susan, a black junior from New York, described an incident in which white friends left a party she brought them to that was hosted by a black sorority at Brown:

> My freshman year me and one of my best friends, who is black, we were going to this party being held by one of the black sororities. We

walked in with a bunch of our friends who were all white behind us, and they were like, "Yeah, yeah, we're coming in." The two of us pay to go in—and, we go in and we turn around and everyone is gone! They just dipped. As soon as they came and saw the space and who was holding it, it was, like, "All right we can't be here. This isn't for us," and they ran. That illustrates what happens at Brown for so many different things. It's just really weird.

While Susan felt upset that whites would eschew a black-dominated space, white students sometimes described minority-dominated spaces they felt they were not welcome to enter. When asked if she's ever experienced racial discrimination, Haley, a white psychology major at Brown, said,

> No, I don't think there have been, except in the sense that I feel like if I put myself in certain situations, like attempting to hang out with a primarily minority friend group here, or attending a function for black students, I feel like I would be unwelcome. So theoretically, yes. But in reality, no.

Haley admits she hasn't attempted to enter minority spaces. She assumes those students would not welcome her, while Susan feels betrayed by white friends who seem to balk at a black-dominated party.[23]

Many students of color explicitly rejected claims that we live in a color-blind society, a result of experiences like Susan's. Marie, a black sociology major at Harvard and the daughter of working-class parents, had this to say about racial inequality in American society:

> Racial inequality is something people ignore now, because we're not to the point where, you know, back in the day you couldn't walk down a certain street without getting yelled at or beaten up or something awful like that. Now, especially since we've elected Obama, people think we're in the postracial era and it's all fine now. It's not all fine! That's something people ignore. Second, if you say something racially motivated, they accuse you of playing the race card, and then it's like, "You're being unfair!" So it's a very sensitive issue, so sensitive I think a lot of people don't talk about it, which is a problem and it helps perpetuate the inequality. We've gotten to a state

of complacency where we think we're fine because we have a black president, which is so completely ludicrous.

Given their experiences with racial discrimination, along with a college culture that tries to address past racial injustices, students of color sometimes claimed a moral authority in matters of race. Christina, a Latina student at Harvard, explained this dynamic:

> I feel like I can talk about race more because I'm not—like if you're black you can talk about race in a different way than a white person can, because if a white person said something then they might be construed as racist, but if you're black and you're talking about your own culture or other people's culture then it's sort of like you have more authority than they do. So I feel like I can talk about things in a way that my white friends can't.

Christina's words show that she identifies with the "black" group even though she describes herself as "Latina" and "mixed." She fears that she sometimes alienates her white friends with her words: "I don't know everything about how to speak in a way that doesn't alienate people, which I'm still learning, and I probably do alienate my white friends when I'm like, 'White people this,' and they're like, 'Why is she generalizing about white people?'" Still, Christina and her peers of color generally held moral authority over matters related to race in many campus situations. Of course, students like Tal Fortgang attempted to question the perspectives of students of color and to assert a different moral compass of outrage toward minorities, but that view was not common. When white students did push back, it appeared more as racial resentment than as moral outrage.

Political Correctness: Not Being Offensive, and Impeding Communication

In 2015, gunmen attacked reporters at the French political satire magazine *Charlie Hebdo*, killing cartoonists associated with satirical depictions of the prophet Muhammad, considered sacrilegious by many religious Muslims. Around the world supporters spoke out to defend *Charlie Hebdo*'s right to free speech, even if they disagreed with the sentiments behind those depictions. The ensuing public debate juxtaposed the need to abstain from offending religious minorities, like Muslims in France, with the right to free speech, which advocates prioritized over what they called "political correctness."

While the term political correctness dates back to the early nineteenth century, it has been used pejoratively since the late 1980s to describe identity politics gone awry.[24] Conservative critics have railed against the "PC police," liberals who are eager to pounce on a speaker's incorrect nomenclature or unknowing offense. Conservatives have used the notion of political correctness to reject the liberal concept that power is embedded in language, and the consequent need to avoid language laden with racist, sexist, and homophobic history. They further suggest that too many peers pander to claims of offense made by disadvantaged groups, including—but not limited to—racial minorities, women, LGBTQ students, non-Christians, and disabled students. In fact, part of the critique is that the number of groups that qualify as disadvantaged is perpetually increasing. Critics argue further that so-called political correctness is dangerous because it limits free speech on campus. These debates have unfolded, to a large extent, on college campuses, particularly elite colleges.[25]

On the Brown and Harvard campuses, the debate over language about minorities was different. Students weighted concerns about maintaining a moral, nonracist identity through inoffensive language with their desire for cross-racial dialogue through open communication. Discussions with students about political correctness illustrate this tension well. We asked students what political correctness is and what they think of it. Overall, their perspectives on political correctness aligned with the importance they placed on collective merit in admissions, and with the diversity frame. Rather than weighing the right to free speech against the desire not to offend, students weighed the importance of intercultural dialogue and open conversation against the need to demonstrate moral beliefs about race and racism. Especially for white students, using "politically correct" language could prevent accusations of racism.

Most students defined political correctness as trying to not offend, by using socially acceptable, "correct" terms for disadvantaged groups. Julie, a white sophomore studying engineering at Brown, said simply, "Political correctness is using the most polite term possible, trying not to offend anybody or step on anyone's toes. . . . I guess it's just trying to be diplomatic and as polite as possible." When asked what she thought about political correctness beyond its definition, Julie said,

> I think it's important, definitely. I think sometimes people can go too far and just be skirting around an issue so much, and it's like, "Just say what you're trying to say!" But there's definitely a spectrum of political correctness. I think if you're about to say a racial slur and you correct yourself to use a more correct version, I think that is a huge improvement. But I think political correctness can sometimes be taken too far, so that you don't even know what they're trying to say. And sometimes issues are important to talk about. So I think as long as you don't use slurs or extremely degrading and rude words, I think you should be able to express what you want to express.

Julie supports the need for moral pressure to prevent others from using racial slurs and derogatory language. However, she weighs the desire for collective suppression of offensive language against the competing desire for open dialogue, especially across groups.

Candice, a Filipino American junior at Brown, emphasized her recognition of the power embedded in language while acknowledging that people sometimes use that language without understanding why some terms are problematic:

> Political correctness is an effort to stray from using language that references racial ideas that have occurred in the past. . . . I like it, because I do think that language is really important to how we think about differences—racial, gender, or class differences in the US. And I think that's the first step. But also I think that sometimes people employ political correctness without actually understanding the inequalities or stereotypes that are operating underneath them.

Candice held a power analysis frame. As a junior ethnic studies major, she probably has read seminal authors such as Antonio Gramsci and Gayatri Spivak, who discuss the importance of language and the power embedded in the words used to describe particular groups.[26] Candice was also involved with the TWC at Brown, and given that center's emphasis on racism and oppression experienced by minority groups in the United States, Candice may have encountered this critique there as well. Indeed, later in her interview Candice told us she had attended some workshops on diversity led by minority peer counselors. She praised those discussions as shaping her thinking, "The MPCs are really well trained at asking questions and facilitating discussion in a good way that gets everybody thinking about things. I liked that." While she credits her discussions in ethnic studies courses, it is peer-led discussions that she feels really opened dialogue:

> Obviously I've had discussions in my ethnic studies classes. . . . But these [peer-led discussions] were different because you didn't have to worry about impressing anyone. And you feel really safe there giving your opinion, because they emphasize that this is a safe space and that we all respect each others' opinions.

These experiences on Brown's campus seem to have given Candice a more positive take on political correctness, even while her analysis is quite similar to those of white and minority peers who expressed more ambivalent or critical views. That is, she appreciates the attention to avoiding offense and also appreciates dialogue about race.

While the predominant view of political correctness among US students was positive, some did have criticisms similar to the ones cited by students with more positive perspectives, related to stifling dialogue. This was important to students of color in particular, because they hoped that dialogue about race would shift some peers' thinking. When peers mask their true colors beneath politically correct language, discussion cannot shift their views, which are never put on the table. Michael, an African American senior at Harvard studying government and sociology, said,

> Political correctness is trying not to use offensive terms, because everyone is not always aware of the history of different terms. You can dismiss it like, "Oh no, it's just words," but it does have cultural resonance. I think part of how it originally started was just being aware of other people's cultures and how something you might think is not a big deal means a lot to them. So I think that in that way the cultural resonance is good, because it would lead to discussions. . . . But now it's just so absurd that people are walking on eggshells. And so rather than discussing it, it's like, "Oh, taboo."

La'Ron, also an African American senior at Harvard, was even more critical of political correctness:

> Political correctness is not talking about something that is real because you don't want to offend anyone. I hate it . . . I hate it. I hate it. You can't have progress without a little friction, and [political correctness] causes us to brush problems under the rug without actually talking about them. So there's a facade of progress. White students will still believe the same thing about black students, but black students will never know because white students will never speak up because it wouldn't be PC to do that. It's not politically correct to say things like that anymore, so you never know and you think you've gotten somewhere but you haven't.

Like their white peers, students of color desired interracial dialogue. However, for many the reason for this interest was different. While white students stood to benefit individually from being exposed to new perspectives, many students of color saw dialogue as an important mechanism to influence their peers to become more sympathetic to minority concerns — a group benefit — in part by opening up their views to critique. So, while inoffensive language might be more important to students of color than to white students, so too dialogue might be more important to them, to promote a deeper understanding of race among their peers.

Overall, while students differed in their evaluations of political correctness, most valued intergroup dialogue and trying not to offend others, goals that are the natural outcome of attention to collective merit in admissions and the moral imperative to not be racist. That is, they value sensitive language so as to preserve interracial dialogue, while also hoping the practice does not stifle the dialogue that is the payoff for campus diversity. Some, like La'Ron, privileged dialogue, while others privileged maintaining a moral sense of self and avoiding accusations of insensitivity.

It is important to remember that students' perspectives described here do not reflect the broader US society; indeed, they may not even reflect the perspectives of most college students in the United States, who attend less selective or unselective colleges. Public debates about political correctness, such as the discussions about *Charlie Hebdo*, tend to revolve around the importance of free speech, and in them political correctness carries a negative connotation. This is also true in Britain, as we will see. But on the Brown and Harvard campuses students thought more about the need to learn from diversity and to maintain one's sense of identity as a morally just, nonracist individual. Students seem to hear about the notion of political correctness from the wider American society, then filter the way they make meaning of it through the race frames on campus, especially the diversity frame. This reveals just how deeply students' race frames shape their understandings of race-related issues.

*   *   *

Despite some similarities in their views of political correctness, it sometimes seems that minority and white students at Brown and Harvard attend different universities. Students of color report profound experiences with racism, often from a young age. Their emotions about these experiences tend to get legitimated in communities of color, institutionalized by the diversity-related infrastructure on campus such as minority students' groups, minority students' centers, and courses related to race. Their moral identities—as people who are not racist—are taken for granted based on their racial identities. Students of color are assumed to have deep knowledge about and understanding of race and racism and hence to hold moral authority to speak about them. The diversity bargain I described in chapter 4 called for students of color to "educate" their white peers, but to do so without recourse to a power analysis frame, ignoring institutional differences in the lived experiences of minority and white Americans, placing them in a precarious position on campus. White students sometimes resented it when peers of color did share their perceptions of racial bias, and at times they denied those accusations of bias. Perhaps because among white students the dominant frames for making sense of race-related observations and events are the diversity frame and the color-blindness frame, students of color found it difficult to explain the full impact of race to their white peers, who mostly understood racism as interpersonal rather than institutional.[27]

Most white students expressed a deep desire to be seen as not racist.[28] Yet, as Pat described it, "No one tells you how to do it." The opportunity afforded them by a diverse college—for many, the most diverse place they have ever lived—was often lost when they didn't learn the skills to overcome the guilt they felt, to accept their moral worth on matters related to race, and to take risks in their interactions with minority students despite the fear of being labeled racist. When their peers accused them of racism, many felt confusion and guilt, or even racial resentment. Sometimes those feelings turned into accusations that minority peers were being "politically correct" and stifling dialogue. Discourse in American society about "reverse discrimination" and criticism of the "PC police" on campus legitimate these feelings. Overall, color-blindness prevented many white students from understanding the qualitative difference between their experiences with racial bias and those of their peers.

By now it should be clear that anxieties about moral worth influence students' interracial interactions on campus. Jan Stets and Michael Carter developed a theory of the relation between individual identities and morality, in which they explained that others' rejections of our moral identities can elicit feelings of guilt and shame.[29] While most whites attempted to behave and speak in ways that maintained their moral identities as not racist, the "reflected appraisals" of their peers of color—that is, whites' perceptions of how minorities view their behaviors, could lead to guilt and shame—moral emotions—about being or seeming racist.[30] In addition, when whites do not speak up in the face of racially offensive jokes, this contrasts with their moral identities as not racist, and they again could experience guilt and shame. While Stets and Carter assume that individuals are comparing their own appraisals of moral identity with their perceptions of others' appraisals, in the realm of a not racist moral identity, students of color are sometimes seen as the main arbiters. Students of color expect to define the boundaries of racism, and whites sometimes defer to the boundaries they draw and at other times seem to resent those assessments, rejecting accusations of prejudice. When they did so, they sometimes expressed hostility or even aggression toward their evaluators.

These negative feelings can lead to social distancing, especially whites pulling away from blacks.[31] So, while an extensive body of research demonstrates that diversity on campus tends to reduce racial prejudice,[32] the dynamics I describe in this chapter attenuate that effect by provoking anxiety and distancing, reducing the power of intergroup contact and thus impeding the goal of diversity that admissions officers and students alike espouse. This dynamic can further lead to segregated social networks for black and white students in particular, common on elite college campuses,[33] with consequences for social inequality in the future. For example, Maya Beasley's study of students at elite colleges shows that black students active in the black community tend not to seek out high-paying professions after graduation, in part because their social networks restrict the connections that could provide job opportunities in those fields.[34] Other research has shown that white students who have contact with black peers tend to have a deeper understanding of race-related issues.[35] Further, they are less likely to hold beliefs associated with "new prejudice," such as disagreeing with affirmative action and thinking the US government already does enough to ensure that blacks and whites have equal opportunities.[36]

In addition to these complex racial dynamics on campus, from time to time overt racism, as students perceived it, made itself visible. When asked about campus controversies related to multiculturalism and diversity, at Harvard students mentioned a controversial article in a student newspaper criticizing the newly formed secondary field (minor) in Ethnic Studies, in which the writer suggested that there are no African civilizations worthy of study.[37] At Brown, one student described a leaflet distributed by campus Republicans that displayed an image of President Obama burning, which provoked perceptions of lynching and cross-burning among some students.[38] Still, overall, when asked about campus controversies, students were much more likely to speak of incidents perpetrated by the police, such as the arrest of Harvard professor Henry Louis Gates[39] or campus police at Brown targeting black students for ID checks.[40] At Brown, students also discussed debates over campus diversity institutions such as the Third World Center or Third World Transition Program. This was not the case at Oxford, as we'll see, where *peers* most often precipitated campus controversies related to racism.

Ultimately, racism, whether overt or subtle, was mostly described by students as the result of individual acts. This perspective assumes that if we could simply root out racism in individuals' language and behaviors toward people of color, our society would truly be equal. This ignores the systematic, institutional racism that continues to affect people of color in the United States. Eduardo Bonilla-Silva calls this "racism without racists."[41] He defines color-blind racism as a mechanism through which whites perpetuate "white supremacy"[42] by emphasizing individualism, highlighting cultural differences between groups, and playing down the impact of race in society. Whites' emphasis on color-blindness in the analysis of inequality legitimates white privilege, consequently denying the importance of social policies to ameliorate black disadvantage.[43] Bonilla-Silva argues that "younger, educated, middle-class people are more likely to make full use of the resources of color-blind racism."[44]

This disregard of institutional racism built into social policies prevents whites from feeling threats to their self-concept that might ensue when they perceive white privilege.[45] When whites identify as not racist and engage in social interactions with peers of color that generally maintain that moral identity (even if those interactions sometimes call that identity into question, leading to guilt and shame, and sometimes defensiveness and hostility), they feel confident that they are not maintaining racial domination. This blinds them to ongoing institutional structures that perpetuate racial inequality in the United States. In addition, the lack of a power analysis frame prevents them from understanding how white identities also have social meaning.[46] Overall, the few students with a power analysis frame seemed to articulate a deeper understanding of the ways race and racism shape life in the United States.

BRITISH
STUDENTS

SIX

RACE FRAMES AND
MERIT AT OXFORD

It is easy for Americans to assume that our way of life is the way of life elsewhere. The dynamics of race in the United States, though complex and contradictory, can seem inevitable. When I moved to Britain in 2003, I expected that my life would change more because I was moving in with my fiancé than because of the country I was living in. Of course I assumed my colleagues at the London School of Economics would have different accents and different mannerisms, perhaps different cultural references, than my colleagues at Harvard. But they were all part of a global elite, embedded in multicultural democracies—how different could they be? Once I figured out how to open a bank account, I thought I was done.

I soon realized I had a lot to learn. By 2003 debates over British multiculturalism were raging. This was two years after 9/11, and there was a growing backlash against multiculturalism. In 2004 David Goodhart, the editor of *Prospect* magazine, wrote a piece that captured these sentiments, questioning whether Britain had become "too diverse," which had everyone talking. A few months later, terrorists attacked the London Underground, also exploding a bus near the Gandhi statue outside my office in Tavistock Square. Many of the editorials in newspapers and magazines after the London bombings questioned Britain's openness to cultural diversity. "What does it mean to be British?" and "Has multiculturalism gone too far?" asked everyone from Labour prime minister Tony Blair to journalists on the left and on the right. I also knew that ordinary British citizens were increasingly wary of multiculturalism. On opinion polls Britons were more likely than Americans to support immigrant assimilation rather than the "adapt and blend" approach, and this preference for assimilation was increasing over time.[1]

Despite these public debates and my keen interest, I had a hard time putting my finger on exactly what *was* British multiculturalism in the first place. I learned that in terms of actual policies, British multiculturalism looked a lot like American multiculturalism. Both countries had adopted a similar number of policies to accommodate ethnic and racial differences, such as multiculturalism in school curricula and exemptions from dress codes, leading Keith Banting and Will Kymlicka to label both Britain and the United States as "moderately" multicultural, in contrast to the "strong" multiculturalism of Australia and Canada and no multiculturalism in countries like France.[2] I learned that British multiculturalism dated back to the 1960s, when immigration restrictions began, alongside the Race Relations Acts of 1965, 1968, 1976, 2000, and 2010. The Race Relations Amendment Act of 2000 in particular required universities to develop racial equality plans to improve access for students and for racial minority job applicants. Still, the impact of these mandates remains unclear, and qualitative studies suggest that the racial equality plans tend to stay in the realm of planning, lacking follow-through in the universities.[3]

To further complicate things, in many ways British multiculturalism never seemed to have made it to the elite campuses of Oxford and Cambridge. To understand why multiculturalism never took hold on the Oxbridge campuses, it is helpful to remember how it *did* take hold in the United States. As I described earlier, in the United States black students recruited to elite college campuses through affirmative action became the leaders of race-based demands on those colleges; later, other ethnic groups made similar group-based demands for greater inclusion, and those movements were inspired by those of their black predecessors. In Britain, the absence of a "leading" minority group that could invoke moral shame among the dominant group and could wield political power, as African Americans did especially during the civil rights movement, meant that minority demands for inclusion in Britain were weaker and less effective, so that affirmative action never took hold there.[4] Further, battles fought by the Labour Party over inequality in Britain emphasized the conditions of working-class life, not equal opportunity and social mobility through access to the likes of Oxford and Cambridge, which were not seen as places that should promote social mobility or even play a civic role more broadly.[5] In contrast, New Left leaders on college campuses in the United States focused on group rights, which later led Todd Gitlin to lament that the New Left was "marching on the English department while the Right took the White House."[6]

In addition, the racial demographics in Britain and at Oxford also differ from those in the United States and on the Brown and Harvard campuses. Recall that Harvard and Brown students transition from neighborhoods that are on average more than 80 percent white to college campuses that are 40–45 percent white American; this shift to a more heavily minority environment, in a society that has long been racially charged, forces students to grapple with racial diversity. In contrast, on average Oxford students encounter a campus that has a percentage of whites similar to their home neighborhoods: 85 percent of Oxford students coming from British schools are white, compared with a young British population that is 82 percent white.[7] Still, black British and British Asian students are underrepresented on campus, with less than 1 percent of students from British schools on the Oxford campus identifying as black, compared with a young British population that is 4 percent black, and 6 percent identifying as Asian, compared with 10 percent in the young British population.[8] In addition, British neighborhoods are not nearly as racially segregated as American ones.[9] On average, then, white Oxford students do not experience a dramatic shift in racial makeup when they arrive on campus.

Given the absence of a race-based social movement in Britain and its downstream effects, different student demographics, and contrasting roles for elite education, I was intrigued by how students at an elite British university might think about merit and race, which led me to this research at Oxford. What do Oxford students think about the role of race in society, and how do they understand the admissions process? What are the implications for race relations? I address these questions in this and the following chapter. As we'll see, I was terribly wrong in thinking that race, meritocracy, and conceptions of justice would be similar in the United States and Britain. I use the material on Oxford students to bring the findings in the United States into sharper relief, so I highlight the contrasting findings between British and American students throughout this chapter and the following one.

Before turning to British students' race frames, I want to point out that long-standing ethnicity-related student groups, called "societies," do exist at Oxford. For example, the Majlis Asian[10] Society describes itself as a "society which hosts cultural, social, and sporting events throughout the year. [Majlis] provides opportunities for people to meet other members of the Asian community in Oxford."[11] In addition, the African and Caribbean Society "aims to explore, promote and celebrate African and Caribbean culture within the University of Oxford."[12] Still, no student we interviewed, whether white or second-generation,[13] spoke of these groups. The only event hosted by an ethnic society mentioned in our interviews was the Diwali Ball, a formal party in the style of Oxford's traditional balls, but in celebration of the Hindu and Sikh festival of Diwali. Three white students, one Sikh student, and one student with African and European ancestry told us they had attended the Diwali Ball. More generally, sixteen of the fifty-two white students at Oxford had attended any diversity-related event on campus, as had eleven of the fifteen second-generation students (UK-born children of immigrants from outside the European Union) we interviewed. At Harvard and Brown, by contrast, attendance at diversity-related events is the norm.[14] Diversity at Oxford simply did not have the same importance in university life as it did for US students.

"Everyone Was Pretty Much the Same": Oxford Students' Race Frames

I begin with Oxford students' race frames. Like US students, many Oxford students frequently employed a color-blindness frame, including fourteen of fifty-two white students (27 percent) and five of fifteen second-generation students (33 percent). William, a white private school graduate studying biology, said, "I just don't see it as an issue of what color skin—as long as you're a nice person or just fun to be around." Poppy, a white private school graduate, was studying history. She spoke positively about racial minorities, expressing a color-blindness frame embedded in a liberal individualist view:

> I don't think [my experiences at Oxford] have changed my perception of ethnic minorities particularly, because I was always of the opinion that everyone was pretty much the same, except for the fact that because of where I lived and the school I went to I didn't particularly know anyone who was Asian, Muslim, or whatever, and I

have actually met them now. But as I expected, they are just like the rest of us.

Poppy spent her childhood in an area of Britain that is 97 percent white. Her use of the language of "us" and "them" in distinguishing herself (and presumably people she grew up with) from ethnic minorities belies her claim that she believes everyone is the same. In fact, she divides the world into people like her and "Asian, Muslim, or whatever."

Ayesha, a state school graduate studying French, grew up in a Muslim household with parents who were professionals from East Africa. She employed a color-blindness frame when asked how diversity affects life on campus:

> I don't think diversity is really an issue. I don't think it really makes a difference . . . . I'm the only Muslim that I really know in this college. But I still get on very well with my neighbors and I'm involved in the JCR[15] and that kind of thing. I don't really find any problem. At Oxford it's possible to just feel integrated by being here. We are all here for the same purpose at the end of the day.

Given the British national context in which public debates about British Muslims and their loyalty to Britain are routinely questioned, Ayesha seems especially intent on color-blindness. Perhaps for Muslim Britons to gain admission to Oxford, they need to embody a particular form of Britishness, which involves adhering to a color-blindness frame that deemphasizes the roles of race and religion in society. Indeed, Ayesha identified as politically conservative. She wore a headscarf and spoke after her interview about making the difficult personal decision to wear it when she was eighteen. Her color-blind perspective, to my American ears, sounded strange given the negative stereotypes that she felt followed her after she began wearing a headscarf. But as I thought more about it, I realized that, lacking exposure to a power analysis frame, Ayesha was left with color-blindness to make sense of her place at Oxford and others' stereotypes about her religious identity.

Some Oxford students employed a diversity frame when asked about the influence of diversity on campus life — this included twenty-three of the fifty-two white students (44 percent) and five of the fif-

teen second-generation students (compared with over 83 percent of
US students overall). These expressions tended to be less effusive than
those from US students. Jasmine, a white private school graduate
studying chemistry, when asked how diversity has influenced campus
life, said, "I think it does enhance—you get to know people from different countries and how they live and what they do. Most of them are
really nice people." Robert, a state school graduate, said,

> I think it makes it quite interesting. We've got Steven, a Chinese
> guy—no he's not Chinese. Sorry, big mistake there. He's a Singa-
> porean guy, and he's a member of the Singapore Society. He invited
> us along to an Asian food festival. So it makes it interesting I think,
> and different people bring different things. . . . It's nice to have differ-
> ence, a nice variety of people from different backgrounds and with
> different stories to tell.

Although Robert confuses his peer's national identity at first,[16] he
nevertheless appreciates the introduction to Asian foods and "different stories to tell." He reports that Steven invited "us" along, signaling a boundary between "us"—presumably his British friends—and
Steven, from Asia. While Poppy used the language of "us" and "them"
despite reporting a color-blindness frame, Robert's diversity frame is
more aligned with that same language, in that he makes a distinction
between his British friends and his foreign-born friends, appreciating those differences. Contrast the responses of Robert and Jasmine
to that of Jean at Harvard, who said that "diversity is at the essence
of Harvard life." While the difference in tone may have something to
do with Americans' proclivity toward exaggeration, the topic of much
mockery in Europe, it also indicates greater commitment to and pas-
sion about diversity than for British students. Thus the diversity frame
had a different texture at Oxford.

Notice, too, that Jasmine and Robert both speak of diversity based
on foreign-born peers. While the percentage of international students
is only somewhat higher at Oxford than at Harvard and Brown (and is
lower if one considers only non-EU students),[17] Oxford students placed
much greater emphasis on the benefits of diversity through their peers
from abroad. US students, by contrast, tended to talk about minority
cultures within the United States. In addition, Oxford did not seem
to influence students' race frames nearly as much as the strong influ-

ence of US universities. When asked about the influence of diversity on campus, Oxford students had little to report beyond exposure to the foods of their international peers' home countries, and sometimes performances and parties put on by ethnic-oriented student groups.

While British students were less likely than American students to express positive feelings about diversity on campus, they were more than twice as likely to employ a culture of poverty frame. This included eleven white students and four second-generation students. Emma, a white student in her final year of studying mathematics, explained the underrepresentation of black students on campus this way:

> From what I know there may be cultural pressures. If you're male and black, working and excelling academically is not the thing to be seen doing. If this could be changed so that people do not feel pressured and can do whatever they want to, and if they want to work really hard then they can, that would work even better.

Emma assumes a lack of strong interest in academic achievement among black youth. While considerable research has discredited this explanation for lower school performance in both Britain and the United States,[18] it endures. Emma grew up in a neighborhood that is 97 percent white and attended a private secondary school, suggesting that she had little contact with black peers either in secondary school or, as we know from the data on Oxford, at the university. Of her five named closest friends, four are white British and one is British Indian. Thus in her explanation of black underrepresentation she may have been relying on accounts of black underrepresentation from media portrayals or hearsay. In fact, private school graduates we interviewed were much more likely to employ culture of poverty explanations for black underrepresentation at Oxford than were state or grammar school graduates, who were more likely to be exposed to black peers in secondary school. This evidence fits with the "contact hypothesis," which states that under certain conditions, interracial contact reduces racial prejudice.[19]

I was surprised to hear some second-generation students also express a culture of poverty frame. When asked what could be done about the racial inequality she acknowledged in Britain, Tisha, whose parents came from Africa and South Asia, shared a story her friend told her:

My best friend was on Cornmarket [a major shopping street in Oxford] the other day and she noticed a group of fifteen-year-old girls just standing for no good reason whatsoever, on a Saturday night. Why of any place to be in Oxford would you stand on Cornmarket? And so there's got to be something that prioritizes young children going out and focusing on alcohol and socializing and not being at home. . . . So what that point highlights is that not everyone wants to be educated. It's all very well to say that everyone should be, but the actions of teenagers would suggest that they don't think education is socially desirable.

Tisha grew up in London with professional parents and attended a prestigious private secondary school. So, although she grew up in an immigrant household, she may be distancing herself from working-class youth cultures, which, as she perceives them, are immersed in a culture of poverty, leading to weak school outcomes and lack of the skills to come to Oxford. As with my response to Ayesha, I reacted with confusion to Tisha's explanation. I concluded that the accomplishments it took for Tisha to become Oxford-eligible, and the outlook necessary to succeed there, may have required her to distance herself from working-class life among ethnic minorities like the teens she described. Unlike minority students in the United States, especially those involved in Brown's Third World Center and its programming, Tisha did not have strong institutional supports for her ethnic identity at Oxford beyond ethnic student organizations, none of which she brought up in the interview. Nor did she have access to a robust power analysis frame, as did participants in Brown's Third World Transition Program, to make sense of racial inequality in Britain.

Given the lack of institutional supports for diversity on Oxford's campus, it will not come as a surprise that a power analysis frame was altogether absent at Oxford, among white and second-generation students alike. When students did seem to invoke elements of a power analysis frame, they were less critical of dominant society than the significant minority of US students who used this frame to judge their universities and the larger society for racial injustice. The two Oxford students who employed a power analysis frame did so with respect to single questions. One of them was Christine, the daughter of two white British professors, who attended a high-achieving state school. When asked whether she had experienced racial discrimination, Christine recognized and called attention to the difference between those in power experiencing discrimination and those with less power experiencing it: "No not at all. But then, because I'm white it would be unlikely for me to experience racial discrimination."[20]

Finally, some Oxford students simply did not articulate a race frame. In their responses they seemed to search for a frame to make sense of the questions. For example, Charles shifted his view on whether Oxford should consider race or ethnicity in admissions in the middle of his answer:

> No. I think they should do everything in their power to encourage lower [class] and ethnic minority communities and to encourage their schools to apply. But as far as saying: "We've got a quota. We've got to do this," that's completely wrong, because that sends the wrong message to these communities as well. . . . Well, actually, no, that's not right at all. Completely [wrong], because what I've been saying is that people from these backgrounds don't have as much time to put into their studies as people like myself. And they don't have as much support to do it on every level. So yes, a complete turnaround! They should take it into account. They should definitely take it into account, because I think that a lot of people who are applying from these backgrounds are not open about the circumstances that they've been in.

Charles recognizes the inconsistency in his answers to different questions and shifts his view. Perhaps because affirmative action has never been an official policy in Britain, whether in higher education or in other sectors, it is not something Charles had previously considered. Like Charles, eighteen of the fifty-two white students we interviewed at Oxford articulated no race frame, as did three second-generation students. During interviews in Britain, it became obvious that the overall time students spent thinking about race and racial inequality was much lower than for American students, only five of whom did not clearly employ a particular race frame. British students often seemed to be searching for ways to make meaning of race in response to questions about diversity, while American students seemed more ready to deploy available language related to the color-blindness frame, the diversity frame, and sometimes the culture of poverty frame or power analysis frame. That is, American students had lenses with which to make sense of the race-related questions we asked them. They were not searching for ways to make meaning of the questions on the spot in the way many British students, like Charles, seemed to do. Students in the United States did frequently employ multiple race frames, but they usually did so in different scenarios, in response to different questions. For example, a US student might employ a diversity frame when asked about affirmative action and a color-blindness frame when asked about racial inequality. Hence, for US students these frames seem to be part of a cultural "tool kit"[21] for making sense of the questions and for responding to situations rather than a sudden brainstorm. Still, I argue that those with unarticulated frames, by virtue of a lack of racial analysis, tend to default to a color-blindness frame. That is, when the role of race in society goes unexamined, the default understanding is one of color-blindness, so that apart from our questions Charles's frame was probably color-blindness, which is how he began his response.

In the United States, as we saw, race frames are closely linked to students' conceptions of merit in admissions. I assumed the same would be true in Britain. However, as we'll see, British students' race frames, or the lack thereof, do not seem to play the same role as race frames do in the United States.

"We Should All Just Be Blank Faces": Individual, Uncalibrated Merit

Given the widely reported disparities in application and admission to Oxford, how do students make sense of the process? To my surprise, like those of the Harvard and Brown students we interviewed, Oxford students' views on merit reproduced official university policies, not the critical perspectives of media commentators and politicians. They believed in clear, simple criteria and goals for the university's admissions system. When asked whether Oxford's admissions process is meritocratic, nearly three-quarters of white British students answered with a simple, unequivocal yes. Theo's response was representative: "Of course! You have to get the best grades. You have to perform the best in the interview. You have to do the best essays. So yeah, of course." John, a grammar school graduate in his final year at Oxford, where he studied history, stated that merit is academic achievement within one's subject:

The interviews are obviously the main part of the admissions process, and I think they are there to see who would be best at the subject. . . . [O]bviously it's in the admissions tutors' interest to let the best people in, because then they will get the best marks [grades] and generally be the most interesting to teach. . . . I suppose it depends on what you define as merit, because obviously it's a very narrow form of meritocracy. . . . Whereas there are obviously other forms of merit, like moral merits, sporting ability, or whatever, which don't get considered at all.

John's emphasis on individual ability suits the Oxford teaching model, which centers on the intimate learning environment of the tutorial—with two students and one faculty member—rather than the discussion-based learning found in many Harvard and Brown courses. Furthermore, John points out that admitting the strongest students in the subject is in the interest of admissions tutors, because they are also the teaching staff of the college and are admitting their future students. Of course, this structure may lead to cultural biases in admissions, because tutors—themselves likely to come from privileged backgrounds—are likely to feel affinity with applicants like themselves. This may explain the documented disparity in admissions rates by class and race even among students with the same national exam grades, as I described in chapter 1. Overall, John's and Theo's perspectives highlight the belief in individual merit that prevails at Oxford, in contrast to the collective merit of the cohort emphasized by both students and admissions offices in the United States. These responses strongly resonated with the official practices of admissions at Oxford. The director of admissions told me, "We're taking students who really only need be really good at mathematics [for the mathematics degree]. . . . It doesn't really matter whether they've got any social skills or have any interest in liberal arts or humanities or whatever, as long as they're good mathematicians" (interview with Warikoo, July 2011). Just as US students' responses strongly reflected the espoused views of the admissions offices at Harvard and Brown, Oxford students' responses echoed those of the Oxford director of admissions.

The singular emphasis on academic skills in a particular subject spills over into students' discussions of whether admissions tutors should consider race, class, or other markers of disadvantage. While nearly half of US white students and a majority of US students of color expressed the belief that evaluations of merit should be calibrated to the opportunities an individual has had, most British students believed that the university should *not* consider background when making admissions decisions, whether related to class, school quality, or race.[22] Interview questions about considerations of race, class, or school type (private or state secondary school) elicited strong emotions in Britain. For example, Olivia, a white private school graduate whose parents held graduate degrees, said when asked whether Oxford admissions is a meritocracy: "Absolutely, I think Oxford strives for excellence, and I think they should always choose a brilliant candidate before looking at where he's from, or what color he is. Absolutely." Olivia's answer, like those of many of her peers, is unequivocal in rejecting any calibration of merit. She was in her final year of study, completing a degree in modern languages. Caitlin, a state school graduate studying European languages, said simply, "Ultimately we should all just be blank faces; we should all just be admitted totally on merit." Second-generation Rafiq, whose parents came to Britain from West Africa, recognized inequality in schooling even while he concluded that Oxford should not take that inequality into consideration. He told us:

> [Oxford is] a meritocracy within an elite in a sense that it's only a meritocracy for people who are able to enter the door in the first place. So if you're like living in an inner-city area [and] go to a really bad school, you are a child of a single parent, and you are really struggling to get anywhere in life, you're never going to enter that door. It's not really—it's not Oxford's fault though, fundamentally. Oxford only works within a system. It's a fault of the social structure itself. It's not a fault of Oxford. It can only do what it can do within its confines.

Rafiq attended an underperforming high school—just one-fifth of the students graduated with grades high enough to make them eligible to apply for *any* university education, let alone Oxford. Soon after Rafiq graduated, the school closed and was replaced by an academy (similar to US charter schools) with a specialization in business. Like many other Oxford students, Rafiq explicitly lays blame for the underrepresentation of disadvantaged groups with "the social structure itself" and supports the admissions system at Oxford. Interestingly, Rafiq recognizes social inequality in British society—it would be hard

to deny given the contrasting educational experiences he had in high
school and university—but this does not disrupt his faith in the fairness of Oxford admissions. Most British students like Rafiq who recognized inequality in either schools or society argued that because the
root of inequality lay outside Oxford's walls, it should be addressed
outside. In contrast, most US students who acknowledged inequality
in American schools and society, whether based on race or on class,
advocated for calibrating evaluations of merit based on that inequality.

Oxford students further believed that calibrating evaluations of
merit would lead to admitting students who could not succeed. Analia, the daughter of South American immigrants, used her own experience to bolster her claim that students with poor training, even owing
to circumstances out of their control, should not be admitted:

> I don't think positive discrimination is a good thing. If black people
> are going to come here and feel left out, then maybe they shouldn't
> come here. . . . The thing about positive discrimination [is that] if
> you give someone a chance because they've had a more disadvan-
> taged background, they're just going to struggle, and that's not a
> good thing. I personally don't think I should have got in! [Laughs.]
> Because I've had such a hard time. I probably would have been a lot
> happier in another university. I feel really left out here and at odds
> with the place.

Earlier in her interview, Analia, who was studying linguistics, told
us she struggled at Oxford because her academic preparation was
much weaker than that of her peers who graduated from private
schools. Still, Analia attended a state secondary school that performs
well above average on national exams. Given that almost half her peers
at Oxford came from private schools and still others from grammar
schools, even a strong state education may feel relatively weak.

Rather than criticize the university for not providing her with supports to succeed and feel included, Analia blames herself.[23] Her view
demonstrates the static understanding of the university that many
students had. Whereas US students expected Harvard and Brown to
adapt to the needs of admitted students with weak academic skills,
Oxford students did not seem to imagine how Oxford might adapt
to students with more variable educational backgrounds, in order to
promote greater opportunities. If nontraditional students could some-

how fit in they were welcome, but students saw those who could not fit in—even if due to no fault of their own—as inappropriate candidates for Oxford. Similarly, Kate, a white private school graduate studying history, told us that Oxford should do nothing about the underrepresentation of black students because

> I have had friends at Oxford who have come here and frankly not been bright enough and have struggled and have had a miserable time. I don't think that's fair. . . . It's miserable being at Oxford if you're not good enough. Oxford isn't the kind of place where your tutor is going to spend extra time teaching you. And if Oxford's tutors aren't prepared to take on the responsibility of getting the people up to scratch, then it's not fair to anyone.

Kate then made it clear that she thinks Oxford should not help struggling students—she doesn't see it as the university's role: "The responsibility, in my opinion, lies with primary schools or the secondary schools. . . . That's where the problem is, not at this level." Ironically, of course, the tutorial system of one-on-one and one-on-two teaching might be most suited to students with a range of academic backgrounds. Still, Kate takes it as given that tutors will not—and, implicitly, cannot be expected to—change to better support students with weaker preparation from their secondary schools.

Similarly, Rose, a white grammar school graduate studying art history, absolved Oxford of responsibility for addressing social inequality. When asked whether the underrepresentation of black students on campus was a problem, Rose said, "I think it's a problem, but it's not Oxford's problem. It's an educational problem that the government needs to address. Oxford has its own criteria to maintain and that's to keep a high level of intellectual ability in education." In other words, considering unequal access to education before applying—a calibrated evaluation of merit—would compromise the goals of Oxford as an institution. Later Rose stated this understanding of Oxford's essential mission even more explicitly. When asked whether the university should consider various social factors in admissions, Rose retorted that it "does not lie with Oxford to choose that," because "Oxford has a very clear, stated aim, and that is to maintain its position in an intellectual society." Given this role for Oxford, Rose can believe that private school graduates have a better chance of admission than state school graduates while also believing that the system is meritocratic. Like Rose, most students viewed the underrepresentation of some groups on campus as a problem, but not Oxford's problem. Hence that inconsistency, though acknowledged, did not contravene faith in the meritocratic process of admission, as it would under the calibrated merit logic common in the United States.

Rose's beliefs about the role of Oxford in British society echo those expressed by many other students we interviewed. They also reflect the perspective of Oxford's director of undergraduate admissions. When asked whether Oxford should consider inequality in secondary education when making admissions decisions, he said,

> I think it's sometimes perceived as being the university's fault that we don't get more students in from particular backgrounds, but all the evidence suggests . . . that a lot of the inequities in society start at a very young age. . . . So part of my job is to try and make people aware that it's not just us who can influence this. This is a big issue for the UK as a whole, and it's a government-led responsibility to deal with this. It's about raising attainment in schools. . . . You can't say "Oxford, Cambridge, it's your job to solve social mobility."

Further, whereas some students suggested the university recruit promising students from working-class and minority backgrounds who otherwise might not apply, he shared his strategy of recruiting mostly at top secondary schools:

> If I'm stuck for a resource, what do I do? Well, logic says put all your eggs in one basket—basically 96 percent of five A-stars [top grades on the national exams] in the UK come from about 50 percent of all the schools in the UK. . . . That's at age sixteen, so this is the first indicator of academic potential. . . . You could say, "Why is it that students from different areas seem to get into Oxford at different rates?" Well actually, that's where many of the really academically able students are. And we can't change that.

In other words, recruiting happens at the most elite secondary schools because that is where the vast majority of students performing well on national exams are.

Just as his explanation resonates with those of Oxford students, it contrasts sharply with the way US students and admissions officers talk about inequality in secondary education and admissions. In interviews with US admissions officers, Michèle Lamont and Graziella da Silva found that most see diversity and excellence as complementary rather than competing interests.[24] The contrasting understandings of elite universities—Brown and Harvard as needing to adapt to students coming from disadvantaged backgrounds and Oxford as a place where *students* must do the adapting—match the overall widely articulated purposes of higher education in the United States and Britain, which I described in chapter 1.

A minority of Oxford students did support calibrating evaluations of merit. Still, those students tended to use the same framework of the primacy of excellence in their arguments. For example, Adam, the son of professionals from a London suburb who studied mathematics, when asked if Oxford should consider school type in admissions, responded, "Yes, I would. I think aptitude is more important than where [applicants are, academically,] at the moment. . . . At the end of the day the university is trying to get the best pupils in the places." Adam implies that individuals have an innate aptitude that can be assessed during the on-campus interview. The difference between Adam and his peers, then, is in how to measure that aptitude, often called "potential" by the university. Adam's view is that grades do not fully measure potential, unlike his peers' assessments based largely on the national exams and the campus interview. Still, his evaluation is based on an understanding of an absolute aptitude scale. Ultimately, Adam had faith in Oxford's admissions process: "From what I've seen, everybody here seems like they deserve to be here," perhaps an indication of his belief that admissions tutors do well at this evaluation of "aptitude" or "potential."

While ultimately even Adam believes that the Oxford admissions system is meritocratic, a few others we interviewed did not. A small group of students cited the underrepresentation of state school graduates at Oxford as evidence that the system was not meritocratic. This group included eight white students and five second-generation students. Of the white students, most had attended state schools. For example, Trevor, one of just three white respondents who was eligible for free school meals at some time during secondary school, said "probably not" when asked if Oxford's admissions process is meritocratic.[25] He went on:

I think it's . . . pretty clear just from being a student at Oxford that a disproportionate amount of people get in because they've had the money to get in and not because—I mean, I'm not saying that they've bought their way in or anything like that, but because they've been able to constantly afford the best education and the best kind of tuition and stuff to prepare them for getting in here. And they know how to do the interview process and things like that. They're coached in it. While that means that they might be the best qualified, I don't necessarily think that means they are the most intelligent people. Also, in the state school [sector] the university clearly prefers people from state grammar schools as opposed to normal state schools, and that's because they are very similar to private schools. So I don't think it is a meritocracy.

Trevor scored high enough on an entrance exam at age eleven to attend his local grammar school—the admittance rate to that school is less than 10 percent, making it more competitive than Oxford admissions. Trevor acknowledged the privilege he enjoyed in attending a grammar school as well as the advantages of peers whose parents paid tuition at expensive private schools.

Henry, a second-generation student studying economics and management, was the first person from his secondary school ever to attend Oxford. He said,

I think it's increasingly becoming [a meritocracy] but I think the fact that there is still a disproportionately large number of private school [graduates] and lack of admissions from state schools—it kind of shows that the system itself is not very meritocratic. It's still quite elitist, in the sense that it doesn't actively go to all schools to encourage people to apply. Like if it had been the intention of getting the brightest students in the country, that's what they would do. But lately they've been trying to do that so . . . I think it is slowly going toward that but in the past I know it's just been all about, kind of, "Oh, he's the earl of this county, so let's just accept him by heritage," basically.

Henry is the son of immigrants from Europe and East Africa. He acknowledges that the university is moving in the right direction. Later in his interview Henry cited a teacher, herself an Oxford graduate, who encouraged him to apply, perhaps persuading him that many qualified students might not think to apply unless they happen to encounter someone with greater cultural knowledge who encourages them to do so. Henry suggests that the solution to underrepresentation of state school graduates is better recruiting in underserved areas. Still, he did not suggest that Oxford should calibrate evaluations of that wider pool of applicants according to the quality of schools they attend. Lacking this calibration, recruiting more applicants is unlikely to yield greater diversity on campus, because recent studies have shown that white students are advantaged in admissions in the interview system— comparing students with the same national exam grades shows that tutors are more likely to select white and private-school students than minority and state-school graduates with the same national exam grades.[26]

Oxford students' perspectives on merit, then, contrasted sharply with those of US students. Given the lack of discussion of "diversity" as an educational (and moral) good in Britain and on Oxford's campus, all those rejecting considerations of race in Britain assume that it would be used for calibration. In other words, when asked whether admissions tutors should consider an applicant's race (or class), British students assess the value of calibrating evaluations of merit and usually reject it. None suggested that attention to difference would contribute to the collective merit of the campus as a whole, the leading justification for affirmative action in the United States. Still, like US students, Oxford students advocated for evaluation criteria that were consistent with the espoused practices of their university.

The British Diversity Bargain

In the United States we have seen the "diversity bargain" at work, in which white students supported affirmative action as long as it benefited them, namely through exposure to new perspectives. This led them to expect black and Latino students to integrate with their white peers and that affirmative action should not go "too far," such that whites begin to feel disadvantaged by it. While all respondents had gained admission to a top US university (either Harvard or Brown), as they looked ahead to internships, jobs, and other competitions, many white students felt anxious about whether, as they perceived it, affirmative action would rob them of a well-deserved opportunity.

The British diversity bargain was different. The students we spoke with in Britain did not support affirmative action, whether by race or by class. One benefit of this perspective was that they did not question the deservingness of their peers on campus. On US campuses, students frequently reported wondering how peers had gained admission. For example, Sheena, an Indian American student at Brown, remarked, "In class one kid said, 'You don't want us to have to use MLA [style] or nothing like that?' and the first thing that popped in my head was 'Oh, he must be an athlete.'" In other instances white students wondered — or assumed — that particular black and Latino peers gained admission or other rewards through affirmative action. In Britain these assessments did not hold. Given the absolute, "blank slate" approach that students advocated and that their admissions tutors supposedly practiced, most fully accepted the deservingness of all their peers. In other words, I did not hear Oxford students talking about whether their peers deserved admission to Oxford, or wondering what got them in, as I did in the United States. Of course, this acceptance came with costs, amounting to a British version of the diversity bargain.

Like the American diversity bargain, the British diversity bargain has two parts. First, students' vision for admissions would keep the number of black British students on campus very low. Even when students recognized that inattention to race in admissions had a circular effect of preventing qualified black students from applying and enrolling, they maintained the primacy of the blank slate approach. That is, students had no vision for how to increase the number of black students on campus beyond more recruiting, a strategy that is unlikely to change the face of Oxford much, since, if we compare students with the same national exam grades, minority students already are more likely than whites to apply to elite British universities.[27]

Second, the lack of attention to inequality or to diversity denied the racialized experiences of minority students at Oxford. While many second-generation students shared perspectives on race and merit with their white British peers, the 2014 "I, Too, Am Oxford" campaign, as we will see in chapter 7, reveals an undercurrent of frustration that many minority students on campus feel.[28] I call this acceptance of minority students as unconditionally equal to their peers, in exchange for uncalibrated admissions and little acknowledgment of racial injustice on campus, the British diversity bargain. Unfortunately, the lack of expectation that the university will accommodate nontraditional students and their needs maintains a model for meritocracy at Oxford that reproduces social inequality. In other words, students imagined no role for Oxford in changing the pattern of minority and working-class underenrollment and left it to the broader British society and education system to address the problem. So white students in both countries adopted a race-related "diversity bargain" with respect to their views on inclusion and admissions, with different consequent costs for students of color.

*　　*　　*

Through Oxford students' perspectives on race, merit, and underrepresentation, we can see how elite British universities shape their students' understandings of who is worthy to enter the elite of society. In contrast to the calibrated evaluations of merit and attention to collective merit that US students advocated, students at Oxford tended to frame meritocracy in the language of absolute, individual merit. Considering any kind of disadvantage was anathema to most British students, so they did not need to employ the color-blindness frame to justify disagreeing with considerations of race in admissions. Rather, in criticizing race-based considerations they rejected the notion of calibration altogether, unlike critics of affirmative action in the United States, who usually argued that calibration should be done through class rather than race. When students did criticize the way Oxford does admissions, those criticisms too were embedded in a frame of merit based on individuals and without calibration. The few Oxford students who supported calibration did so by class; to them, current achievement and the admissions interview alone cannot assess an individual's potential to succeed—they believed these assessments would overlook deserving working-class and poor students who have the intelligence and motivation to succeed in their chosen fields of study.

Overall, I found that, like students in the United States, students in Britain are deeply embedded in their universities' cultures, both past and present. Students in the two countries perceived different institutional goals in admissions, and they supported those different goals. In the United States, universities seek to craft a diverse cohort of students who have made the most of whatever opportunities they had in high school. In Britain, universities seek to admit those with the most potential to succeed in their subject matter, and that potential stems from both intelligence and cultivation in elite schools and families. These different priorities are reinforced by the difference in the people who make admissions decisions. In the United States, decisions are made by an independent admissions office, while at Oxford interviews are conducted by tutors teaching the subject for which they interview candidates.[29] Tutors have their own teaching interests in mind, because they will be conducting tutorials with those admitted, while admissions offices in the United States don't have much interaction with admitted students but must respond to a much wider variety of demands—athletic coaches, the university's concerns about public image, alumni, demands of the faculty, and more. Students' perspectives on admissions are also reinforced in the United States by the prevailing race frames on campus. American students most commonly relied on the diversity and color-blindness frames to develop their ideas about admissions and affirmative action. British students had less articulated race frames, and their individual, uncalibrated approach meant they did not rely on race frames for making sense of admissions. In other words, Oxford students' race frames do not inform their perspectives on merit in the same way.

Students' views on admissions also rested on particular understandings of the role elite higher education should play in society. As we have seen, elite US universities tend to be "socially embedded," envisioning a more civic role for themselves, while elite British universities, despite being public, tend to be "socially buffered" from the broader society, focusing on students' academic achievement in one subject rather than on civic purposes.[30] Most students seem to have adopted these understandings of the roles of their respective universities, and they employ them to imagine solutions to underrepresentation. So US students imagine that their universities should play a role in reducing underrepresentation, even if they lay blame for it outside the university's gates. This view of the role of elite higher education, along with students' race frames, led them to beliefs about calibrating evaluations of merit and about the importance of diversity on campus. Oxford students, on the other hand, see underrepresentation as an important social problem but not Oxford's problem.

Given that the students we interviewed on all three campuses had recently fared well in the admissions process, perhaps it is not surprising that they maintained the legitimacy of those contests. They worked exceedingly hard in secondary school. Many, with the aid of

their parents and schools, deliberately crafted themselves into individuals poised to gain admission to the likes of Harvard, Brown, and
Oxford. At Oxford this means developing the cultural know-how to
impress tutors in the Oxford interview, alongside the academic preparation for national and university exams. In the United States it means
developing into "well-rounded" individuals with leadership qualities.

Recent changes suggest that in the future Oxbridge and the Ivy
League may converge in their admissions processes. Elite universities
around the world are part of a highly institutionalized global system
of higher education, and with greater globalization has come greater
convergence of their missions, organizational structures, and even curricula.[31] Drew Faust, president of Harvard University, in fact calls on
Harvard graduates to become global leaders.[32] In addition, Oxford and
other British universities are moving toward American-style attention
to greater access. The British Office for Fair Access (OFFA) opened in
2004; since 2006 the British government has required most universities to develop an "access agreement" with OFFA. This move may be a
shift toward more emphasis on equal opportunity. It may also signal a
Labour Party shift toward an emphasis on social mobility rather than
improving working-class life.[33] Social mobility requires a meritocratic
system with legitimate opportunities for students of all social backgrounds, hence the turn toward greater access at a time when support
for generous government benefits, even in the Labour Party, has declined. Still, change is slow. Students in this study, from the first cohorts to be admitted under this new system, seemed unaware of government requirements, and their words suggest they would disagree
with them. In terms of the actual admissions process, at least for now,
the effect of this information on admissions tutors' decision making is
also unclear.[34]

Fundamentally, aside from their *universities* converging on a global
system of higher education, most of the *students* we interviewed also
seem to be joining a color-blind global elite that emphasizes using
meritocracy as a fair system of rewards. That is, if they did support
attention to race, as many US students did, it was usually through a
desire for collective merit, in which groups are seen as different but
equal. Ongoing racial inequality, apart from the correlation of race
and class, is virtually ignored as a thing of the past, despite research
evidence of ongoing implicit prejudice, racial bias in housing markets
and employment, and more.[35] In addition, their version of meritoc-

racy seems to be what Joseph Soares calls an "ultrameritocracy." As the competition for spots at elite universities grows more and more fierce—in the United States the most elite have admittance rates close to 5 percent, and Oxford's rate is about 20 percent, and both grow smaller each year—so too does the belief that the system is truly competitive. Students coming from elite private high schools no longer see most of their peers gaining admission to Harvard, Brown, and Oxford;[36] they take this as evidence that the system is fair, even while ignoring the fact that students like them and their high school peers are vastly overrepresented at elite universities. Research shows that the more competitive admissions become, the greater inequality there is in who gains admission to elite universities.[37] Despite the history of student protest and the propensity of young people to disagree with what the adults around them do, when it comes to admissions students fall in line with their university administrators.

SEVEN

RACE, RACISM, AND "PLAYING THE RACE CARD" AT OXFORD

In the spring of 2014, as part of an independent study project, Kimiko Matsuda-Lawrence, a black student at Harvard, made the "I, Too, Am Harvard" site on Tumblr. She posted pictures of black Harvard students holding placards with messages responding to offensive comments they had heard on campus. "Having an opinion does not make me an 'angry black woman,'" for example, and "You're *not* blacker than me because you can rap more Jay-Z lyrics." The moving campaign quickly went viral. Less than two weeks after the original Harvard campaign, Oxford minority students started a parallel "I, Too, Am Oxford" blog on Tumblr, citing the inspiration they took from Harvard black students.[1] "'Back home' is London, not India!" and "Yes, you CAN pronounce it!" are some of the statements they announced on their placards. The speed with which Oxford students echoed their Harvard peers, as well as the similarity of their campaigns, suggests a globalizing of protest at these elite universities. However, the origins of the campaigns, as well as the responses of peers of these disaffected students and their university administrators, were remarkably different at Harvard and Oxford.

Institutional supports allowed the Harvard project to take place in the first place. The site arose out of Matsuda-Lawrence's independent study project, for which she interviewed peers and which culminated in a theater production. The independent study was supervised by a professor of African and African American studies.[2] The play was staged as part of an annual Black Arts Festival at Harvard, organized by Kuumba, a singing group that performs music of black heritage and that "proclaims and celebrates the creativity and spirituality of black people."[3] The dean of Harvard College responded supportively to "I, Too, Am Harvard" in an opinion piece for the *Boston Globe*: "Harvard is . . . about inclusion. This photo campaign . . . is a great example of students speaking about how we can become a stronger community."[4] At the end of the related theater performance, the dean further "pledged to work closely with students to make Harvard a more inclusive environment."[5] A few months later Harvard's president, Drew Faust, acknowledged students' sentiments: "Its creators have reminded us that America is far from a post-racial society and that our national heritage and history of racial injustice persists." She added, "It is time for Harvard to ensure the fundamental justice that guarantees every member of this community an honored seat at the welcome table. Every group that makes up this richly diverse institution must feel confident in affirming, 'We, Too, Are Harvard.'"[6]

Especially when contrasted to Oxford University's response, Harvard administrators seem inclusive and supportive. Oxford's response to "I, Too, Am Oxford" was silence—I could not find any public statements or interview quotations about the campaign by university administrators in the press. Further, some peers were critical of "I, Too, Am Oxford." A group of Oxford students took on what they saw as a marginal group of peers complaining about the university. Three days after "I, Too, Am Oxford" appeared, those critical peers launched "We Are All Oxford," using their own placards to articulate their positive experiences as minority or working-class students on campus: "I have mates of all colors. Never have we been made to feel different," and "We enjoyed celebrating diversity at the OUSU [Oxford University Student Union] International Fair."[7] In an interview, the young black woman who started the critical response campaign spoke of the negative image she felt was portrayed by "I, Too, Am Oxford," which contravened her own and others' positive cross-cultural experiences.[8] These responses, whether those of the universities, the students, or the press, highlight important differences between elite higher education in the United States and in Britain. Institutional supports in America empower students to develop minority identities and affirmation, and they uphold the importance of students' speaking up when they are dissatisfied with their university experiences. At Oxford, as we'll see, there is little speaking up.

In this chapter I discuss Oxford students' perspectives on race and interracial interactions. One difference between American and British students is that Oxford students do not foreground their university experiences when speaking about race, as American students do. Whereas American students spoke about shifts in how they think about race and race-related issues after arriving on the Brown and Harvard campuses, Oxford students spoke of no such shifts and instead, in response to questions on race and diversity, drew almost seamlessly on experiences during childhood as well as on campus. Further, they did not speak of the campus as a special place in which particular ideas about race and diversity flourish, as American students did. Questions about the influence of diversity on campus mostly fell flat at Oxford; students responded with statements like, "Not very much" and "I don't think it has any effect at all, really."

"Playing the Race Card" and (Mis)Perceptions of Racism in Britain

While many white US students lamented the guilt they felt about their white identities, a result of the moral failures of racism in US society that they were taught about in school from early on, feelings of guilt were never mentioned by British interviewees. Many British students, in fact, saw tolerance and multiculturalism as endemic to their identities. For example, Adam, when asked how his racial or ethnic identity shapes his views on race and ethnicity, replied,

> As a result of being white and British I do feel that all races should be accepted. . . . I think it's not the fact that my skin is white that makes me that way. I think it's what comes with growing up in Britain and growing up in school and society here, where all faiths and races are considered equal.

A grammar school graduate studying mathematics, Adam shifts the question to one of national identity and declares Britain an accepting, multicultural society. Others similarly reported that their racial identities had little relation to their views on race and ethnicity or, like Stephen, that they "don't have very strong views on race and identity, ethnicity."

Belief in British tolerance did not preclude criticism of minorities' reports of racism. Olivia, a private school graduate studying modern languages, expressed irritation at minority claims of injustice. After identifying as "white and British," she said,

> I'm slightly irritable when it comes to people crying wolf, and by that I mean doing what they do best, which is, you know, playing the race card, saying, "Is it because I'm black?" That really annoys me, because it is so unfounded in England. It's so untrue. You see racism so much in other countries which we don't have here.

Like Adam, Olivia conceptualizes British society as tolerant and multicultural, going even further by contrasting Britain to other countries where she believes greater racism exists. Olivia's sharp words provide a startling contrast to the reactions of white US students who, even when pushing back against political correctness or affirmative action, were very careful. Even in one-on-one interviews with a white graduate student, in the United States I heard hesitant language, peppered with phrases such as "I feel like someone is going to gnaw at my neck right now, but I feel like it has to do with cultural differences rather than racism" and "I'm not racist but . . . ," attempting to mitigate the accusation "that's racist." Olivia's tone suggests she does not fear moral judgment; indeed, she rejects such accusations of racism as spurious, given her understanding of British society. Unlike white students in the United States, she does not defer to the judgment of her minority peers in questions of racism. Moreover, without the diversity frame and a desire to learn from the collective merit of her peers, Olivia does not seem to see value in attempting to understand why some ethnic minorities may claim to experience racial discrimination.

Nicole, a white grammar school graduate studying biology, also described her frustration with situations in which her minority peers "play the race card." When asked to describe a negative experience with someone of another race, Nicole said,

> They would play the race card if something happened. . . . It would be, "Oh, is it because I'm, you know—" And [I] would be like, "No!" And that would get really annoying. I guess it's probably just like a defense mechanism. Maybe they somehow feel like they are this group in society that is a minority, so they feel like they need to stick together a bit more.

Nicole's comments lack specificity about *when* her minority peers "play the race card," or even who "they" are—she does not name any particular person, group, or situation. In other words, "playing the race card" is a script for making sense of situations in which minority peers bring up race and acknowledge racial differences, which Nicole and Olivia implicitly reject. Cultural scripts are based not necessarily on particular experiences but rather on stock ways of understanding that are "independent of individual experience."[9] This claim of "playing the race card" is a script that students are ready to deploy, just as the "reverse discrimination" script exists in the United States.

Given the confidence white British students feel in their views and their own readings of interracial situations, there were fewer opportunities for them to feel victimized by "reverse discrimination." Indeed, when asked if they had ever experienced racial discrimination, most white British students said no or else shared experiences they'd had while traveling abroad, in which they'd been yelled at or mugged or harassed because they were British, or they told of witnessing the racism of British National Party supporters. Perhaps because they reject their minority peers' accusations of racism, they don't experience those claims as discrimination, unlike US whites, many of whom talked about reverse discrimination in which minorities seemed to be favored.

Just as students of color in the United States reported disturbing experiences with racism, so too did minorities in Britain. For example, Tisha, a South Asian private school graduate studying history, spoke of multiple disturbing experiences from her childhood:

> When I was five someone was making racial slanders and I went home and I was just telling my mum about my day and then my mum realized it was quite racist. She informed the school and then the teacher dragged me in and told me I was being a silly little brown girl and I ought not to go telling my mum silly little things. I didn't know any better so I didn't really understand it. I can give you countless things like that.

Tisha's experiences with racism at school did not stop in primary school. She went on to describe offensive comments both in her secondary school and at Oxford:

At school there were always jokes. There is a lot of comic discourse about ethnic minorities. Like one of my friends [once joked], "I can't believe you're wearing your [bike] helmet! Only Asian students wear their helmets." And I was like, "Oh, I don't care. I'm wearing my helmet." But that doesn't change what I think of him. . . . At Oxford I was at a dinner party and a grandmother of a friend turned around to me and was just like, "Oh, so what are you going to do after university?" And I was like, "I don't know. Get a job, I presume. I haven't decided what I want to do." "Well, are you going to go and help your people?" And I was like, "Sorry, what people?" "Well, *your* people." The implication was obviously that I was not English, not British, and all the rest that goes along with it. . . . Another friend of mine who does history here, he makes really silly comments all the time. Like he lives in the countryside, and he came to visit me in London and I was working behind Oxford Street, and so he was like, "Ah, I've seen so many darkies!" . . . That was more about him trying to be a "lad" than it is about him being rude. And he had a girlfriend who was from Iran, so I know he's not racist.

Tisha's Oxford friends take liberties, perhaps because they are her friends, in ways that most US whites did not, especially around their minority peers.

White students, too, remembered incidents like those Tisha described. Lily, a white student in her second year studying modern languages, spoke about overt racism at her private secondary school:

At school there were some kids that really gave a lot of the boarders a really hard time. . . . There was a group of [boarders] who were from Nigeria, and they quite often were the brunt of a lot of jokes. These were the really, really nasty guys that thought it was fine and it was funny to just keep hammering away, until it got to the point where it was just racism and it was a little out of control.

We asked Lily how she reacted in those situations. She said,

I tended to let other people deal with it, because I didn't want to stand up to these people any more than most other people did. We always had to wait for a teacher to deal with it. There were very few

people that used to say, "Shut up, that's racism!" because you knew
you were asking for it if you did.

Given the nature of interviews, we cannot know for sure whether
Lily ever spoke up or whether the US students who *say* they speak up
actually do. Regardless, the contrast between Lily and US students
suggests less moral stigma to inaction in the face of racism in Britain.
Lily gives what she feels is a reasonable explanation for her inaction—
that peers may have retaliated if she accused them of racism. In contrast, I didn't hear US students explaining inaction in the same ways,
perhaps because in the United States silence in the face of racism is
viewed as a moral failure and hence not as easily excused by fear of
retaliation.

Henry, the son of an East African father and a European mother,
shared his experience with racial profiling:

One time when I was coming back from school, I got stopped by the
police. Some guy started grabbing me on the street saying, "Come
here! Come here!" He didn't show me his police badge, so I thought
he was just grabbing me. But basically some police surrounded me
and said that I matched the description of someone who had stolen
something. Then they let me go. I know my father has been attacked
by racist youths. . . . We used to live in a really, really bad estate [pub-
lic housing] when I was younger, where at the time there was a lot of
racism and violent crime.

Aside from these public experiences, Henry went on to describe
racism in his secondary school: "There was always casual racism in
my secondary school, like white people using the N-word, but it was
accepted as the norm. It was very strange. 'We don't really mean it.'
That's what they said."

The experiences shared by Henry and other second-generation
respondents, as well as the observations of a few white students like
Lily, suggest that the perception that racism is uncommon in multicultural Britain, although hopeful, is wrong. Even beyond what students shared in the interviews, I heard and read about multiple incidents of overt racism perpetrated by students at Oxford, students in
secondary schools, and adults during the period of this research. For

example, students dressing in offensive ways was common, including students attending a party in blackface and an athletic team's party themed "bring a fit [sexy] Jew," in which at least one person came in caricatured Jewish attire and carrying moneybags.[10] Other students mentioned a campus party where some students wore T-shirts bearing racial slurs, including the N-word.[11] Outside of social events, several Oxford students discussed a controversy in which the student debate team had invited Nick Griffin, head of the far-right nationalist British National Party, along with Holocaust denier David Irving, for a campus discussion.[12] Certainly there were highly publicized racialized incidents at Harvard and Brown as well, but they were fewer, and only one on each campus was led by students. The gravity of the incidents at Brown and Harvard was remarkably different as well, even if offensive. Recall that at Brown students mentioned a flyer with an offensive picture of President Obama and Harvard students mentioned a student newspaper article criticizing the new ethnic studies area. Overall, then, while racism played a role on the Oxford campus, most white students there did not feel the same moral imperative to appear not racist as US students did, and so they did not fear the accusation "that's racist" in the same way.

"People Don't Need to Be Wrapped in Cotton Wool": Political Correctness

In chapter 5 I described how US students used the concept of "political correctness" to reinforce the importance of not being offensive, while also expressing a desire for interracial dialogue. Given that white students at Oxford did not fear the moral judgment of "that's racist" as white American students did, political correctness had a different meaning there. These differences highlight the contrasting ways US and British students think about race. Many at Oxford saw political correctness as silly; some students actually responded to the question, "What is political correctness?" with laughter. British students were concerned that political correctness sometimes "goes too far," leading to absurdities: one student complained about not being able to sing the nursery rhyme "Baa Baa Black Sheep"; several complained about needing to say "Happy Holidays" instead of "Happy Christmas." While the most common definition of political correctness was, as in the United States, trying not to offend other groups when speaking or using terms for social groups that those groups prefer, one-third of white and second-generation students at Oxford described political correctness as a problem. Lily, quoted above about the racism she witnessed in her secondary school, said political correctness has "gone too far":

> [Political correctness] can get to the point where you worry too much about offending someone, where you can like imagine problems where there normally wouldn't be problems. . . . I think in principle it's a really good idea to be able to not discriminate against everybody. But then again I think that you need to appreciate that people don't need to be wrapped in cotton wool and some stuff is just having a sense of humor or is just disliking people sometimes. I think it's gone a bit far now and you can really . . . you can get in trouble for stuff that you really didn't mean in any kind of racist, sexist, homophobic way. Because people can say, "Oh, that's not politically correct, you can't like sack this person because they are a woman." Well maybe it's just because they are not good at their job. I think it has gone a little bit far now.

At first Lily recognizes the value of trying not to offend others. However, she seems to feel that sometimes there are false accusations of racism, sexism, and homophobia—playing the race, gender, and sexuality cards. Further, she insists on evaluating a speaker's intent rather than the offense taken by someone.

Dylan, a white private school graduate studying French, also declared that political correctness sometimes goes too far. He attempted to define the boundary between not discriminating and going too far:

> Political correctness is attempting, usually on the level of language, to not discriminate [against] minorities. Quite a lot of it is widely derided and mocked, for being mostly superficial aesthetic changes pandering to very loud, complaining minorities. . . . I think in essence it's a very good thing, but it's very badly applied in a lot of cases. Things like suppressing "Happy Christmas" to be replaced with "Happy Holidays" is an example of fairly thoughtless political correctness, because people will always see through holidays and read

Christmas without really distinguishing between the two. Whereas there are other things, like replacing "his" with "his/her" or a singular "they" to degender the language—slightly more thought has gone into that.

Many second-generation respondents shared the belief that political correctness can be a good thing but that it can "go too far." Jian, a medical student whose parents immigrated from South Korea, said,

> Political correctness is not offending people with different backgrounds and different cultures. . . . Sometimes people go a bit over the top, and sometimes it's just a bit funny. Like the other day I was walking past the cake shop and they had a wedding cake, and on top of the cake were two men. I thought that was quite funny, and that was someone saying they are trying to be politically correct and not always just have a man and a woman. . . . [But] sometimes it's not really necessary to be too over the top.

Contrast these students' assessments with those of US students, most of whom deferred to disadvantaged groups to determine the boundaries of acceptable language. British students were more interested in discussing where the boundary was between positive language shifts—for example, gender-neutral language—and seemingly absurd language shifts—for example, saying "Happy Holidays" in place of "Happy Christmas." The problem, of course, is that what seems absurd to some is reasonable and important to others. Yet students did not identify this issue. Instead, they used examples that were obviously beyond the boundary of reasonableness to themselves—and, they assumed, to others—to demonstrate that in Britain political correctness had gone to absurd lengths. They easily relied on their personal moral compass, unlike many white students in the United States.

Other students rejected the attempt not to offend altogether, emphasizing the seeming absurdity of political correctness. Nick, a white private school graduate studying chemistry, said, "Political correctness is when you are not allowed to have an opinion because it may offend someone. . . . I think it's a load of rubbish, because it's just gone a bit too far. It's like, I know in schools you're not allowed to sing the old nursery rhyme, 'Baa Baa Black Sheep' because it may have racist connotations. I think it has just been going a bit too far."[13] Nick stops there rather than explaining why going too far is troubling. Interestingly, he uses passive voice and does not explain where the limits on speech come from. When pressed about why it's troubling, he stated that "it almost stifles people's opinions, whereas you could face problems if you're not politically correct." While Nick describes the absurdity of political correctness in detail, including an example, any actual negative consequences seem more of an afterthought. Second-generation Henry said, "Political correctness is silly. It's just the term that people who get offended really easily use. . . . I think most people have common sense not to offend people right in their face, but I disagree with political correctness in general." Unlike US students, who felt anxiety over the accusation of racism, Henry rejects taking offense, claiming that those who take offense "get offended really easily." In addition, while US critics worried about political correctness preventing dialogue on diversity, British students emphasized its seeming absurdity.

Overall, the students we interviewed in the United States and Britain used different language to talk about political correctness, whether they supported or criticized it. American students emphasized the importance of dialogue about diversity on campus and the potential for political correctness, even if well-meaning, to derail that dialogue, while British students expressed frustration about others' apparently unlimited capacity to feel offended, which could "go too far," a problem in itself rather than tied to particular consequences. The contrast illuminates students' different concerns related to race and racism. American students feared the moral judgment of racism and hoped to learn from campus diversity, shaping their perspectives on political correctness. British students, by contrast, did not share those same fears.

"It's Just a Joke!" Race-Related Humor on the Oxford Campus

When I sat down to coffee with a leader of Majlis, Oxford's South Asian students' organization, I expected to finally hear the criticism of Oxford that I had expected of students from non-elite families but that we had not heard in our interviews so far. Imagine my surprise when the conversation was upbeat and positive about the university—

he told me that race relations on campus are great; that everyone gets along famously; and that peers of all backgrounds are respectful of difference. I asked probing questions, but the story did not seem to change. Then I told him that many Oxford students reported in interviews that they frequently hear and participate in racial jokes. He nodded, as if I had just mentioned something utterly banal, and dismissed my concerned look by saying, "It's a joke that anyone could be racist!"[14] He told me that he himself engaged in this banter, with South Asian and non–South Asian peers alike; during the remaining hour of our conversation, he said, "It's a joke that anyone could be racist" four or five times. The phrase perplexed me — and it continued to haunt me for some time. To my American eyes and ears this was evidence that he was brainwashed by Oxford. I tried to remove my American lens, reflecting on this conversation for many months, recounting it often. Now, in retrospect, I see I was mistaken. What does it mean to say "it's a joke that anyone could be racist"?

Paying attention to what racial jokes *do* for white British students may help to explain why they engage in this banter, and why they reject others' objections when offense is taken.[15] In the United States, avoiding racial humor signals a desire to learn from diversity on campus and to be morally just, whereas in Britain no parallel desires push students to avoid racial humor. If we take their words at face value, British students understood racial jokes to signal an understanding that some people in society continue to hold racist beliefs, but that one is unlike those people and finds those beliefs absurd. Hence, the president of Majlis telling me, "It is a joke that someone could be racist!"

When asked, "Have you witnessed racial prejudice, in the form of discrimination, racial jokes, or other ways?" three-fourths of British students brought up racial jokes. Many, like the president of Majlis, defended those jokes, claiming that in fact they have antiracist intent. White students made similar claims. For example, Daniel said, "People tell jokes that could be deemed as racist but because of the attitude that's [expressed] in them, they actually become satirical of people who would tell those jokes. So instead you laugh at the attitude rather than the joke." Daniel describes this as "ironic humor." The joking thus demonstrates the speakers' willingness to broach sensitive topics while signaling their own antiracist attitudes. Ultimately, many students found this banter funny and consequently were willing to take the associated risks. Moreover, the risks were lower in Britain than in the United States. American students take very few risks in talking about race, because the consequences of landing on the wrong side of the hurtline are greater and the boundary is less clear, and sometimes defined by the person who takes offense, not by the offender. As a result, British students were much more likely than Americans to report hearing or telling racial jokes.

British students defended racial jokes in several ways. One technique for deflecting criticism was to make jokes about *all* groups, or at least to claim that jokes are made about all social groups—a color-blind approach. For example, Paige, a white private school graduate studying biology, told us,

> I've probably heard racist jokes, but I've also heard blonde jokes and sexist jokes. . . . I think as long as you can laugh at something and not agree with it—like, if someone makes a sexist joke sometimes they can be funny. As long as I don't think the person saying it is a sexist— I heard a racist joke from someone who's not racist, and there's been someone of that minority [group] there as well who's laughed along. If it was too extreme, then I would say something.

Paige explains the rules around race-based humor: laughing is a sign that you disagree with the content of the joke—that you are laughing at the kind of person who would actually believe such a thing. She takes a color-blind (and gender-blind) approach to racist humor by equating blonde jokes, racist jokes, and sexist jokes. This defense, however, ignores the very real fact that racial jokes are most often made not about dominant groups but about oppressed groups— women, racial minorities, Irish, and Jews were mentioned by students, and not men, whites, or English people.[16]

The second way students mitigated perceptions of offense was to identify good intentions. The boundary Adam, a white student, identifies for the hurtline is intention: "If it is *designed* to cause offense then that's a problem [my italics]." Similarly Jasmine, a white private school graduate, told us, "I guess there are racial jokes. People do say them. I mean, they don't mean to be racist or anything. . . . I know the people [who tell the jokes] and I don't think they are racist people generally." White students in Britain, like Adam and Jasmine, were more likely to identify *intent* as determining the boundary between funny and offensive, compared with white American students' emphasis on *others' feeling offended* as determining whether a speaker had crossed the hurtline.

Third, just as comedians in Raúl Pérez's study of stand-up comedy training mitigate offense by making jokes about their own groups,[17] British students claimed that jokes can't be racist when members of the target group participate in the banter. For example, Joseph, a white private school graduate studying English literature, said,

> The odd thing about racial jokes is that very often friends of mine to whom the butt of the joke applies are the ones that have told them or haven't minded them. So this Nigerian friend would participate in a joke about a black man or my Muslim friend wouldn't actually mind a joke of that kind. So yes, certainly it's happened, but not always hurtfully.

While we didn't ask Joseph about the evidence that his friends "don't mind," from his description it seems to be that either the minority person is participating in the joke or that person does not protest. When asked about racial jokes, Niamh, whose name is Irish, identified "Irish jokes," clarifying, "I don't have a problem with them . . . because I don't feel sore about the fact that I'm Irish. . . . Like I know some black guys who tell horrific black jokes and it's absolutely fine because they are black."

While many claimed that silence means acceptance of the humor, other British students, especially second-generation respondents, noted the difficulty of intervening when they did find peer behaviors offensive, because doing so would violate the cultural practices of the group. That is, intervening turned lighthearted interactions into heavy claims of moral transgression and consequently altered the meaning of the conversation, ultimately stigmatizing the offended speaker for violating the group culture.[18] For example, Rafiq, a second-generation student with parents from North Africa, told us,

> If there is a group of friends and one of them is black and you pick on that person, and you specifically attack in racial terms as a joke, that's still racism. And that's still to be utterly condemned, because that person feels isolated. [On the other hand] if there were three black people and you were having cross-jokes between the groups— if there is an exchange of jokes and if everyone is fine with it and

everyone is laughing then it doesn't really matter. It's only if you start to pick on an individual where it starts to get out of hand.

At first Rafiq suggests strength in numbers—that is, if the target group is not isolated and no one in that group complains, it might be OK. However, he goes on to point out that, given the social milieu at Oxford, it is very difficult to protest even if one feels uncomfortable or offended:

> You should immediately stop if any individual feels uncomfortable with it. And that's the problem with this idea—when will anybody say that they feel uncomfortable with it? Will people actually say that they feel uncomfortable if everyone else is having a laugh? If everyone is just enjoying themselves will someone say that they are not comfortable and spoil the fun for everyone else? That's the problem.

Rafiq points out the difficulty of expressing discomfort in the situation. Thus, even if the implicit rule about racial jokes is that they should stop if someone perceives them to cross the hurtline, in practice such accusations were rarely expressed.

Sylvia, a second-generation student whose parents are from India and China, also noted the difficulty of expressing offense among friends:

> [You hear racial jokes] mainly with your friends, and that's after you've known them for a long time so it's kind of fun. But then they can take the joke a bit too far. I do think it's strange that they would do that, because [I would think] they would feel it's too impolite to do that.

I asked Sylvia how she responds in those situations. She said,

> I just kind of laugh uncomfortably. But then, different people have a different threshold of humor, so it's kind of hard to know what's right and what's not right. . . . I don't think they are racist.

Unlike students of color in the United States, Sylvia feels unsure about moral judgment—"It's hard to know what's right and what's not," deferring to the views of her peers who tell the racial jokes, even when they make her uncomfortable.

When students did try to intervene, despite the group culture requiring silence, they were frequently sanctioned. Laura, a private school graduate studying history and French, reported,

> I've been quite shocked while I've been at Oxford that some people think it's okay to make racist jokes, because they don't think it's offensive or racist. They think it's being risqué and not being politically correct, whereas actually I find it quite offensive to hear people making racist jokes. I was labeled politically correct by some of these people because I took offense to some of the jokes that they were making. . . . Jokes against Chinese people, against black people.

Laura said racist jokes were most evident from her boyfriend and his peers, who had attended an elite British boarding school. Among these students, according to Laura, race-related jokes were common, and criticism or expressions of offense were not taken seriously:

> I had a boyfriend who went to [elite boarding school] and it's him and his friends. . . . Very, very posh school. They've not had much exposure to diversity. In that situation you can try and point out to them that they shouldn't really say things like that, [but] they will be like "Ah, it's politically incorrect! It's fine! It's funny!" It's not just racist jokes, they can also make very sexist jokes, and jokes about different classes. They just like to shock in any way they can, to get a reaction. . . . I don't think it's discrimination particularly. I don't know how they'd act with people who fulfilled the stereotypes that they were joking about.

Laura reports that her objection violated the norms of the group and further isolated her as someone who is "politically correct" and perhaps lacking a good sense of humor. So, rather than the hand-wringing of US students accused of racism, British students usually rejected that accusation, almost defiantly. This stance effectively silences dissenting students, whether minority or white, who attempt to identify offense. While US students did not describe the same banter from the culture of elite secondary schools, if students did bring those cultures to higher education, they would likely be muted on US campuses, given their diversity cultures and the espoused desire to learn from racial diversity.

In these ways British students insisted on a color-blindness frame in the realm of race-related joking. If "everyone knows" racism is terrible, then jokes about it are permissible, especially if jokes are told about *all* races, as well as about other social groups. This allowed students at Oxford to claim that racial jokes are jokes about racism, as the president of Majlis did. I learned after the interviews with dozens of other Oxford students that the Majlis president was making a point that illuminates Oxford students' perspectives on race and racism, "It's a joke that someone could be racist"—despite evidence of overt racism on campus. Following the cultural rules at play related to racist jokes allowed students to maintain a stance against racism while simultaneously telling racial jokes and, at times, rejecting peers' suggestions that some are offensive. I now understand the joke, and I also more clearly understand the ways it silences dissent.

* * *

In the lives of Oxford students, diversity and race are palpably different than they are in the lives of students at Brown and Harvard. Many Oxford students were quite blunt in discussing racial differences and inequality. Not only did the boundaries of moral behavior and words around race and diversity differ between British and American students, so did the referee—that is, *who* defined those moral boundaries. White Britons felt free to define the limits of offense and morality related to race. Their white American counterparts, who frequently feared the moral stigma of being called "racist" by their peers, tended to work to use language preferred by marginalized groups so as not to offend, often following those peers' moral boundaries rather than their own. These attempts could sometimes lead to feelings of racial resentment or that they were experiencing reverse discrimination. In Britain, white students are much more willing to *reject* accusations of racism, claiming that minorities are being too "politically correct," that they lack a sense of humor, or that they are "playing the race card." Thus the white students are the ones who define the boundary between offensive and inoffensive speech and behavior. That is, rather than experiencing the accusation of racism as an unexpected moral transgression rife with guilt (and sometimes, leading to racial resentment), in Britain, students usually reject that accusation and do not feel an assault to their sense of moral self-worth and heightened emotions.

The difference between British students saying "it's just a joke" and US students saying they find racial jokes offensive is instructive. It stems in part from the diversity frame that predominates at Brown and Harvard, which prioritizes collective merit, along with the particularly heinous history of slavery and racism in the United States that students learn about in school. Lacking the diversity frame, British students didn't assume that minority peers had different and important perspectives that whites should seriously consider before evaluating whether a word or phrase is offensive. Moreover, the lack of emphasis on collective merit meant that British students didn't see their university experience as an opportunity to learn from differences related to race or ethnicity. Further, British students' color-blindness frame prevented them from seeing the ways skin color and race more broadly hinder the life chances of some racial minorities.

Overall, the students in both countries are employing particular scripts for making sense of race-related experiences. When describing "reverse discrimination" in the United States or "playing the race card" in Britain, students sometimes could not think of specific examples. Instead, they relied on the scripts for making sense of diversity. These scripts are embedded in the larger contexts of nation-specific race frames and conceptions of merit. They suggest that the ways universities, and the larger society, defend the legitimacy of admissions criteria, affirmative action, and more shape the ways students make sense of fairness, inequality, and justice in admissions and beyond.

CONCLUSION

Over the past eight years I have spent countless hours talking to undergraduates and thinking about them. My goal in all this talking and thinking has been to understand how winners in this "postracial" generation make sense of the admissions process that has rewarded them, and what that tells us about race in the twenty-first century. Elite universities and their students are in the spotlight—these universities are national symbols of academic excellence, and many see their students as the most promising young adults in the country, no less than the future of our world. The students we talked to, more often than not, have internalized that perception. This is not surprising—after all, they have gained status through that perception, whether or not they came from privileged backgrounds. Just as important, students and the general public alike, especially in the United States, see elite universities as embodiments of foundational values, as proof that meritocracy and equal opportunity are flourishing.[1] So those students who do gain admission see themselves as part of an elite that has been fairly chosen through an inclusive and democratic process. The increasing competition for seats—admissions rates to the most selective universities decline almost every year—means that most of their high school peers did *not* get into Harvard, Brown, or Oxford, whether they came from an urban high school where a majority of students do not graduate or an elite New England boarding school. This increasing competition and exclusivity fuel students' belief that the system is fair; many fail to see how their upbringing, and its privileges, has helped them get into college. Students assume that applicants who do not get into Harvard, Brown, and Oxford may be bright and accomplished but are not as much so as them and their college classmates. On the other hand, the long history of student criticisms and protest, with students seeing themselves as liberal, along with loud public discussions about under-representation of working-class students and some minorities, made me expect to hear more critical perspectives than I did.

I am far from the first to uncover such blind spots. Mary Jackman and Michael Muha, for example, have revealed how dominant groups in society maintain their advantage in the face of public criticisms of inequality by defending the legitimacy of the system that led to their advantage.[2] Jackman and Muha report that these dominant groups tend toward two responses: they privilege individual rights over group rights, much the way our students advocated individualistic, and sometimes race-blind and class-blind, assessments of candidates, and they advocate symbolic rather than substantive concessions. Such concessions include Oxford students' support for outreach programs to disadvantaged youth that *encourage* their applications to Oxford rather than policies that *ensure* their presence on campus, and US students' support for affirmative action that admits just enough black and Latino students to create a "diverse" learning environment rather than striving for representation proportionate to the US population.[3]

This support for the status quo, even while simultaneously ac-knowledging the disadvantages of others, is also in accord with re-search on white Americans' views on racial inequality. Specifically, white Americans often recognize African Americans' disadvantages while opposing social policies to remedy them, such as affirmative action, aid to poor families with children, and busing to promote school integration.[4] Similarly, Americans often support multicultural-ism in the abstract, but not social policies to promote it, such as bilin-gual education.[5] Some have termed this combination of acknowledg-ment and refusal the "new prejudice."[6] In an era when overt racism is no longer socially acceptable, such attitudes perpetuate the en-trenched disadvantages that come with being a minority. Still, while much of the research on new prejudice analyzes when and why white Americans do *not* support race-based policies, in this book I show that we should also be looking more closely at when and why they *do* sup-port them. That is, which rationales are acceptable, and which are not? Further, we should be paying attention to how institutions influence those views, because therein lies hope for influencing a more inclu-sive society.

Given their position as young adults attending college and, in the United States, living on campuses with institutional supports for diversity, I expected my respondents to differ somewhat from these discouraging findings on racial attitudes. In the United States, elite students do support affirmative action more than ordinary Americans. Indeed, in America affirmative action serves in part to assuage the criticism that the competition may not be fair.[7] Still, when they do support it, it is, as Jackman and Muha predict, through attention to personal benefits rather than group rights, and that support is generally ambivalent. In Britain, support for increasing the number of minority students on campus is symbolic rather than substantive—students had no suggestions for how to correct underrepresentation of blacks, even when they articulated why it is a problem.

The problem with this understanding of the admissions process is that it blinds students to the numerous sources of inequality in admissions. First, countless studies have documented unequal achievement in high school, fueled by unequal resources in children's homes and schools and much more. Second, even among students with the same level of achievement, working-class, black, and Latino teens in the United States are less likely than well-off white youth to apply to elite colleges.[8] The same is true for working-class and Afro-Caribbean youth in Britain.[9] Third, in Britain, among students with the same grades on the national exams, working-class, black, and Asian students are less likely to gain admission than white middle-class applicants.[10] These sources of inequality lead to unequal outcomes of the admissions process. In Britain, while only 7 percent of the population attends private schools, nearly half of Oxford students come from private schools.[11] Black students are also underrepresented in elite British universities.[12] In the United States, black, Latino, and working-class and poor youth continue to be underrepresented at elite universities, and this inequality in admissions outcomes appears to be increasing rather than decreasing.[13] Studies of the most selective colleges in the United States have demonstrated that their student bodies have become wealthier over time, and even among wealthy Americans, whites are increasingly more likely than blacks to attend these colleges.[14] In addition, the percentage of students who were black at the most selective colleges in the United States *declined* from 1982 to 2004.[15]

Why should we care? Inequality in the United States and Britain will never be solved solely by changing the admissions process of elite universities, which, after all, educate such a small fraction of the population. We should care because these colleges matter a lot. They hold symbolic value in their respective societies and arguably around the world. Everyone seems to know Harvard and Oxford. Lower-tier colleges often look toward higher-status colleges when thinking about their own policies, on admissions and otherwise, so elite university policies trickle down.[16]

Second, we should care because going to a selective college provides important advantages to students. It increases income in adulthood.[17] And, elite US firms in banking, consulting, and law assume that the most talented graduates can be found on elite college campuses, and they consequently focus their recruiting efforts, often exclusively, on graduates of those colleges.[18] In Britain, Oxford is known as the breeding ground for Britain's politicians and media leaders. Over one-fourth of members of Parliament graduated from Oxford or Cambridge (commonly referred to as Oxbridge).[19] More specifically, thirty-seven of the current members of Parliament—over 5 percent— including Britain's prime minister and another three cabinet ministers, studied a *single* major at Oxford (politics, philosophy, and economics).[20] Although the percentage of graduates from Oxbridge has declined since the 1970s,[21] the universities remain an important pathway to leadership in Britain. While graduates of other colleges can make it to the top, an elite college degree acts as a kind of "social status insurance," dramatically increasing the likelihood that a graduate will take up a high-status or high-paying job.[22]

Finally, we should care because as these students turn into independent adults, many making important decisions in their professions and in the world at large, they will take with them their conceptions of what is fair, of what is (and is not) unequal, of what race means (and doesn't mean). How they think about these questions now, while they're still in college, tells us something about the way many of our future leaders will lead. These students' faith in their universities' admissions systems, alongside the blindness to inequality that those systems perpetuate, leads me to see their perspectives as part of a process that Shamus Khan calls "democratic inequality": an ostensibly democratic process with inevitably unequal outcomes.[23] The vast gulf between those few who get into an elite university and those many who do not isn't seen as a problem because that system of entry is seen as fair.

Other scholars, too, have recognized the ways students at elite educational institutions legitimate their status through belief in the meritocratic process by which they gained admission. Shamus Khan and Rubén Gaztambide-Fernandez showed this in their studies of students attending elite boarding schools in the United States.[24] In terms of college admissions, Mitchell Stevens has shown that admissions systems fuel a belief in their fairness while virtually guaranteeing privileged youth a seat at a selective college.[25] Lauren Rivera has shown how this democratic inequality operates in hiring at elite consulting, banking, and law firms.[26] My contribution to this growing chorus is to show that this legitimation of status operates quite differently in the United States and in Britain, and how race matters in these systems.

Let me begin with race. Any effort to understand how we think about merit today must, whether we like it or not, confront the way we think about race. The past shows that in the United States the definition of merit in admissions has long been intertwined with questions of race and ethnicity. In the 1920s, concerns over Jewish boys, seen as "greasy grinds," overtaking Ivy League colleges led to admissions quotas for Jewish applicants. The Ivies also changed their definition of merit, deemphasizing test scores in favor of "character," as measured by photographs, teachers' recommendations, sports participation, and more. This holistic review allowed for subjective judgment of applicants. Those seen as "too Jewish" were excluded. Even earlier, eugenicists of the late nineteenth and early twentieth centuries embarked on a quest to classify races according to their levels of intelligence. This was the sordid precursor of intelligence testing, which led to the SAT in admissions. The SAT was first used in the 1930s to identify students for scholarships at Harvard.[27]

Today merit and race remain as intertwined as ever. Social psychologists in the United States have demonstrated that our beliefs about racial inequality and our beliefs about meritocracy are entangled. For example, Frank Samson has shown that whites' beliefs about the importance of the SAT in college admissions decisions seem to shift when they are reminded that Asians do better than whites on the SAT (they say the SAT should matter less) and when they are reminded that blacks do worse than whites on the SAT (they say the SAT should matter more).[28] In addition, Eric Knowles and Brian Lowery have shown that whites who express strong beliefs in meritocracy are more likely to deny racial inequality than those who do not, in order to maintain a sense of themselves as high in merit.[29]

So how *do* students think about race, and what are the implications for their views on merit? Most students we talked with in the United States, across racial lines, saw the role of race in society through a *diversity frame*, which emphasizes positive aspects of cultural differences between racial groups. They appreciated diversity on campus for the enrichment it brought to their own educational experience rather than for its impact on racial justice or on the lives of students benefiting from affirmative action. This diversity frame led most students to believe that admissions should consider the *collective merit* of the university cohort, so that they could have a richer college experience. Following this emphasis on personal benefit, many white students expressed what I term the *diversity bargain*: ambivalent support for affirmative action as long as they benefited through a diverse campus, and as long as black and Latino peers didn't seem to deprive them of success in other competitive endeavors. Ultimately, then, most US students tended to hold individualist understandings of diversity and race rather than the "hard" multiculturalism espoused by many proponents that insists on state support for ethnic and racial identities[30]—let alone an understanding of power and resource differences between racial groups in society through a *power analysis frame*.

Students' appreciation for diversity is part of the "culturally omnivorous" sensibilities they are developing as part of their burgeoning elite American identities—that is, an appreciation for a range of genres of music, literature, and more, rather than tastes limited to traditionally elite cultures such as Western classical music and abstract art.[31] In addition to the need for the elite to be comfortable with a range of taste cultures, being familiar and at ease with diverse *peers* also signals a moral self in the contemporary United States and was an important part of the college experience as students described it.[32] We might also think of these students as budding cosmopolitans—individualists who draw from an array of cultures and who ultimately see themselves as citizens of the world.[33]

Related to their individual emphasis, many whites and Asian Americans in the United States held a *color-blindness frame*. The contradiction between the color-blindness and diversity frames—one views race as insignificant and the other views race as highly significant—leads many students to ambivalence and confusion over race-related issues. Still, while the two frames differ in their assumptions about the importance of race in society, they share a lack of attention to differences in power and resources between racial groups. This leads to a partial understanding of race. In other words, an emphasis on diversity and color-blindness, without a power analysis frame, will always be a limited view, because it does not recognize the racial inequality that is embedded in our institutions.[34] As Ellen Berrey describes it in her account of the rise of "diversity discourses" across a range of organizational contexts,

> Selective inclusion—especially the *symbolism* of selective inclusion—is surprisingly low risk for the high-status white people who do the managing of diversity. It does not necessitate that leaders address racial inequalities. . . . When diversity is confined to a small proportion of those who attend elite universities . . . it helps lessen the risks of radical, race-class transformation that social justice may require.[35]

Without a nuanced understanding of race in society that considers power, how will this generation address the race problems that continue to plague us?

Black and Latino students also supported affirmative action, but more frequently through a power analysis frame in which they recognized the often-invisible power differences between race groups and the implications of that inequality. Moreover, they did not view themselves as present on campus to enrich the experiences of their white peers. Instead, their diversity frame led them to appreciate differences *among* students of color, in addition to differences between minority and white peers. Many Asian American students shared their white peers' beliefs about affirmative action, while others embraced institutions such as the Third World Center at Brown; these students were more likely to criticize the status quo.

Diversity shaped the college experiences of all American students in one way or another. Talk of race is ubiquitous on American campuses, even if not always considered in enough depth. Most students were influenced, at least a bit, by the diversity of their peers, campus events centered on diversity, and formal and informal conversations about diversity. Many reported shifting their views on issues like affirmative action after they arrived to campus and experienced its benefits. They developed a robust diversity frame in college. A select few were deeply influenced and were emboldened at Harvard, and especially at Brown, by campus institutions such as centers promoting diversity, departments of African American and ethnic studies, and for some at Brown, a freshman orientation event targeting students of color that focuses on oppression. Most, but not all, of the students most influenced by these diversity efforts were black or Latino. They frequently analyzed issues related to race through a power analysis frame, raising questions of inequality embedded in the very fabric of their universities. Still, most of their white peers remained perplexed by these questions and wondered if these more vocal students were too quick to judge others for supposedly "racist" behaviors or expressions. Overall, students in the United States expressed a lot of concern with being not racist, which was a moral imperative, sometimes making white students very anxious.

A comparison with conceptions of merit and race in Britain throws the US case into relief. While in both countries students expressed strong belief in the functioning of admissions as a fair meritocracy, in the United States that belief is more pervasive, and more consequential, because our faith in and desire for equal opportunity through meritocracy is stronger.[36] Alexis de Tocqueville, in his nineteenth-century study of American democracy, contrasted Americans' belief in rugged individualism and democracy with life under the French aristocracy.[37] Seven decades later, German sociologist Max Weber identified the roots of American-style capitalism in the Protestant ethic, which he described as driving belief in hard work and asceticism in order to affirm God's grace in the individual.[38] That foundational American belief—that the opportunities we have and the rewards we earn are based on our individual merit—remains strong. A recent study showed that Americans today are more likely than Britons to believe that merit *should be*—and *does get*—rewarded with higher earnings.[39] Further, Americans tend to believe that a strong democracy rests on individualism, combined with equal opportunities for all Americans, rich or poor, black or white. Our belief that the United States is meritocratic undergirds our national identity as a land of democracy and equal opportunity.[40] To question whether American meritocracy is fair is to question the very basis for our sense of what is good about America. In contrast, European elites tend to embrace the distinctions associated with being part of the elite class, identifying themselves based on exclusive cultural knowledge—everything from classical music to the difference between a fish knife and a cheese knife—that explicitly differentiates them from the majority of society.[41]

I found that Oxford students did not express the same insistence on the fairness of their university admissions systems as American students did. They, like their university, advocated for admission to be based simply on achievement in the intended subject of study. Many, in fact, spoke comfortably about unequal schooling that led to unequal chances of admission to Oxford; moreover, despite this awareness, most did not perceive this as a problem for the university. It did not contravene deeply rooted beliefs about equal opportunity and meritocracy as it seemed to do in the United States. Most Oxford students, when asked about the underrepresentation of minority and working-class students on campus, saw this as a problem, but not as Oxford's problem. Instead, they expected the British primary and secondary education system to correct unequal opportunities, by helping minority and working-class students achieve the necessary credentials for admission to Oxford. Most second-generation students agreed with this approach. The problem is that it provides no vision for how to alter the status quo of unequal outcomes in the admissions process.

Oxford students were also less likely to acknowledge racial discord. They tended to reject expressions of racial offense as taking jokes too seriously and lamented what they saw as unnecessary "political correctness" that inhibited casual banter. Those British students who were critical of their peers' racial jokes had difficulty convincing them that such jokes were troubling. On the one hand, the ability of Oxford students to bluntly express their views on race was promising, compared with the emotionally fraught interracial encounters described by many white students in the United States. However, at many moments I wondered what good this open expression could do in a climate in which students' vision for their universities was not one of including learners from all walks of life, but rather one that does not concern itself with the unequal social processes of the world outside its hallowed gates. Indeed, while students in Britain were open about their views and didn't fear being labeled racist, there was little room for honest discussions about difference and racial offense. Some, mostly second-generation students, complained of the lack of space to object to offensive racial banter, but even those critics did not tie that banter to a larger system that almost guarantees a paucity of black (and

working-class) students on campus. In other words, the ways most
students at Oxford thought about admissions and race provided no
solution for ensuring broader inclusion of underrepresented groups
on campus, whether by race, class, or type of high school, or even
for an inclusive climate that made students from disadvantaged backgrounds feel they belonged.

Ultimately, despite the important differences between American
and British students, they all shared a trajectory into an increasingly
global elite that is largely color-blind and that is legitimated—despite
the differences between countries—by meritocracy. Most students
maintained a liberal individualist perspective, maintaining the sanctity
of individual choice, agency, and autonomy in what they assumed is
a fair system that rewards individual excellence. White American students also embraced diversity, but this was not a strong multiculturalism that recognizes group identities and provides resources to support
them.[42] Instead, white American students talked about multiculturalism as important for their *own* fulfillment rather than that of their minority peers. In both Britain and the United States, color-blindness is
the foundation for students' individualism.

In the end, if we care about being an inclusive democracy we need
to rethink our conceptions of merit and race and what we implicitly
teach our children and young adults. What would this vision look like?
What would it mean to dismantle the inequality embedded in our admissions policies and the meanings related to fairness, race, and inequality that those systems rest on? There must be a better way forward. Below I highlight three domains in which we can address merit
and race for a more inclusive democracy: defining the goals of meritocracy; framing affirmative action and race on campus; and recognizing that meritocracy is always incomplete.

Defining the Goals of Meritocracy

Merit pervades our modern world; indeed, we can see Western culture today as an amalgam of multiple merit-based systems. The most
obvious is higher education, but merit also shapes who gets jobs,
who gets promoted, and even who gets a spot in a coveted preschool.
While the ways we define merit often appear objective, they are in
fact always embedded in socially defined goals, whether implicit or explicit. What is a fair means of distinction, of deciding that one person

deserves something and another person does not? Can we use inborn intelligence? (And do we have any way to measure our innate abilities that is not biased by race, or gender, or class?) Can we judge who is deserving based on who works the hardest? Or who is best able to focus? There are no obvious answers here, and philosophers have debated these questions for decades, if not centuries. Still, as Amartya Sen reminds us, we can't know whether our definition of merit is just until we are clear on the purposes of evaluating merit and the incentives we want to create.[43] In US higher education, admissions officers consider multiple interests, from manning athletic teams, to encouraging alumni donations, to creating an environment conducive to learning, to selecting those students they think will be the leaders of tomorrow. Moreover, these purposes may sometimes conflict. For example, creating a diverse learning environment requires more racial diversity, but legacy admissions decrease racial diversity.

Thus, to effectively define merit, we must clearly articulate what we are aiming for. I argue for what might seem to some a radical perspective on the role of universities in society. I believe universities can and should play a civic role and concern themselves not just with improving the minds of young adults, but also with improving our democracy, in part through increasing opportunities.[44] I believe our elite universities need to harness their culture-influencing role toward greater ends. They need to be more adamant, and more intentional, about the ways they are able to shape the next generation of leaders and thinkers in terms of who they are, how they think about social inequality, and what they do in the future. I am not the first to advocate such a mission. Stanford University's founding charter, for example, calls for "service to the children of California."[45] More recently, Harvard president Drew Faust, in the wake of the 2009 economic crisis, argued that "universities might well ask if they have in fact done enough to raise the deep and unsettling questions necessary to any society."[46] She wondered further, "Should universities—in their research, teaching and writing—have made greater efforts to expose the patterns of risk and denial?"[47] In other words, Faust was advocating a civic role for universities. One way to achieve this is to train the leaders of tomorrow to help solve the world's most pressing problems. Another is to encourage further research toward a better society. And a third, most relevant to the content of this book, is to expand opportunities.

Increasing opportunities and making our beliefs in democracy and equal opportunity more legitimate means investing greater commitment to affirmative action—by race, but also by other forms of disadvantage like class. By this point it should be clear that I support a robust, ongoing affirmative action policy by calibrating admissions decisions according to a student's opportunities, much more than is done today. Calibration should be according to class, race, and other circumstances; moreover, it should consider the racial history of the United States and its ongoing effects. This calibration can be buttressed by extra academic and social supports for students coming from weaker academic backgrounds. Perhaps some colleges will opt for an additional college year for some admitted students to bring their skills up to those of their peers who attended more privileged schools. Increasing opportunities also means ending, or at the very least dramatically decreasing, the considerations that exacerbate inequality—most obviously, athletic recruiting and legacy considerations.[48]

Since retiring, former US Supreme Court justice Sandra Day O'Connor has argued that the "pathway to leadership" in American society needs to be open, supported by affirmative action when necessary, so ordinary Americans can see that leadership as legitimate.[49] In other words, a monochromatic leadership will be viewed with suspicion by an increasingly minority citizenry. She further argues that children need to see leaders that look like them, again to encourage high aspirations.[50] O'Connor's emphasis on civic inclusion demonstrates an important rationale for affirmative action that is rooted in the functioning of our democracy but that I rarely heard from students. Their emphasis on individual advancement, rather, led students to a narrow form of support, the diversity bargain, in the United States and none at Oxford. If a former US Supreme Court justice can put forth this rationale, then surely universities can also move beyond the diversity rationale to help students understand the importance of a diverse leadership, for legitimacy *and* for democracy.

While the goal of promoting democracy through social mobility via higher education has deeper roots in the United States, it is not unique to America. The 1997 Dearing Report on Higher Education in Britain supported Tony Blair's "Third Way" politics, in which he emphasized equality of opportunity as a foundation of a just society.[51] A sustained and broadened vision for what role Oxford and Cambridge can and should play in British society and, more broadly, in the world is imperative. Remember that British universities are publicly funded.

As with any other branch of government, they must be accountable to a public that looks very different from the students they are currently subsidizing. Given that elite universities serve privileged Britons, their public funding is arguably a regressive tax whereby Britons of all walks of life pay for privileged youth to attend university and gain further advantages. And those advantages matter, as we have seen.

Indeed, increasing access to higher education in Britain, or "widening participation," as it is called there, has become an important goal for the government and for universities since the start of the twenty-first century. Government mandates since 2006 require publicly funded universities to enter into "access agreements" with the government's Office for Fair Access, in which they outline how they will promote greater access, despite charging tuition fees (up to £9,000 per year). Attention to class and geographic representation, called "contextual information," dominates these access agreements, compared with the attention to race along with class in the United States.[52] The British government's efforts are laudable, but they can be improved on. For example, we need closer examination of the interview system of admission to Oxford and Cambridge. Interviews allow for displays of cultural ways of being that signal to admissions tutors "smartness" and deservingness of an elite education and can bias admissions toward students from privileged backgrounds.[53] Indeed, when minority and white students with the same national exam scores apply to Oxford and other elite British universities, the white students are more likely to be selected after the on-campus interview.[54] This suggests that greater attention to implicit bias and other forms of elite cultural markers in the training admissions tutors undergo can increase equity in admissions decisions.[55] Still, these changes will be impossible to implement without a discussion—among students, faculty, and administrators—about the role Oxford can and should play in British society today and, relatedly, about the goals of the admissions process.

Framing Affirmative Action and Race on Campus

In 2014 cultural critic Ta-Nehisi Coates published a widely read article, "The Case for Reparations," in the *Atlantic*. Coates provides a painstaking history of the systematic ways African Americans have been excluded from engines of social mobility since the time of slavery. He calls for a national reckoning that would lead to spiritual renewal. Reparations would mean the end of scarfing hot dogs on the Fourth of July while denying the facts of our heritage. Reparations would mean the end of yelling "patriotism" while waving a Confederate flag. Reparations would mean a revolution of the American consciousness, a reconciling of our self-image as the great democratizer with the facts of our history.

This reckoning, and the reparations that might follow, acknowledge the unequal life experiences that African Americans have had in American society. Over the past year, when I have thought about my vision for future students at elite universities, I keep coming back to lessons in history. Most American students were unaware of the history of racial exclusion in the United States beyond legal segregation and slavery. They did not learn about the systematic exclusion of African Americans from first-time homeowner loans that laid the foundation for today's racial segregation in our neighborhoods. Nor did most learn about racial exclusion from unions that kept down wages for African Americans, or about government scholarships for college through the GI Bill that did not force those colleges to admit African Americans.[56] Most were unaware, too, of the systematic incarceration of vast numbers of black men and the social policies leading to this "New Jim Crow," as Michelle Alexander calls it.[57] Some students learned this history in college, and they developed a power analysis frame as a result. This leads me to believe that with a better understanding of racial exclusion in American history, as well as lessons from social psychology about how race shapes our views on particular social policies, meritocracy, and much more, students will more fully understand race in America. In Britain, too, students would benefit from understanding why certain minorities are underrepresented on campus, the differences between the average state school and private and grammar schools in preparation to study at the likes of Oxford, and, more generally, how race and class shape opportunities and life experiences in Britain.

Most US students of all racial backgrounds, as I came to understand, are eager for this education. The moral weight of racism looms large for American students. Those we talked with were eager to better understand race in the United States, and lessons in history will bring all students closer to that understanding. Journalist Jose Antonio Vargas made a documentary for MTV exploring this education. In *White People*, he confronts young white Americans with racial realities and documents their shifting ideas. Developing a sharper power analysis frame that illuminates how differences in status and resources have affected white and black Americans throughout history—as well as Native Americans, Asian Americans, and Latinos—will allow white students in particular to see why the "Black Lives Matter" movement should come as no surprise. The race frames American students encounter most frequently in their lives—color-blindness, diversity, and sometimes the culture of poverty frame—provide only a partial understanding of the role race plays in American society. Currently, the small spaces in which students learn about the history of racial exclusion—most prominently from places like Brown's Third World Center—are not enough to shift the dominant narratives on their campuses. This is why the frames they use to make sense of race and affirmative action are so limited, and why we need a systematic education about America's racial history.

When more Americans have a better understanding of the role race has played and continues to play in our society, we will be better able to reframe how we justify affirmative action to emphasize unequal opportunities and historical exclusion, especially of African Americans. That is, we need to emphasize why calibrated evaluations of merit should consider not just class but also race, and why collective merit is not the only—or even the most important—reason we need affirmative action.

When white students understand affirmative action instead as a policy implemented for their own benefit, the moment a situation arises where they feel excluded—for example, by assuming they did not get a job or internship owing to affirmative action, or just that they don't feel invited when they see a table of black students sitting together in the dining hall—they reject it. As they grow older, these successful young adults will inevitably face setbacks—being rejected in job interviews, seeing peers win awards over them, and more. Affirmative action is an easy scapegoat in those situations. I fear that although millennials have come of age while affirmative action was the norm and thus many accept it as a fact of life, as they age and inevitably do not win every competition, their support will wane. Data from the 2004 General Social Survey, for example, suggest that while young college graduates may be more sympathetic to multiculturalism than other Americans, among older Americans the difference in support between college graduates and those with less education is not as large.[58] My hope is that a better understanding of the ways social policies have led to racial injustice in the United States today might compel students to support affirmative action for its emphasis on promoting racial equality and thus to maintain their support beyond college.

Some might argue that our hands are tied because of Supreme Court decisions from the past thirty-five years that allow affirmative action only when it is used to create a diverse learning environment.[59] But this has not stopped some public intellectuals from elaborating more far-ranging, and arguably more urgent, defenses of the policy.[60] In addition, judicial implementation theory—a theory that court decisions dictate future policy-making—cannot alone explain how universities have handled affirmative action.[61] It does not explain why, for example, universities did not simply end it after the 1978 *Bakke* decision, and why they continue to search for race-neutral alternatives even in the face of bans on affirmation action in eight states.[62] In another domain, employment law, the US Supreme Court has rejected altogether considering race to increase workforce diversity (for example, to increase the number of teachers of color); however, this has not stopped employers and professional associations from openly discussing diversity in hiring.[63] As much as we like to think the courts stand outside society, they do not. We know that conversations in the public domain shape decision making even in the US Supreme Court. Hence I argue that when making admissions decisions universities need to be bold—as employers often are—in taking a stand about the importance of addressing racial inequality and the ongoing effects of racial exclusion on minorities in the United States.

Aside from affirmative action, how can colleges and universities help students learn about the realities of race in our country? In addition to offering classes about race-related history, sociology, and psychology, promoting interracial interaction and dialogue can play an important role in developing students' understandings about race. Elite US universities have an incredible opportunity to bring together students of different backgrounds and facilitate conversation. Indeed, although many students are yearning for more opportunities to talk about race,[64] we have no clear consensus on *how* to do this important work. In the United States, how do we get students of color and white students to trust one another—to move past the fears of racial aggression and of being accused of racism? In Britain, how can we help second-generation students voice their concerns without being accused of political correctness or seen as disrupting supposedly harmless race-related banter?

In chapter 4 I outlined Harvard's and Brown's attempts at diversity-related programming. As universities consider such programming, it is important to keep in mind these two models and their concomitant considerations. Not all diversity-related goals and outcomes are compatible. Universities need to deliberate carefully on what goals they are trying to further through their diversity-related programming. How, then, can other colleges learn from the different experiences of these two elite universities? If a university seeks to implement strategies for developing self-confidence, solidarity, and resilience among students of color, it should draw from Brown's power analysis model. But if it is concerned with campus divisions between white students and students of color, it should draw from Harvard's diversity model.

Still, the real challenge is to develop a model that incorporates both these worthy goals. Students of color and white students alike need to think deeply and critically about racial inequality, discrimination, social justice, and power. They both need to develop tools for engagement and dialogue across racial lines, in order to take full advantage of their deliberately integrated campuses. One model for this is Patricia Gurin and Biren Nagda's *intergroup dialogue* (IGD), which integrates social psychological research suggesting that intergroup harmony requires downplaying group identities or shifting group identities (for example, from racial identities to dorm identities), with full recognition of the importance of group identities.[65] IGD programs bring students of two identity groups together—for example, black and white students, or men and women—with an explicit aim of "learning that involves understanding social identities and group-based inequalities."[66] The program's explicit focus on "social justice through education" makes its power analysis frame explicit and distinguishes it from most programming on diversity at Harvard.[67] Still, unlike Brown's Third World Center and the Third World Transition Program, IGD deliberately includes the dominant group, requiring half of training group participants to be from the dominant group and the other half from the marginalized group. This program has had much success, and a recent study found "improved intergroup understanding, positive intergroup relationships, and intergroup action" among participants compared with nonparticipating peers.[68]

Other scholars have investigated extracurricular activities on campus that tackle racial issues across ethnic and racial boundaries. For example, Julie Park demonstrates how the InterVarsity Christian Fellowship at a California university moves beyond a color-blindness frame and promotes racial reconciliation.[69] Sherry Deckman documents the same among the Kuumba singers of Harvard, an interracial singing group that performs music of black heritage.[70] Both of these studies show that greater interracial understanding unfolds when students confront race rather than ignore it, and when minorities feel they are important members of the group.[71]

Each of these examples teaches us that promoting interracial understanding in the United States is not easy. The short sessions most universities currently devote to diversity, though well-meaning and at moments revelatory, are unlikely to have the impact necessary to promote true, ongoing dialogue. American students are not warned that the racial diversity they look forward to in college might sometimes be difficult and even painful—that they will be forced to examine their assumptions and the beliefs passed down by their elders back home. Our interviews gave a taste of this discomfort again and again. Often my white graduate student interviewer in the United States came to me after interviews wondering whether she had probed too deeply, or whether she should follow up with students she interviewed. Take Megan. Megan sat back comfortably and smiled a lot at the start of her interview, but as it progressed she grew agitated, prompting my research assistant to write in her field notes, "By the end of the interview, during the last section, she appeared obviously uncomfortable to the point that I found myself wanting to lean over and hold her hand or give her a hug." Other students seemed to "lean in" to the interviews, hungry for open conversation about race and diversity, and asked if we could recommend readings that would help them think about the issues even more. At times the interview itself seemed like an intervention, precisely the kind of (difficult!) conversation students longed for on campus yet felt acutely uncomfortable with.

In Britain, it remains to be seen how universities like Oxford will approach the expanded access required by the government in recent years. As I listened to interviews, I wondered whether elite British universities would eventually follow the path of American ones, increasing attention to and sensitivity around diversity in order to more fully include students from disadvantaged backgrounds. Or, instead, might they find their own path toward greater inclusion and support for those students? How will universities ensure that students admitted through attention to their "contextual information" have positive experiences on campus? Will the universities provide emotional, academic, and cultural supports to ensure those students make it to graduation? I believe that British universities too need to consider programs like intergroup dialogue, to break the stronghold of Oxford and Cambridge's traditional notions of worthiness and foster respect and inclusion among students. The backlash against multiculturalism in Britain, along with color-blindness, denies the ways race (and ethnicity and religion) affects British society. White students at British universities enjoy a general lack of anxiety around race, yet with that freedom comes a lack of attention to how comments, jokes, or behaviors might harm or offend ethnic minorities. White students' reliance on the "playing the race card" script, that often knee-jerk reaction to the uncommon moments when minorities claim racial injustice is at play, suggests that whites in Britain lack a language for making sense of racial inequality. Here British universities might take cues from US universities' attention to diversity and difference, whether through the Harvard model of integration or Brown's emphasis on developing minority students' power analysis frames, or through a more syncretic emphasis like intergroup dialogue.

Recognizing That Meritocracy Is Never Complete

Increased access to higher education—while undeniably an important development—should not fool us into thinking it is, or perhaps ever will be, truly equal. Our seemingly bone-deep belief in meritocracy ignores the tangle of disadvantages that many continue to face. We may not live in the dystopia of inherited status, legitimated by the illusion of fairness and mobility that Michael Young envisioned more than sixty years ago when he coined the satirical term meritocracy, but meritocracy will never truly be completely democratic: it will always be partial. The notion that we can ever create completely equal opportunities for all children, I argue, has little basis in reality. "Pure" meritocracy means that everyone has exactly the same life chances. When in history has that happened? What would it take to make that happen? The underrepresentation of disadvantaged groups at elite universities in both countries is not a coincidence, as we know, nor is it a result of innate differences in youth of different social origins. Rather, it stems from life in an unequal society. Justice Sandra Day O'Connor's exhortation that the need for affirmative action should end in the next twenty-five years is a hopeful one.[72] But even if we do eliminate the underrepresentation of black, Latino, and Native American students at selective colleges by 2028, as O'Connor famously suggested we must in her 2003 affirmative action decision, what new forms of inequality will emerge?[73] Our world will probably always be unequal in one way or another.

We are better off doing all we can to promote equal opportunity—and let me be clear that I believe addressing inequality in access to elite universities is vital—while also recognizing unequal outcomes. And given those outcomes, we should place a little less faith in the illusion of meritocracy and give more support to those who do not rise to the top, no matter how much we theoretically believe we can all do so. This means not assuming that Oxford and Harvard students are necessarily better than students at UCL (University College London) and Berkeley. It also means supporting a generous welfare state—more financial assistance for the poor, health care for all Americans, a higher minimum wage, and much more—because it recognizes that success is not simply a matter of hard work, intelligence, and determination. So, while I applaud British developments in widening participation in higher education, I hope they do not lead Britain to an American-style faith in meritocracy and equal opportunity, to the detriment of a strong welfare state. We must acknowledge that the system is imperfect—and in turn that there is no such thing as a completely fair system of admissions when children have unequal opportunities in their lives, when there are more qualified students than seats available, and when admissions serves a variety of goals. One simple way universities can support this understanding is by ceasing to publish acceptance rates, which would signal that rejecting more applicants does not mean those accepted are even better. Students attending selective universities need to understand their extraordinary luck in the education they experience, as well as to recognize the smarts, determination, and drive of students outside the likes of Harvard and Oxford.

Given these problems with meritocracy, I propose a thought experiment for selective universities. Why not scrap the notion of meritocracy altogether and go with an admissions lottery? At the very least, why not simply identify criteria for selection and enter everyone who makes it over that bar into a lottery? A lottery would force us all—admitted students, rejected students, parents, university faculty and administrators, and society as a whole—to rethink our faith in meritocracy and the inequality that it inevitably produces. In other words, it would change the *meaning* of admission to universities like Harvard and Oxford, signaling that studying there is a valuable opportunity, but one that is gained somewhat by luck. If admission were defined by universities as at least somewhat random, then admitted students, employers, and others could not assume they are the best of the best and that those who didn't gain admission are not. In our conversations about admissions, underrepresentation, and fairness, just eight respondents in the United States, and none in Britain, commented that there are more qualified applicants than there are spots at Harvard, Brown, and Oxford. This blindness to others' merits that selection inevitably produces suggests to me that we need to disrupt the selection process so that students are forced to reckon with the privileges that led many, perhaps most, of their peers to an elite university.

Criteria for inclusion in the lottery could include particular accomplishments, obstacles overcome, GPA or SAT scores in the United States and national exam grades in Britain. These could be calibrated by social context, perhaps zip code, high school attended, class, and race. To ensure the collective merit of the cohort, the lottery could even select proportionately from particular groups the university cares about. For example, universities might commit to having a certain percentage of students from every income quintile, or a certain percentage of black and Latino students, and enter students into separate lotteries based on these (or other) categories. Many high schools in New York City, for example, encourage all students to apply but commit to a student body in which 16 percent of students are top performers on standardized tests, 16 percent are low performers, and the remaining 68 sixty-eight are in the middle range.[74] While this may seem like a crude method of allocation, under the current system family income and other aspects of privilege and disadvantage play a major, if unseen, role in the likelihood that a student will apply to and be admitted to selective universities.

Philosopher Peter Stone points out that when there are more candidates than positions and all those candidates have an equal claim to those positions, a lottery is the most just solution.[75] Moreover, Stone points out, not having a lottery can be unjust when a system of selection does not "track merit rather than extraneous arbitrary factors (such as race, gender, or class). Fairness thus requires random selection under the right circumstances."[76] Given the increasing competition for admission to universities like Harvard, there are plenty more students qualified to study than there are seats. The past has shown us that when this happens, privilege wins, in part because elites pour more and more resources into ensuring that their children get those few seats—this is precisely the situation Stone points out that we want to avoid, in which an allocation system selects on unjust criteria. My suggestion, then, is that universities consider a lottery as a baseline and then use a discussion of university purposes to outline goals in admissions.[77] I recognize that a lottery for selective colleges may be unrealistic, for a variety of reasons.[78] Still, considering a lottery in order to make clear just what distinctions admissions officers are making, why they are making them, and the implications of those decisions is an important exercise that I hope all selective colleges will engage in, if only as a thought experiment.

We know what we need to do—as educators, as parents, as concerned members of university communities and of society. Most important, we need to cultivate a willingness to engage in difficult discussions about meritocracy, race, and inequality. Each of us must listen to others with different worldviews. We must challenge each other's understanding of inequality and consider how privileges we have enjoyed and continue to enjoy prevent equal opportunity and promote inequality. We must learn the skills necessary to promote racial justice. The work is difficult and requires a great commitment of time, emotion, and humility. If we are to learn anything, we must acknowledge all we do not yet know; we must admit our mistakes, recognize our blind spots, and be willing to expose our own shortcomings and our privileges in the pursuit of a better world. Without that commitment, we will remain a society divided by race and by class, a society that is shockingly unequal. And, of course, the terrible irony is that we'll remain blind to that division and to the innumerable inequalities that result from our hopelessly hopeful faith in meritocracy.

RESPONDENT CHARACTERISTICS AND RACE FRAMES

Harvard University Students

White Students at Harvard

Pseudonym	Year	Type of High School	Concentration	Race Frames
Anna	Junior	Public	Religion	Color-blindness Diversity
Charles	Junior	Private	Environmental science and Government	Diversity
Craig	Senior	Public	Biology	Color-blindness Culture of Poverty Diversity
Daniel	Sophomore	Parochial	Literature	Diversity
Dylan	Senior	Private	Economics	Diversity
Elizabeth	Junior	Public	Economics	Color-blindness Diversity
Eric	Junior	Public	Biology	Color-blindness Diversity
Genevieve	Senior	Public	Sociology	Diversity Power analysis
Jean	Senior	Private	Social studies	
Jeremy	Senior	Public	History	Power analysis
Karen	Junior	Public	Economics	Color-blindness Diversity
Katherine	Senior	Public	Biology	Color-blindness Diversity
Lauren	Sophomore	Public	Psychology	
Naomi	Sophomore	Public	Diversity	Color-blindness Diversity
Natalie	Senior	Public	Literature	Power analysis
Noa	Senior	Parochial	History	Diversity
Orin	Junior	Public	Social studies	Color-blindness Culture of poverty Diversity
Rachel	Junior	Public	Biology	Diversity
Renee	Sophomore	Public	Postcolonial history and literature	Culture of poverty
Serena	Junior	Private	Psychology	Color-blindness Diversity
Stephanie	Junior	Public	History	Color-blindness Diversity
Thomas	Sophomore	Public	Biology	Color-blindness Diversity
Tim	Sophomore	Public	Linguistics	Diversity

Students of Color at Harvard

Pseudonym	Year	Type of High School	Race/Ethnicity (self-reported)	Concentration	Race Frames
Afi	Senior	Public	Black	Economics and English	Diversity
Christina	Senior	Private	Latina	Sociology	Diversity Power analysis
David	Sophomore	Private	Chinese	Neuroscience	Color-blindness
Dexter	Sophomore	Private	Black	Sociology	Diversity
Elaine	Senior	Public	Asian (Chinese)	English	Diversity
Grace	Sophomore	Public	Korean	Social anthropology	Color-blindness Diversity
Joanne	Sophomore	Public	Asian American	Sociology	Diversity
Justin	Junior	Public	Indian American	Computer science and Sociology	Diversity
Kimberly	Senior	Public	Black/African American	Statistics	Diversity
La'Ron	Senior	Private	Black	African American studies and Sociology	Power analysis
Marie	Sophomore	Public	Black (mixed Haitian and American heritage)	Sociology	Diversity Power analysis
Maya	Sophomore	Public	Native American and Hispanic	Anthropology and History of Science	
Michael	Senior	Public	African American	Government and Sociology	Diversity
Shuyi	Senior	Private	Chinese	Social studies	Color-blindness Culture of poverty Diversity
Sophie	Senior	Public	Multiracial	Folklore and mythology	Diversity Power analysis

Brown University Students

White Students at Brown

Pseudonym	Year	Type of High School	Concentration	Race Frames
Alex	Sophomore	Public	International relations and Mechanical engineering	Diversity
Angelica	Not reported	Public	Geological sciences	Diversity
Brianna	Sophomore	Public	Business and Religious studies	Color-blindness Diversity
Ellen	Junior	Private	Architectural studies and Economics	Diversity
Elliot	Sophomore	Public	Religious studies	Diversity
Haley	Sophomore	Public	Psychology	Diversity
Hannah	Senior	Private	Comparative literature	Color-blindness Diversity
Hunter	Sophomore	Public	Biology	Diversity
Jack	Junior	Private	Economics and Physics	Color-blindness
James	Junior	Public	International relations	Diversity
Jeff	Sophomore	Public	Applied mathematics and Computer science	Color-blindness Culture of poverty Diversity
Johanna	Junior	Public	Biomedical engineering	Diversity
Julie	Sophomore	Private	Engineering	Diversity
Kirk	Junior	Public	Literary arts and Psychology	
Kyle	Junior	Public	Neuroscience	Diversity Power analysis
Lissa	Sophomore	Public	Commerce, Organizations, and Entrepreneurship	Color-blindness Diversity
Maggie	Senior	Private	Biology	Color-blindness Diversity
Megan	Junior	Public	Economics and History of art and architecture	Color-blindness Diversity
Meredith	Sophomore	Public	Education studies and Public policy	Color-blindness Diversity
Pat	Sophomore	Public	Modern culture and media	Color-blindness Diversity
Rebecca	Sophomore	Public	Development studies	Diversity
Sarah	Not reported	Private	Sociology	Color-blindness Diversity
Summer	Junior	Public	Urban studies	Color-blindness Diversity

Students of Color at Brown

Pseudonym	Year	Type of High School	Race (self-reported)	Concentration	Race Frames
Brandon	Sophomore	Public	African American	Commerce, organizations, and entrepreneurship	Diversity
Byron	Senior	Private	Chinese American	Political science	Color-blindness
Candice	Junior	Public	Filipino American	Ethnic studies and International relations	Diversity
Christopher	Junior	Public	Multiracial	Biology and International relations	Color-blindness Diversity
Ernesto	Senior	Private	Hispanic	Ethnic studies	
Imani	Senior	Public	Black and multiracial	Africana studies	Diversity Power analysis
Jeniece	Junior	Public	Biracial (Hispanic and white)	International relations and Media studies	Power analysis
Jenny	Junior	Public	Multiracial (Asian and Caucasian)	Cognitive science	Diversity
Jessica	Junior	Public	Mexican and United States, multiracial	Africana studies and Latin American and Caribbean studies	Diversity Power analysis
Kelly	Junior	Public	Asian	English	Diversity
Nisha	Junior	Public	South Asian	Community health and Sociology	Diversity
Nuri	Junior	Private	African American	Psychology	Diversity
Sheena	Freshman (second semester)	Public	Indian	Community health and Public policy	Diversity
Susan	Junior	Private	Black	Africana studies and Education studies	Diversity Power analysis
Zak	Freshman (second semester)	Public	Black and Mexican	Education and English	Color-blindness Diversity

University of Oxford Students

White Students at Oxford

Pseudonym	Year	Type of School	Course of Study	Race Frames
Abbie	Year 3	Grammar	Law	Color-blindness Culture of poverty Diversity
Adam	Year 1	Grammar	Mathematics	Diversity Color-blindness
Alice	Year 2	State (nongrammar)	Biology	Color-blindness
Anne	Year 3	Private	Biological sciences	
Bethany	Year 4	State (nongrammar)	French	
Caitlin	Year 4	State (nongrammar)	French and Italian	
Charles	Year 2	Private	English literature	
Christine	Year 2	State (nongrammar)	Modern languages (German and Spanish)	Color-blindness
Connor	Year 2	Private	Classics	Culture of poverty
Daniel	Year 4	Private	English and Modern languages (Italian)	Diversity
Dylan	Year 4	Private	Modern languages (French)	Diversity
Ella	Year 2	Grammar	Biochemistry	
Ellen	Year 2	State (nongrammar)	Biological sciences	
Emma	Year 4	Private	Mathematics and Statistics	Color-blindness Culture of poverty
Ethan	Year 2	Grammar	Philosophy, politics, and economics	Diversity
Harry	Year 2	State (nongrammar)	Physics	Color-blindness
Hazel	Year 3	State (nongrammar)	English literature and language	
Holly	Year 4	State (nongrammar)	Mathematics	
Jake	Year 4	State (nongrammar)	Mathematics	
Jasmine	Year 4	Private	Chemistry	Diversity
John	Year 3	Grammar	History	Color-blindness
Joseph	Year 3	Private	English	Diversity
Joshua	Year 3	State (nongrammar)	History	Color-blindness Culture of poverty Diversity
Julie	Year 2	State (nongrammar)	Experimental psychology	
Kate	Year 2	Private	History	
Kyle	Year 2	Private	Engineering, economics, and management	Color-blindness Diversity

Pseudonym	Year	Type of School	Course of Study	Race Frames
Laura	Year 4	Private	History and Modern languages (French)	
Leah	Year 2	State (nongrammar)	French and German	Diversity
Lewis	Year 3	State (nongrammar)	Physics	Culture of poverty
Liam	Year 3	Private	English literature and language	Culture of poverty
Lily	Year 2	Grammar	Modern languages	Diversity
Lucy	Year 4	Private	Modern languages	Diversity
Melissa	Year 4	Private	Classics	Color-blindness Culture of poverty
Nathan	Year 2	State (nongrammar)	Engineering science	
Niamh	Year 4	State (nongrammar)	Physics	
Nick	Year 3	Private	Chemistry	Color-blindness Diversity
Nicole	Year 3	Grammar	Biological sciences	Culture of poverty
Olivia	Year 4	Private	Modern languages	Diversity
Paige	Year 2	Private	Biological sciences	Diversity
Phoebe	Year 3	Grammar	Experimental psychology	
Poppy	Year 3	Private	History	Color-blindness
Rachel	Year 3	Private	Classics	Diversity Color-blindness
Robert	Year 2	State (nongrammar)	Chemistry	Diversity
Rose	Year 3	Grammar	History of art	Culture of poverty
Sara	Year 4	State (nongrammar)	Modern languages	
Scarlett	Year 2	Private	Physiological sciences	
Shannon	Year 2	State (nongrammar)	Jurisprudence	Diversity
Stephen	Year 2	Private	Economics and management	Culture of poverty
Theo	Not reported	Not reported	Not reported	Diversity
Trevor	Year 2	Grammar	Economics and management	
Violet	Year 2	State (nongrammar)	Linguistics and French	Diversity
William	Year 2	Private	Biological sciences	Color-blindness Diversity

Second-Generation Students at Oxford

Pseudonym	Year	Type of School	Race/Ethnicity (self-reported)	Non-UK Parent(s)' Birthplace(s)	Course of Study	Race Frames
Abigail	Year 1	Grammar	Mixed (white and Asian)	China	Human sciences	Diversity
Analia	Year 2	State (nongrammar)	Other	South America	Linguistics	Diversity
Ariagne	Year 2	State (nongrammar)	Turkish	Turkey	Law	Diversity
Ayesha	Year 4	State (nongrammar)	North African Arab	North Africa	French	Color-blindness Diversity
Gurminder	Year 3	Grammar	British Asian	India	English	Color-blindness
Henry	Year 2	State (nongrammar)	Mixed	Europe, East Africa	Economics and management	Color-blindness
Jason	Year 3	Grammar	Mixed (British and Asian)	India	History	Color-blindness
Javed	Year 1	Grammar	Iranian	Iran	Biological sciences	
Jian	Year 1	Grammar	South Korean	South Korea	Medicine	Diversity
Jordan	Year 2	Private	Anglo Indian[a]	East Africa[b]	History and Economics	
Rafiq	Year 2	State (nongrammar)	Arab	North Africa	History	Culture of poverty
Shanta	Year 2	Grammar	Sri Lankan	Sri Lanka	Medicine	
Sylvia	Year 2	Grammar	Chinese	China and India	Biology	Culture of poverty
Tisha	Year 2	Private	British Asian	North Africa and Sri Lanka	History	Color-blindness Culture of poverty
Valerie	Year 1	Grammar	Mixed (white and Asian)	East Africa and Europe	Medicine	Culture of poverty

[a] Anglo-Indian refers to a community in India descended from British traders and colonists in India, dating to the eighteenth century, many of whom partnered with Indian women. See Caplan 2001.

[b] Given Jordan's Anglo-Indian identity, this parent is probably part of the migration from India to East Africa dating back over a century.

A NOTE ON METHODS

The Interview Process

My analysis of student perspectives on race, admissions, and meritoc-racy is based on 143 interviews with undergraduates at Harvard Uni-versity, Brown University, and the University of Oxford (see table 1 in chapter 1). In chapter 1 I shared details of the research process. In this appendix I focus on additional considerations of the research for those readers who are especially interested in methodological questions. The qualitative and comparative approach I took allowed for a deeper understanding of the influences on students' perspectives as well as the complexity of those perspectives than is possible with survey data. I knew that in matters related to race, I was more likely to get insights into the murky details of how students think through interviews, as other researchers have found in the past.[1] On the other hand, some have criticized the use of in-depth interviews in favor of participant observation.[2] But in this research interviews were particularly useful because I wanted to understand students' own framing of issues of race, merit, and inequality.[3] I assumed that, given many whites' desire to be seen as not racist and as racially aware, any concerns about social desirability would lead white students to express greater support for the concerns of racial minorities and for affirmative action. Overall, given several, especially white, students' unsolicited comments about the positive experience they had in talking freely about the issues, I be-lieve that social desirability did not shape most comments. Still, I pre-sent students' perspectives not as the unencumbered truth about their beliefs but as the way they make sense of their social worlds and com-municate that sense-making to others.[4] Among students of color in the United States and second-generation students in Britain, I wondered whether I would hear from a disproportionate number of radical students interested in sharing their views on diversity with a researcher. The moderate views most students of color and second-generation students expressed put my fears to rest.[5]

As I embarked on this research, I wanted to avoid essentialist analyses of racial identities and their impact on student perspectives. I knew, for example, that as high achievers Asian Americans might share some perspectives with their white peers, but as fellow racial minorities in the United States they might share other perspectives with black and Latino peers. I also knew that many black students on elite college campuses are the children of immigrants and not descendants of slaves in the United States, the intended beneficiaries of affirmative action as it was first conceived in the 1960s. To avoid essentializing students and their racial identities, at the start of this project I decided we would interview any students who signed up for the interview within the small pool who were invited.[6] I did require students we interviewed to have grown up in the United States or Britain, because I wanted respondents who could reflect on the transition from childhood to college within the same national environment.

As the interviews unfolded, however, I realized that students of color in the United States had perspectives that did not map onto those of their white peers, especially on racially charged issues like Brown's Third World Transition Program or, more generally, affirmative action. Moreover, those differences seemed to be about racial categories in the United States—primarily black, Latino, Asian, and white. I wanted to be able to say something meaningful about these differences, so I asked my research assistants in the United States to ensure that we included significant numbers of black, Latino, and Asian American students. I did not limit respondents to one racial category but allowed students to name their own racial identities. In the end, in order to recognize patterns in students' perspectives, I decided to include seventeen students in the United States who identified as black or Latino and another thirteen Asian Americans.

In Britain, boundaries of race are different, often linked to immigration and ethnicity. The British Census, for example, separates black Britons into Afro-Caribbeans, Africans, and "other black" in its measure of "ethnic group," akin to race on the US Census. I therefore decided to oversample children of immigrants in Britain, with the criterion that the student's parents must be from outside the European Union. In Britain I asked my research assistant to include fifteen second-generation respondents. Other students interviewed were born and raised in Britain with British-born parents. In addition, I wanted to hear from a quorum of Oxford students who came from private, state, and grammar schools, given public outcries about differences in Oxford admissions for graduates of different kinds of British schools. Overall, about one-third of students interviewed at Oxford came from each type of school. In this book I have distinguished students by race, ethnicity, generation, and school type only when those differences coincided with significant differences in their perspectives, to avoid essentializing their perspectives.

Before being interviewed, students filled out a short online survey that captured information on their family backgrounds, how they identified on a number of factors such as race, political orientation, and socioeconomic status, and their views on a variety of issues related to multiculturalism and diversity. However, I draw most of my conclusions in the book from the interviews, conducted between 2009 and 2011.[7] Most students were interviewed in their second year of college or later, with a handful of second-semester freshmen included.

Although in my previous projects I have done all the interviewing myself, this time I felt it would be unwise to do so with white students. I wanted to hear students' perspectives on race, and I knew that although I was a skilled interviewer, as an Indian American I could not conduct interviews on this topic with white US students and gain reliable information about their views on diversity and race. The United States is a highly racialized society, and cross-race discussions of diversity can be difficult to engage in,[8] so I knew students were much more likely to share their views on race and diversity with an interviewer they felt shared their background.[9] Hence, in the United States white students were interviewed by a white doctoral student trained and experienced in qualitative methods. To maintain consistency and not bias my lens toward greater empathy for students of color by having interviewed them myself when white students were interviewed by someone else, I decided to also have students of color interviewed by a (minority) doctoral student. American students of color were interviewed by one minority doctoral student at each site, both of whom had training and experience using qualitative methods. Both happened to be light-skinned black, which I believe helped them put black, Latino, Asian, and multiracial students at ease. Let me be clear:

I am not advocating racial matching in every research project. In fact, some benefits can ensue from cross-group interviewing, and US students of color who were not black experienced this. However, in this particular project, given the questions I wanted to ask, I felt strongly that matching white students with white interviewers and students of color with minority interviewers, while a crude form of race matching, was important.

In Britain I also worried about students' responses to my skin tone and features that mark me as South Asian. Given the colonial history of Britain, I did not believe white students would speak openly with me about race. In the end, the findings of my study suggest that white students might have been comfortable expressing to me views critical of multiculturalism, or views unsupportive of minorities, at least more so than their US counterparts. However, I chose to exercise caution in this regard, given the nature of my research questions and the importance of understanding their perspectives as expressed to in-group members. An additional issue in Britain was accent, because there a person's accent reveals class background. I needed an interviewer who would make both working-class and wealthy students feel comfortable. I did so by hiring an interviewer without a clear British class identity, a Western European doctoral student in sociology trained in qualitative methods. Her lack of a British class identity, along with her Western European identity and identity as an Oxford student, I believe, put white Oxford students at ease regardless of class. Also, her outsider status within Britain seemed to put second-generation respondents at ease. In other words, she was able to draw on her class-neutral European identity with white respondents and her outsider-to-Britain identity with second-generation students. She made her shared identity as an Oxford student clear in the interviews as well. This proved to be a remarkably effective strategy at Oxford, and most students quickly opened up in interviews.

All four interviewers were extensively trained by me, beyond their previous formal training in the qualitative methods courses they all had taken previously at Harvard and Oxford. Interviewers did multiple pilot interviews, and I listened to recordings, read and reread transcripts, and gave feedback, especially on follow-up questions, maintaining a neutral stance and pace. I spent considerable time in meetings explaining to interviewers the rationale behind each question, so that they could ask useful follow-up questions where relevant.

The interviewers contributed to the work in extremely productive ways. They pointed out when questions were unclear, when a question was misinterpreted and needed to be rephrased, and when questions did not address my underlying question, helping me strengthen the interview protocol in many ways. They also wrote detailed field notes after every interview, and after groups of interviews they wrote memos highlighting any key insights, surprising and unsurprising responses they heard, and any other analytical observations or puzzles they noticed. We met monthly during the research, often much more often, to compare notes, discuss findings, and more.

Interviews lasted one to three hours, with an average of 120 minutes.[10] All interviews were transcribed. I and a team of research assistants, some of whom were also interviewers, coded the transcripts in ATLASti, a software program that allowed us to sort student responses by particular questions, analyzing them by race or ethnicity, university, and more. ATLASti also allowed me to autocode for particular themes like spontaneous discussions of words like *multiculturalism* and *postracial*. I and my research team read and reread transcripts, reviewed students' responses to particular questions across transcripts in search of themes and patterns, wrote dozens of analytic memos, and discussed patterns of responses by country, by university, and by race, ethnicity, and generation. Through this process, students' meaning making around merit emerged quite differently in the two national contexts, but we saw how students at all three sites seemed to legitimate their own status as part of the elite attending elite universities. Moreover, their particular ways of understanding race, related to the overall national contexts as well as to the particular cultures of elite higher education, seemed to inform students' understandings of merit in admissions as well. Finally, we noticed that these race frames and understandings of merit seemed linked to students' experiences on campus. Thus emerged the central findings of this book.

Naming Names

As I embarked on this study of some of the most elite universities in the world, I thought hard about whether to name the universities. On one hand, I hoped readers would recognize some of the social processes and meaning making I describe as happening in places beyond the particular universities whose students I interviewed. This argued in favor of keeping the universities anonymous, as several recent qualitative studies in higher education have done.[11] Eliminating the names of the universities might have focused readers' attention on the broader social processes and meaning making I document, rather than on scrutinizing whether my representation of these particular universities is accurate. On the other hand, the spirit of academic research asks the investigator to make the research process as clear as possible, to fully allow others to scrutinize the findings. In that spirit of full transparency, I decided to name the universities whose students we interviewed. Ultimately, I believe researchers should provide as much detail about their research settings as possible, which means naming names when it will not compromise ethical considerations and raise other logistical blocks.[12]

Naming the universities also allowed me to capture the particulars of campus organizations and events that support diversity. Brown in particular is somewhat distinctive. For example, I felt the name of Brown's Third World Center—changed since this research—and its related Third World Transition Program were important to understanding that context. In Britain, Oxford and Cambridge, or Oxbridge as they are collectively known, are widely considered the top universities. They have their own admissions process, and they are the only British universities to include an interview. Hence, not naming Oxford would simply have had readers wondering whether the university was Oxford or Cambridge. Readers can compare my portrait with news accounts, language from the Internet, conversations with recent graduates of the universities, and even discussions on College Confidential about Harvard, Brown, and Oxford. I hope those comparisons bolster confidence in what I present in this book.

I leave it up to readers to decide which aspects of what I found are unique to these particular universities and which might be true of other elite, second-tier, or even nonelite universities or of other kinds of organizations. I hope that naming the universities allows readers to understand the particular mechanisms of universities' influence on students, as well as how gaining admission to these very top places shapes them. I also hope readers will think about what processes and meaning making exist beyond universities in the United States and Britain as well. I have tried to articulate my sense of what is unique to elite higher education and what we can see in the broader societies in which those universities are situated.

INTERVIEW QUESTIONS*

1. Would you say Harvard/Brown is a meritocracy in terms of its admissions? [If they ask: Meritocracy is a system in which achievement and success are based on merit rather than, for example, what school you went to, your class, whom you know, etc.]
   a. In what ways?
   b. In what ways is it not?
2. Do students of different ethnic and racial backgrounds at Harvard/Brown mix in general?
   a. Do any groups self-segregate? To what extent? What do you think of that?
3. How does diversity affect life on Harvard/Brown's campus, if at all? [If they ask what kind, leave it open—race, ethnicity, class, geographic, etc.]
   a. How has diversity enhanced life at Harvard/Brown, if at all?
   b. What problems has it created for the university and university life?
4. How have events at Harvard/Brown shaped your views on multiculturalism and diversity?
   a. What about controversies that have come up? Tell me about those and how they shaped your thinking.
5. How has diversity influenced your college experience?
   a. How has your college experience changed your understanding of blacks, Latinos, Asians, Muslims, other minority groups, or multiculturalism in general, if at all?
6. Have you taken any courses in African American studies [Brown: Africana or ethnic studies]? If so, how has that course shaped your thinking, if at all? Have you thought about taking any/any more? Why/why not? [not asked in Britain]
7. Have you attended any diversity-related workshop at Harvard/Brown? What led you to it? Was it mandatory? Describe the workshop and your experience in it. Who led it? What did you do in it? How did you experience it? How did it influence or affect you, if at all?

* I include here only questions drawn on in the book, rather than the full interview guide. I also include only the US version of the questions; Oxford students were asked parallel questions, with "Oxford" substituting for "Harvard/Brown" and "Britain" for "United States."

8. Some people see ethnic and racial organizations in college as divisive and leading to separatism, and others see them as important support networks that also promote cultural diversity. What do you think?

9. Have you attended any events sponsored by one of the ethnic or race groups at Harvard/Brown, like a party, cultural event, lecture, or anything else? What was it, and how was that experience?

10. Does Harvard/Brown do a good job of supporting its minority students and promoting multiculturalism on campus? In what ways? In what ways could it improve? Does the university go too far?

11. At Harvard, 15 percent of students [14 percent of Brown students] are black or Latino, but 28 percent of the United States population is black or Latino:
    a. How do you explain this difference?
    b. Do you think it's a problem?
    c. Should the university do anything about it—if so, what?

12. Do you think that college admissions should consider racial or ethnic background when deciding whether to admit students to Harvard/Brown? [if yes] Why?
    a. What about public vs. private school?
    [if yes] Why?
    b. What about social class?
    [if yes] Why?
    c. What about athletic ability?
    [if yes] Why?
    d. What about parents being Harvard/Brown alumni?
    [if yes] Why?

13. What is "political correctness"?
    a. What do you think of it?

14. *White students*: What has been your exposure to ethnic minorities and immigrants? *Students of color*: What has been your exposure to ethnic and racial groups other than your own?

15. Tell me about a positive experience you've had with someone of another ethnicity or race.

16. Tell me about a negative experience you've had with someone of another ethnicity or race.

17. Have there been situations in which you feel you experienced racial discrimination? Tell me about one of them.

18. Describe to me a situation involving race or ethnicity in which you had to make a difficult decision.

19. Have you witnessed racial prejudice [discrimination, racist jokes]?
    a. How did you react in that situation?

20. What is your racial or ethnic identity?
    a. How does your identity shape your views on race and ethnicity?

21. What led you to sign up for this interview?

NOTES

Introduction

1. Throughout this book, by *affirmative action* I mean race-based affirmative action as it is usually understood in US higher education. In the United States *affirmative action* is also used for gender-based considerations, especially in the workplace. In other countries, affirmative action policies have been based on other forms of disadvantage or discrimination as well, such as ethnicity or caste; see Sowell 2004.
2. Schuman and Scott 1989.
3. Donnelly 2013.
4. Karabel 2005; Reuben 2001; Stulberg and Chen 2014.
5. For example, see D'Souza 1991 and Sander 2004. Findings from a study by William Bowen and Derek Bok (1998) show that affirmative action, in fact, has numerous long-term benefits to its beneficiaries and to society.
6. Bowen and Bok 1998.
7. Reardon, Baker, and Klasik 2012.
8. Lammy 2010; Vasagar 2011.
9. Vasagar 2011.
10. Kahlenberg 2014.
11. Carnevale and Strohl 2013.
12. Johnson 2006. Pierre Bourdieu (1996) suggests further that higher education is used by elites as a cultural vehicle to legitimate class reproduction.
13. Hochschild 1996; Johnson 2006.
14. Duru-Bellat and Tenret 2012.
15. Boren 2001; De Groot 1998; Lipset 1975; McAdam 1988; Newcomb 1943; Sidanius et al. 2008. Some scholars point out that the mechanism for liberalization in college is unclear. For example, the extent of faculty liberalism does not seem to be associated with the extent of students' liberalization (Mariani and Hewitt 2008); and students who *enter* college tend to be more liberal than eighteen-year-olds who do not (Jennings and Stoker 2008).
16. Pew Research Center 2009; Schildkraut 2011. This general support for racial equality and multiculturalism often does not translate to support for social policies

that will ensure equality of outcomes (Bell and Hartmann 2007; Bobo, Kluegel, and Smith 1997). In fact, Bonilla-Silva (2003) argues that well-educated Americans are more likely to mask racist belief systems through their greater tendency to employ the tools of "color-blind racism."

17. Sauder (2006) demonstrates that universities respond to public rankings such as those listed in *US News and World Report* by looking toward what higher-ranked universities are doing, in attempts to increase their own rankings.

18. Binder 2014; Ho 2009; Rivera 2011.

19. Individual students at private elite universities are more likely to graduate than those at lower-status colleges; they also earn more (Hoekstra 2009; Long 2008) and are more likley to hold top corporate and government positions (Dye 2014). Dale and Krueger critique these findings; nonetheless, they still find that college selectivity matters for working-class, black, and Latino students (Dale and Krueger 2002, 2011). Some have pointed out that elites are not produced exclusively by elite universities. For example, Brint (2015) finds that leaders of Fortune 500 companies as well as members of the US Senate have college degrees from a wide variety of universities; see also Bruni 2015. Indeed, because of their relatively larger size, public universities produce more leaders overall (Brint 2007). Still, it remains clear that an elite college degree provides greater opportunities and income than a degree from a lower-status college.

20. UK Social Mobility and Child Poverty Commission 2014.

21. Kelsall 1955.

22. Schuman and Scott 1989.

23. Pew Research Center 2014.

24. Ford 2008.

25. Mariani and Hewitt 2008; Sidanius et al. 2008.

26. Massey 2003.

27. Schuman, Steeh, and Bobo 1997.

Chapter One

1. Lemann 1999, 156.

2. Kett 2013.

3. Karabel 2005; Kett 2013.

4. Daniel Bell 1973; see also Baltzell 1964 and Bender 1997. Baltzell (1964) was hopeful that the Harvard model of admissions, which by the 1960s recruited more students who were not Anglo Protestants than other elite universities, would serve as a model of promoting democratic inclusion based on meritocracy for other elite universities as well as for corporations. Baltzell (1958) noted that Harvard in particular groomed nonelite students for inclusion in a democratic aristocracy. Still, he warned of the dangers of class reproduction that turned class into a caste status; he particularly noted the exclusion of Jews and African Americans (Baltzell 1964).

5. For example, see Lipset and Bendix 1992.

6. For example, see Bourdieu 1984; Bourdieu and Clough 1996; Bowles and Gintis 1976; and Karabel and Halsey 1977.

7. Bourdieu and Clough 1996; Bourdieu and Passeron 1977; Lareau 2011.

8. Karabel 2005, 5.

9. Karabel 2005.

10. Alon 2009; Carnevale and Strohl 2013; Soares 1999.

11. Hoxby 2009.

12. Demerath 2009; Kaushal, Magnuson, and Waldfogel 2011; Lareau 2011; Stevens 2007; Weis, Cipollone, and Jenkins 2014.

13. Little and Westergaard 1964.

14. Christopher Jencks (1972) similarly argued in the United States that greater emphasis should be placed on enhancing working-class life than on ensuring equal opportunities, given the role that luck plays in shaping socioeconomic outcomes.

15. Carson 2003; Lemann 1999; Zuberi and Bonilla-Silva 2008.

16. For example, see Herrnstein and Murray 1994; Wilson and Herrnstein 1985.

17. Reuben 2001; Skrentny 2002; Stulberg and Chen 2014. Stulberg and Chen (2014) point out that Harvard instituted affirmative action in 1961, three years before Brown did so. Still, they group Harvard and Brown together (along with other Ivies) as elite private universities that adopted affirmative action before widespread campus protests and urban riots, in contrast to Princeton and Yale.

18. Grodsky 2007. Overall, this is a case of organizational response to threats to legitimacy. Similarly, Lamont (2009), in a study of decision making on academic funding panels, found that decision makers made sure that a range of universities, rather than simply top research universities, were represented among grant winners, out of their own concern that they might miss strong candidates with nontraditional backgrounds for prestigious fellowships. For a detailed history of affirmative action in admissions, see Karabel 2005; Reuben 2001; and Stulberg and Chen 2014.

19. In many respects the federal government paved the way for this resolution to the contradiction between a supposedly meritocratic system distributing opportunity fairly and the poor performance of African Americans on these supposedly fair tests of merit. Rather than rethinking the notion of meritocracy, the government instituted an adjustment, affirmative action, that would maintain the legitimacy of the meritocracy (Lemann 1999). Affirmative action requirements first appeared in federal contracts during the early 1960s; universities then took up this policy to promote diversity on campus.

20. Regents of the University of California v. Bakke 438 US 265 (1978).

21. Fisher v. University of Texas at Austin 570 U.S. (2013); Grutter v. Bollinger 539 U.S. 306 (2003); Regents of the University of California v. Bakke 438 US 265 (1978). Multiple cases challenging affirmative action have gone to the US Supreme Court. Most recently, in the 2013 *Fisher* decision, the court upheld affirmative action but required that universities be able to prove that no other, race-neutral mechanisms could achieve the goal of diversity. The Supreme Court reheard the *Fisher* case in 2015 and will probably announce its decision in June 2016. The court may insist that universities go further to justify their claims that affirmative action is the only way to create a diverse learning environment. Unlike state bans, which affect only public universities, US Supreme Court decisions affect both private and public universities. Beyond the Fisher case, legal scholars predict that future challenges

to affirmative action in higher education will be coming to the US Supreme Court (Kahlenberg 2014); personal conversation with Jim Ryan, December 1, 2015. Already a suit against Harvard's affirmative action policy is on hold until the *Fisher* case is settled (Students for Fair Admissions, Inc. v. President and Fellows of Harvard College 11-14176 (2015) [order on motion to stay]).

22. Berrey 2105; see also Green 2004.

23. Dobbin 2009; Stevens and Roksa 2011.

24. Stevens and Roksa 2011.

25. Kennedy 2013; Rothstein 2014.

26. Cashin 2015; Kahlenberg 2012.

27. Guinier 2015.

28. For example, see Sander 2004.

29. For example, Delbanco 2012; Deresiewicz 2014; Golden 2007; Lemann 1999; Steinberg 2002.

30. Lemann 1999.

31. Bowen and Levin 2003; Kahlenberg 2010.

32. For a review of this literature, see Radford 2013, introduction. Stacy Dale and Alan Krueger (2002, 2011) have criticized this finding, citing unobservable differences in students attending elite versus nonelite colleges before they even start college as the real driver of different outcomes. In other words, Dale and Krueger claim that education at elite colleges does not matter as much as we assume, because students bring to college skills that help them succeed later in life. To address this issue, they study the socioeconomic outcomes of students who gained admission to higher-ranked universities but did not attend them. However, this method too is flawed, in that students choosing to attend a college ranked lower than the most selective college to which they gained admission are likely to be a unique bunch. Nevertheless, under their method Dale and Krueger find that working-class, black, Latino, and first-generation college students *do* benefit from higher-status colleges in terms of future earnings.

33. US Department of Education, National Center for Education Statistics 2009. The colleges where students even choose to apply are stratified as well. Caroline Hoxby has shown that high-achieving low-income students tend to apply to lower-ranked colleges than well-off peers with the same SAT scores; her simple intervention of sending high achievers from low-income families application fee vouchers and information on where they are likely to gain admission boosts those students' application rates to and enrollment in higher-ranked colleges (Hoxby and Avery 2012; Hoxby and Turner 2014).

34. Kopicki 2014.

35. Lamont and da Silva 2009; Lipson 2007. Lipson (2007) finds that US universities have converged in their emphasis on "diversity management," so that a near consensus arises when speaking with admissions officers about whether affirmative action should continue, in contrast to public debates about the practice. Lipson finds that admissions officers converge not only on the importance of affirmative action, but also in justifying it as contributing to campus diversity rather than as promoting social justice.

36. For a review of this literature, see Milem, Chang, and Antonio 2005.
37. Gurin et al. 2002; Milem, Chang, and Antonio 2005; Sidanius et al. 2008; McClelland and Linnander 2006; Stearns, Buchmann, and Bonneau 2009.
38. Gurin et al. 2002; Hurtado 2005. Still, Antonio (2001) finds that diversity-related workshops have a weaker association with cultural knowledge of other groups than do frequent interracial interactions.
39. For a discussion of the development of affirmative action in the United States and its absence in Britain, see Lieberman 2005 and Teles 1998.
40. Foner 2005; Katznelson 1973.
41. Lamont 1992; Schildkraut 2011.
42. Bender 1997.
43. Kerr 2001, as cited in Bender 1997.
44. Lemann 1999.
45. Ramirez 2006; Soares 1999. From the 1970s, however, Soares (1999) describes a shift at Oxford to an "ultrameritocracy," a system in which admission is based on demonstrated capabilities, but those capabilities are fostered most by the cultural and economic resources held by privileged families.
46. Harris 2011.
47. Office for Fair Access 2015.
48. The Office for Fair Access notes increased participation in higher education among working-class Britons since the access agreement requirement began, though working-class students remain underrepresented, especially at the most selective universities. See Office for Fair Access 2015.
49. UK Department for Education 2011.
50. University of Oxford 2015a.
51. Boliver 2013; Noden, Shiner, and Modood 2014; Parel and Boliver 2014.
52. Delbanco 2012; see also S. Khan 2010.
53. Gaztambide-Fernandez 2009; Johnson 2006; S. Khan 2010; Lareau 2011.
54. Gaztambide-Fernandez 2009.
55. S. Khan 2010.
56. Gaztambide-Fernandez 2009; S. Khan 2010.
57. Samson 2013.
58. For details on the historical development of this infrastructure, see Chen 2000; Lipson 2007; Reuben 2001; Rojas 2007; Stulberg and Chen 2014; Lipset 1975.
59. Grodsky and Kalogrides 2008; Karen 1990.
60. For example, see Arthur and Shapiro 1995; Bloom 1987; D'Souza 1991; Gitlin 1995; Taylor 1994.
61. Banerji 2005.
62. Pollock 2004.
63. Berrey 2015; Dobbin 2009; Skrentny 2013.
64. Mariani and Hewitt 2008; Sidanius et al. 2008. This has been consistent over time; Lipset (1975) provides evidence that Harvard students during the postwar period tended to identify as liberal and that more Harvard students than students on other campuses participated in radical student groups.
65. Boren 2001; De Groot 1998.

66. Duru-Bellat and Tenret 2012; see also Johnson 2006.
67. Bobo and Fox 2003; Ford 2008; Heath and Tilley 2005; McLaren and Johnson 2005.
68. Bobo and Kluegel 1993; Bobo 1999; Bonilla-Silva 2003; Citrin et al. 2001; Feagin and O'Brien 2003; Kinder and Sears 1981; Quillian 2006; Sears and Henry 2003.
69. Sears and Henry 2003; see Sniderman and Carmines 1996 for a critique of this argument.
70. Bobo at al. 2012.
71. Schuman, Steeh, and Bobo 1997.
72. Citrin et al. 2001.
73. Greenwald et al. 2002.
74. Gaddis 2014.
75. Schuman, Steeh, and Bobo 1997.
76. Zúñiga, Nagda, and Sevig 2002.
77. Richeson and Shelton 2007.
78. Goff, Steele, and Davies 2008.
79. Torres and Charles 2004. Walton and Cohen (2007) show that black college students are more susceptible to "belonging uncertainty" than white students.
80. Laar et al. 2005; Page-Gould, Mendoza-Denton, and Tropp 2008; Shook and Fazio 2008.
81. Stevens 2007.
82. Steinberg 2002.
83. Lamont and da Silva 2009.
84. Espenshade, Chung, and Walling 2004.
85. Brown University Office of College Admission 2014.
86. Fitzsimmons 2009a.
87. Hill, Corbett, and St. Rose 2010.
88. Bowen et al. 2005.
89. See Consortium of Higher Education Lesbian Gay Bisexual Transgender Resource Professionals 2015.
90. Fitzsimmons 2009b.
91. Brown University Office of College Admission 2014.
92. Unz 2012, appendix C. In fact, these remarkable similarities have been fodder for criticisms of affirmative action (Unz 2012).
93. Brown University Office of Institutional Research 2010; Harvard College Office of Admissions 2011.
94. In 2009, 16 percent of eighteen-year-olds were black, 18 percent were Latino, and 60 percent were non-Hispanic white. See US Census Bureau 2012.
95. Brown University Office of Institutional Research 2010; Harvard College Office of Admissions 2011.
96. Reardon, Baker, and Klasik 2012.
97. Reardon, Baker, and Klasik 2012.
98. *U.S. News and World Report* 2011a, 2011b. Though the percentage of students receiving financial aid represents a 16 percent difference, the percentage of students applying for financial aid who received it is quite similar: 65.9 percent applied for

need-based financial aid at Harvard for the 2011–12 academic year, and 61.5 percent received it; at Brown 48.8 percent applied for need-based financial aid and 45.5 percent received it (*U.S. News and World Report* 2011a, 2011b).

99. See Mountford Zimdars (2016) for details on admission to elite British universities. Before the 1950s, Oxford mostly trained the sons of elite families, much as Ivy League universities did in the United States (Soares 1999).

100. Students take the A-level exams in a minimum of five subjects, each a separate exam.

101. University of Oxford 2014.

102. Harvard College 2014.

103. Brown University Office of College Admission 2014.

104. Some international students are interviewed remotely.

105. University of Oxford 2011a.

106. Higher Education Statistics Agency 2009/2010.

107. Office for National Statistics 2013.

108. Boliver 2013.

109. Zimdars 2010.

110. In addition, cultural knowledge seems to play a role in admission decisions to Oxford based on the interview, especially in the arts (Zimdars, Sullivan, and Heath 2009); see also Burke and McManus 2011.

111. Ramirez 2006, 130; see also Lipset 1975.

112. Flexner 1930. See Lipset (1975) for a history of the shifting purposes of higher education, in particular at Harvard, over the past three centuries. Lipset contrasts the US model of the university and its relation to civil society (for example, in faculty governance) with the model at Oxford and Cambridge.

113. Ramirez 2006, 135.

114. At the same time, the Gilded Age saw the growth of an American aristocracy, served by the new New England boarding schools that were founded in the same era (Karabel 2005).

115. Soares 1999.

116. Ramirez 2006.

117. Mountford Zimdars 2016.

118. Bobo 1983; Kluegel and Smith 1983.

119. Massey 2003.

120. Unz 2012. While this argument is increasingly common, in opinion polls Asian Americans tend to support affirmative action; see Ramakrishnan and Lee 2012. A current lawsuit against Harvard, filed in November 2014 by Students for Fair Admissions, the organization funded by Edward Blum, alleges that Harvard discriminates against Asian American applicants.

121. Zeng and Xie 2004.

122. For example, in the recent past there have been numerous incidents at University of California campuses, as well as on Harvard's campus (Gordon 2014b; *Huffington Post* 2011, 2012).

123. Banks 1991; Pollock 2004.

124. There are a significant number of British-born young adults whose parents are

British-born children of immigrants—the immigrant third generation. However, I did not encounter any of them in this study.

125. UK Department for Education 2014.

126. Colloquially, those who trace their heritage to England are often called English (and for Wales and Scotland, Scottish and Welsh). However, these terms are less satisfactory for whites with British-born parents, because only 68 percent of white residents of England and Wales identify as English or Welsh. On the other hand, nearly all residents who identify as English or Welsh identify as white (96 percent and 99 percent, respectively), so white seems to capture English and Welsh identities. In addition, some foreign-born residents in Britain identify as English: 8 percent of residents of England and Wales who were born in Africa, the Middle East, or Asia identify as English. While some may have white British heritage, a remnant of colonialism, most are likely to be ethnic minorities. British, too, is an unsatisfactory term; just 14 percent of whites in Britain identify as British, compared with 49 percent of ethnic minorities, many of whom are immigrants or the children of immigrants. (All data are from my calculations from the 2011 UK Census, adapted from data from the Office for National Statistics licensed under the Open Government License v.3.0.)

127. I use many techniques to protect the identities of students interviewed, including changing their names and obscuring the actual interview year. In addition, when students' characteristics might make them easily identifiable, I have obscured details such as gender or major.

128. Harvard College Office of Admissions 2009.

129. Binder and Wood 2013.

130. Nine black students had at least one parent from the long-standing African American community, and four had at least one immigrant parent; six of the twelve black students had two nonimmigrant parents. Among Asian American students, nine are East Asian, three are South Asian, and one is Filipino.

131. University of Oxford 2015c.

132. Lawrence-Lightfoot 1997.

133. Now called the Brown Center for Students of Color. Because the name change happened after I completed this research, throughout the book I use the name at the time of the research, the Third World Center.

Chapter Two

1. Brief for Amici Curiae, Retired Military Leaders, in Grutter v. Bollinger 539 U.S. 306 (2003).

2. Blake 2013.

3. See King 1964.

4. Small, Harding, and Lamont 2010.

5. Irving Goffman (1974) first developed the notion of frame analysis, conceptualizing frames as the ways people organize or make sense of the social world. According to Goffman, frames affect how individuals interpret social phenomena by making some aspects prominent and obscuring others. Scholars in the field of so-

cial movements have taken up the notion of "collective action frames" to describe the ways a social problem and collective action are constructed by activists and by others, in order to mobilize constituencies (Benford and Snow 2000). Frame analysis, in contrast to the concept of ideology, suggests that activists actively construct those frames, often in contrast to dominant ideologies (Benford and Snow 2000). Ideologies also tend to entail values, unlike frames (Ferree and Merrill 2000). For my purposes here, defining these as race *frames* rather than *ideologies* allows space for analyzing how those frames shift through personal experiences and institutional influences, and it especially helps account for their contingent nature. George Lakoff (2004), a cognitive linguist, has used the concept of frames to explain how people of different political views understand the world differently. Lakoff powerfully argues that the language used to discuss political issues—their framing—shapes people's views. Similarly, in subsequent chapters I discuss how race frames seem to shape students' views on, in particular, college admissions. However, whereas Lakoff is especially interested in how frames develop in the political sphere and the media, I emphasize the role that institutions like higher education play in developing (race) frames.

6. Small 2004.
7. Telles 2004.
8. More recently some scholars have begun to identify influences on individuals' understandings of race, including transnational ties (Roth 2012); teaching in higher education (Morning 2011); K–12 teachers' avoidance of race talk in classrooms (Pollock 2004); and media exposure to positive portrayals of black Americans like President Obama (Goldman 2012).
9. Lawrence and Kane 1995.
10. Ely and Thomas 2001; Foldy and Buckley 2014.
11. Lewis 2003.
12. Lewis 2003; Pollock 2004.
13. Hochschild and her colleagues (Hochschild, Weaver, and Burch 2012) trace the roots of the idea that the United States is "postracial" to 2008. Some scholars espouse a postracial society as something the United States should aspire to. For example, see Appiah 1996; Hollinger 1995.
14. Ferree and Merrill 2000.
15. For example, US Supreme Court justice Clarence Thomas and writer Shelby Steele have employed a color-blindness frame to oppose affirmative action. See Fisher v. University of Texas at Austin 570 U.S. (2013); Steele 1990. Knowles and his colleagues find, however, that invoking color-blindness as an ideology is often rooted in perceptions of intergroup threat (Knowles et al. 2009).
16. For example, see Sniderman and Carmines 1997.
17. For example, see Bonilla-Silva 2003; Gallagher 2003; Moore and Bell 2011. I want to distinguish my use of the term race frames from Bonilla-Silva's. He argues that race frames are "set paths for interpreting information," serving to prop up color-blind racism. In other words, for him race frames serve to maintain the racial order in US society. Bonilla-Silva's critical view, as well as those of Feagin (2006) and Gallagher (2003), assumes negative intent and consequences of the color-blindness

frame. I do not take a stance on its ideological role; rather, I focus on the kinds of frames students espouse and their relation to experiences with race on campus and perspectives on affirmative action. The "abstract liberalism" and "minimization of racism" frames that Bonilla-Silva identifies can be seen as part of the color-blindness frame in that both hold that race has little social meaning.

18. Bobo, Kluegel, and Smith 1997; Kinder and Sears 1981. While I focus on race frames themselves rather than on the policy preferences they suggest, I consider my analysis compatible with this literature.

19. At Harvard and Brown students' fields of study are called their concentrations, akin to a major at other universities.

20. Orfield, Kucsera, and Siegel-Hawley 2012. Americans commonly base their residential decisions in part on the racial makeup of particular neighborhoods; white parents are even more likely than white adults with no children to choose predominantly white neighborhoods when they buy their homes, net of other characteristics like school quality, crime level, and house prices (Emerson, Chai, and Yancey 2001). Even more so than in neighborhoods, school segregation is an ongoing feature of American education (Orfield, Frankenberg, and Lee 2003; Orfield, Kucsera, and Siegel-Hawley 2012).

21. Staiger 2004; Tyson 2011.

22. Espenshade et al. 2009.

23. Brown University Office of Institutional Research 2010; Harvard University Office of Institutional Research 2009. This finding is similar to Espenshade and Radford's 2009 finding that, on average, 82 percent of high school peers of white students attending elite US universities are white, and 13 percent of their peers are black or Latino.

24. Sharkey 2013, 2014. Sharkey writes, "[Black] households making more than $100,000 per year live in communities that have greater levels of disadvantage, and that are surrounded by communities with greater disadvantage, than even low-income white households making less than $30,000 per year" (Sharkey 2014, 935). See also Pattillo-McCoy 1999.

25. For example, see Carnevale and Strohl 2013; Skiba et al. 2002.

26. For example, see Bonilla-Silva 2012; Frankenberg 1993; Hughey 2009; Lewis 2004; McDermott and Samson 2005.

27. Alba and Nee 2003; Kasinitz et al. 2008.

28. Hartmann and Gerteis (2005) distinguish three models for multiculturalism, one of which logically leads to the diversity frame. An "interactive pluralist" model of multiculturalism emphasizes both group identities and the importance of interaction across groups. Whereas Hartmann and Gerteis are identifying normative stances with respect to multiculturalism, my analysis identifies cultural frames for understanding race in society. Still, the diversity frame and interactive pluralist model for multiculturalism are compatible in the perspectives they call for on difference and interaction.

29. We might think of a negative view of pluralism as a culture of poverty frame, which I describe below.

30. Alba and Nee 2003; Berrey 2015. John Skrentny (2013, xi) highlights the development among US employers of "racial realism"—that is, "employer perceptions that workers vary by race in their ability to do certain jobs and contribute to organizational effectiveness, and/or in the kinds of signals their racial backgrounds send to customers and citizens."

31. Similarly, Espenshade and his colleagues found that 40 percent of students attending eight of the top colleges/universities in the United States have taken at least one course in African American, Asian American, or Latino studies (Espenshade and Radford 2009, 178). This includes a majority of all minority groups and nearly one-third of white students.

32. Regents of the University of California v. Bakke 438 US 265 (1978). Powell is citing another case, Keyishian v. Board of Regents 385 U.S. 589 (1967).

33. See also Feagin 2006.

34. See, among others, Cornell and Hartmann's (1998) racial formation theory.

35. For example, see Bonilla-Silva 2003; Feagin 2006; Moore and Bell 2011; Yosso et al. 2004.

36. Hunt 2007.

37. Of course, I cannot say whether students predisposed to a power analysis frame were more likely to attend TWTP. In addition, not all TWTP participants expressed a power analysis frame. Still, the evidence suggests that even if students came to TWTP sympathetic to a power analysis frame, through the TWTP experience they developed the language to express their opinions in confident and persuasive ways.

38. No Asian Americans employed a power analysis frame.

39. Derrick Bell 1973.

40. Bourdieu 1996; Young 1958.

41. For example, see Bonilla-Silva 2003; Modood 2005.

42. Huntington 2004.

43. Bobo and Charles 2009; Schuman, Steeh, and Bobo 1997. Scholars sometimes call these views color-blind for their belief in color-blind *policies*, even while the *frames* with which they understand race are culturally embedded.

44. Recent scholarship on culture and poverty develops more sophisticated theories about the influence of culture on poverty (see Small, Harding, and Lamont 2010 for a review). However, most lay understandings are not these kinds of explanations, but rather simple explanations resting on assumptions about group values and priorities.

45. Recall that the sample of students may have a liberal bias, hence there may be more students on campus who sometimes employ a culture of poverty frame than captured in this research. Other scholars have shown evidence for the culture of poverty frame in greater proportions in the larger, adult population in the United States; in fact, cultural explanations for black disadvantage have grown in recent years, among both black and white Americans (Bobo 2001; Hunt 2007). For example, in 2000 to 2004, half of whites explained socioeconomic differences between white and black Americans as due at least in part to a lack of motivation

or willpower among blacks, as did 45 percent of black survey respondents (Hunt 2007).

46. A wide range of research shows that under certain conditions, intergroup contact reduces racial prejudice (Pettigrew and Tropp 2006).

47. While a minority of Americans hold other race frames, these four are the most commonly discussed among scholars, employed by ordinary Americans today, and expressed by students in this study. Other race frames include a *biological* understanding of the significance of race, which was more common in the past, and a *cultural nationalist* frame, which prioritizes one's own culture over others and entails belief in its superiority. No students in this study employed a biological or a cultural nationalist frame.

48. Swidler 1986.

49. Swidler 1986.

50. Peterson and Kern 1996; see also Johnston and Baumann 2007; Peterson and Simkus 1992.

51. S. Khan 2010.

52. Karabel 2005.

53. Binder 1993.

54. Johnston and Baumann 2007.

55. Savage, Wright, and Gayo-Cal 2010.

56. Somewhat relatedly, political philosophers have developed the idea of cosmopolitanism—a belief in the importance of group-based identities alongside a desire to engage with and learn from groups outside one's own identity (Appiah 2006; Hartmann and Gerteis 2005; Hollinger 2001; see Lamont and Aksartova 2002 and Warikoo 2004 for examples of ordinary rather than elite cosmopolitanism). Certain multiethnic spaces in contemporary societies are places where individuals hold distinct ethnic and racial identities yet interact across them in meaningful ways (for example, see Anderson 2011; Appiah 2006; Gilroy 2005; Warikoo 2004). Many have noted that cosmopolitanism can be a form of elite identity, even if not explicitly so (Carson 2003; Lemann 1999; Zuberi and Bonilla-Silva 2008). This suggests, too, that this engagement with multiple group cultures—what I'm calling the diversity frame—can be a way of becoming elite.

Chapter Three

1. Mitchell Stevens and his colleagues describe universities as "incubators for the development of competent social actors." They argue that sociologists have not paid sufficient attention to the lived experiences of college students, "leaving us with an incomplete understanding of just how college attendance impacts so many arenas of life" (Stevens, Armstrong, and Arum 2008, 132). A burgeoning line of research on the organizational influence of universities demonstrates that how universities are organized—from the nature of campus housing, to the size of the student body, to parties with alcohol being thrown mostly by fraternities—shapes students' experiences, affecting outcomes as disparate as styles of political protest (Binder and Wood 2013); to the pathways through and dropping out of college (Armstrong and Hamilton 2013); to gender norms and violence (Armstrong, Hamilton, and

Sweeney 2006; Holland and Eisenhart 1990); to class-based ways of being (Reay, Crozier, and Clayton 2009; Stuber 2011).

2. Allport 1954. For a review of research on contact theory, see Pettigrew and Tropp 2006.

3. A third goal for diversity work exists, especially on elite campuses. Some argue that elite colleges should help build a diverse leadership for American society, in part through affirmative action. Former US Supreme Court justice Sandra Day O'Connor made this "pathway to leadership" argument in the Grutter v. Bollinger 539 U.S. 306 (2003) affirmative action decision (see also O'Connor and Schwab 2009).

4. Mica Pollock (2004) describes most primary and secondary schools as "color-mute"—avoiding discussions about race at all costs. Frank Dobbin (2009) demonstrates how corporate human resources departments defined compliance with equal opportunity law by, among other things, formalizing hiring practices and developing "diversity management" programs. Andrea Voyer (2011) examines those corporate programs, finding that most corporate (and nonprofit) diversity training emphasizes intercultural sensitivity at an individual level, ignoring institutionalized privilege and inequality in society. Alexandra Kalev and her colleagues show that the kind of approaches corporate firms take to promote diversity has important influence on whether those activities are associated with organizational change (Kalev, Dobbin, and Kelly 2006).

5. Karabel 2005; Stulberg and Chen 2014.

6. Reuben 2001.

7. Rojas 2007. Brown changed the department name from Afro-American Studies to Africana Studies in 2001 (Brown University News Service 2001). Harvard changed its name from Afro-American Studies to African and African American Studies in 2003 (Harvard University Department of African and African American Studies 2015b). Both are meant to signal the inclusion of studies of Africa.

8. These positions and the roles those play are often established in part by looking at what other universities are doing, through a process of institutional isomorphism (DiMaggio and Powell 1983). This process is aided by a great deal of movement by individuals occupying the positions. For example, the head of Brown's Office of Institutional Diversity as of 2015 previously held positions as Harvard's assistant provost for faculty development and diversity and as director of the Office for Diversity and Equal Opportunity at Yale's Graduate School of Arts and Sciences (Brown University Office of Institutional Diversity 2015). Harvard's chief diversity officer as of 2015 previously was the director of Tufts's Office of Institutional Diversity (Harvard University Office of the Executive Vice President, 2015).

9. Jesper Pedersen and Frank Dobbin (2006) describe two influences on organizations: the need for legitimacy, which leads to similarity between organizations, and the need to develop an identity, which leads to the development of unique organizational cultures. Similarly, Brown and Harvard share much related to diversity yet have developed unique campus cultures.

10. Brown University–Tougaloo College Partnership 2011; Campbell 2011.

11. McLaurin-Chesson and Pong 2004.

12. McLaurin-Chesson and Pong 2004.

13. Brown University Third World Center 2011.
14. I base this estimate on two hundred first-year students attending each year, and approximately five hundred students of color from the United States per cohort.
15. Brown University Third World Center 2011.
16. Brown University Third World Center 2012.
17. Brown University Third World Center 2010.
18. Brown Center for Students of Color 2015.
19. Brown University TWC Strategic Planning Committee 2014. I use the TWC name throughout because the name change happened after the conclusion of this research, so the name TWC parallels the experiences of students whose voices we hear.
20. Almandrez 2013. When Brown's TWC inquired into centers at the seven other Ivy League universities, four universities replied, three of which have smaller budgets and less space for their similar cultural centers. The fourth reported a budget over $1 million, with offices all over the university, suggesting a different model altogether (Almandrez 2013).
21. McLaurin-Chesson and Pong 2004.
22. Brown University 2015a, 2015b; Brown University Center for the Study of Slavery and Justice 2015; Brown University Steering Committee on Slavery and Justice 2011.
23. Brown University Black Student Union 2011.
24. Brown University Office of Residential Life 2011.
25. Nickens 2014.
26. Personal communication with house representative, March 13, 2015.
27. BearSync 2015.
28. Brown University 2015d.
29. One of the two dissenters was a white student who was ambivalent about the valorization—as he perceived it—of oppression at TWTP. The other was Nuri, an African American woman, who felt TWTP fostered segregation and focused too much on racism rather than on integration.
30. Note that this is a misperception, since white students are not barred from participating. However, students of color do receive special invitations to TWTP. Many white students said they knew about this practice.
31. There were a number of other concerns that weren't shared as widely across students, including that the programs lead to a sentiment on campus that feeling oppressed is "cool," akin to a status marker, and that the focus on race is misdirected.
32. Note that there are other preorientation programs at Brown, including an orientation for international students, a program to improve writing skills, and a program focused on community service (Brown University 2015e).
33. Personal communication with Shane Lloyd, assistant director at Brown Center for Students of Color, April 23, 2015.
34. The question was, "Some people see ethnic and racial organizations in college as divisive and leading to separatism, and others see them as important support networks that also promote cultural diversity. What do you think?"

35. The TWC does indeed have rooms for different racial and ethnic communities (personal communication with TWC administrator, June 6, 2012).

36. It may not be surprising that the students of color who tended to level this criticism of the TWC identified as biracial. Prior research has demonstrated that biracial college students may feel more social distance from and less closeness with their monoracial peers of color. See Smith and Moore 2000 for a discussion of this phenomenon among black undergraduates.

37. Chen 2000.

38. Harvard Foundation for Intercultural and Race Relations 2015a.

39. Harvard Foundation for Intercultural and Race Relations 2015a.

40. Harvard Foundation for Intercultural and Race Relations 2015c.

41. Harvard Foundation for Intercultural and Race Relations 2015b.

42. Harvard College Office of Student Life 2015; Harvard Foundation for Intercultural and Race Relations 2013.

43. Waite 2008.

44. Phillips Brooks House 2015.

45. Phillips Brooks House 2015. In the 2010–11 academic year, Harvard implemented Sustained Dialogue, which acted as a follow-up to Community Conversations. Interns at the Harvard Foundation ran the program, which was a voluntary, small-group, discussion-based diversity initiative that took place throughout the school year, with each group meeting for an hour and a half each week. In the first year of the program, sixty to seventy students across racial lines participated (Underwood 2010). More recently, Sustained Dialogue transitioned to Harvard Dialogues, based on the Sustained Dialogue Institute model (www.sustaineddialogue.org).

46. Quoted in Kumar 2010. Indeed, Thomas Espenshade and his colleagues find that living with a roommate of a different race during the first year of college increases the likelihood that students will socialize with, have close friendships with, or date peers of a different race in subsequent years (Espenshade and Radford 2009).

47. Guren 2005.

48. Personal communication with Committee on EMR administrative director, March 16, 2015.

49. Harvard University Department of African and African American Studies 2015a.

50. Harvard College Freshman Dean's Office 2014.

51. Harvard Foundation for Intercultural and Race Relations 2015b.

52. For a discussion of the complexity of arts education and its goals and impact, see Gaztambide-Fernandez 2013.

53. This is half the number of first-year participants in TWTP.

54. Harvard First-Year Urban Program 2014.

55. Oliver and Shapiro 1995. The GI Bill did not require colleges to admit black students; hence black men had a harder time availing themselves of it (Katznelson 2005).

56. Allport 1954; Pettigrew and Tropp 2006. In particular, Robin Ely and David Thomas (2001) have shown that the most effective diversity perspective for promoting group functioning in corporate firms is an "integration-and-learning" per-

spective, in which diversity is valued for contributing to the work of the organization, beyond access to markets, legitimation of the firm by visible diversity of personnel or a sole focus on discrimination and justice.

57. See, for example, Sleeter and McLaren 1995.

Chapter Four

1. Fortgang 2014.
2. Schonfeld 2014.
3. A majority of students on these campuses are liberal—I found this in the survey students completed before our interviews. Large data sets measuring US college students' political views also find that residential college students tend to identify as liberal (Mariani and Hewitt 2008; Sidanius et al. 2008). After they arrive at college, students tend to become even more liberal (Mariani and Hewitt 2008; Sidanius et al. 2008), and college-educated adults tend to be more liberal than those with less education (Pew Research Center for the People and the Press 2005).
4. Bowen et al. 2005; Kahlenberg 2014; Massey et al. 2007.
5. Binder and Wood 2013.
6. Sears 1993.
7. I also expected a minority who identified as conservative to disagree with affirmative action in particular, taking issue with the liberal view that Fortgang rejects.
8. Douthat 2005; Golden 2007; Ho 2009; Karabel 2005.
9. Fitzsimmons 2009b.
10. Brown University Office of College Admission 2014.
11. This was 33/46 whites, 9/13 Asian Americans, and 11/17 black and Latino students. The differences between racial groups in considering diversity an important dimension of admissions are not statistically significant.
12. Less than 10 percent of the student body was black or Latino, and less than 5 percent of Sophie's peers were eligible for free or reduced-price lunch.
13. While Harvard and Brown, like their sister Ivy League universities, do not offer athletic scholarships, recruited athletes on those campuses do go through a special admissions process. Once coaches identify their preferred players, if those players have a minimum GPA and SAT score, the admissions office will usually admit them (Bowen and Levin 2003). Perhaps as a result, recruited athletes' SAT scores tend to be lower than those of other students on campus. While some high-profile sports like basketball can increase racial diversity on elite campuses, sports recruiting overall *decreases* racial diversity on campus because of recruiting to elite sports like lacrosse and crew (Bowen and Levin 2003).
14. How far universities consider legacy status in admissions has been debated. At many elite colleges, including Harvard and Brown, admissions officers are given information about applicants' alumni parents' histories of donations to the college. Universities generally describe legacy status as a factor that can merely "tip" an applicant into the "admitted" pile, and they note that most legacy applicants are not admitted (Worland 2011). While this is true, the legacy "boost" has been esti-

mated at 160 SAT points (Espenshade, Chung, and Walling 2004) or as increasing the odds of admission by more than three times (Hurwitz 2011). Why admit legacies? Universities claim that legacy preferences build loyalty, with the implication that loyalty encourages donations to the university. Indeed, the Yale dean of admissions, among others, has said that rates of legacy admissions are correlated with levels of alumni donations (Worland 2011). Brown University states that "Brown takes into account the natural affinity for the University that often emerges among family members of our graduates" (Brown University Office of College Admission 2014). Others have forcefully criticized the practice, citing the reproduction of privilege it engenders and questioning its impact on alumni donations; for example, see Kahlenberg 2010.

15. This finding resonates with a poll conducted by the Brown student newspaper, which found that 50 percent of Brown students agree with legacy admissions (Lanney 2014).

16. Brown University 2015c.

17. Fitzsimmons 2009a.

18. DiMaggio and Powell 198.

19. Kymlicka 2013, 109; see also Berrey 2011. John Skrentny (2013) calls this "racial realism" when employers use it to justify making race a job qualification.

20. It may be that Dexter imagines himself to be the black colleague faced by someone white and hopes the white colleague will treat him equally and with respect. Still, this benefit is quite different from one that ensures he has particular skills for advancement, as the neoliberal logic of collective merit applies to white students.

21. It further means that, just as low numbers of black or Latino students on campus would be a problem, so too might the overrepresentation of Asian American students be a problem.

22. DiMaggio likens sociological conceptions of "scripts" to psychological conceptions of "schemata," which he describes as "representations of knowledge and information-processing mechanisms. As representations, they entail images of objects and the relations among them" (DiMaggio 1997, 269); see also Fiske and Linville 1980. Research in psychology shows that people recall events more accurately and precisely when they fit with existing schemata, and that we sometimes even falsely recall events in line with existing schemata (Freeman, Romney, and Freeman 1987).

23. Beyond college campuses, ordinary white Americans believe there is more antiwhite bias than antiblack bias in the United States today. The reverse is true for African Americans (Norton and Sommers 2011).

24. Kinder and Sanders 1996, 293.

25. Schuman, Steeh, and Bobo 1997.

26. Lowery et al. 2006. The same study finds that support does not shift when whites are reminded of black gains due to affirmative action.

27. It is unclear whether Anna's perception is a realistic picture of campus life. Aries (2012) and Smith and Moore (2000), in their studies of undergraduates, find important differences among black students, including whether they sit at the "black tables" in the cafeteria. Many black students, in fact, do not sit at tables with all

black peers. However, black students who do participate in black-identified campus organizations, cafeteria tables, and more, are clearly racially marked, unlike minority peers in integrated groups. Further, Aries (2008) finds that whites *arrive* on campus with concerns that minority peers will "self-segregate." Hence, seeing some minorities together may fuel that concern, despite the evidence to the contrary of other black students associating with whites or across minority groups.

28. Sidanius et al. 2008.

29. I draw here from the literature on the "patriarchy bargain," in which women give up independence to secure financial or emotional security or accede to poor treatment as young wives to gain power later as the elder matriarch (Kandiyoti 1988). Scholars of immigration have discussed the "immigrant bargain," whereby immigrants sacrifice to give their children additional life opportunities (Louie 2004; Smith 2006). While the patriarchy bargain and immigrant bargain pertain to disadvantaged groups attempting to gain status or to experience intergenerational mobility, the diversity bargain illustrates how an advantaged group—whites at elite universities—maintain their advantages while supporting a policy that purports to help others.

30. Lewis, Chesler, and Forman (2000) find that students of color also perceive that whites have essentialized understandings of minorities that shape their interactions with them.

31. For example, in Aries's study of undergraduates at Amherst College, she found that three of every four black students interviewed "felt they were regarded as representatives of their race" (Aries 2012, 66).

32. Kahlenberg 2014.

33. Jackman 1994; Jackman and Muha 1984.

34. Delbanco 2012; see also S. Khan 2010.

35. For example, see Kymlicka 2007.

36. Coates 2014.

37. Jackman and Muha 1984; see also Bonilla-Silva 2003.

38. Bell 1979.

39. Bell 1979.

40. Aries 2012.

41. Berrey 2011; Yosso et al. 2004.

42. Brown University 2015b.

43. Diamond, Randolph, and Spillane 2004; Farkas 2003; Orfield, Frankenberg, and Lee 2003; Orfield, Kucsera, and Siegel-Hawley 2012.

44. Lucas 1999.

45. Skiba et al. 2002.

46. Lacy 2007; Pager and Shepherd 2008.

47. Alexander 2010.

48. Pager and Shepherd 2008.

49. Woo 2000.

50. Sharkey 2013.

Chapter Five

1. In the school, among peers there was no particular negative stereotype of Dominicans that I heard. The phrase was spoken to another Dominican student, and the context—laughter, and the search for a co-ethnic—made it clear to me that Dominican was not used pejoratively.
2. Lamont 1992, 2000.
3. Bush 2010, 325–26.
4. Richeson and Shelton 2007.
5. Goff, Steele, and Davies 2008.
6. Steele and Aronson 1995.
7. Goff, Steele, and Davies 2008. This research has not been done with respect to Latinos and Asian Americans.
8. See Hitlin and Vaisey 2013 for a discussion of the relation between individual identity and morality as socially embedded. I cannot distinguish between instances where individuals see "not racist" as part of their moral identities and those where they are simply performing a "not racist" identity, as symbolic interactionists emphasize (Collins 2004; Goffman 1959). Whether the motivation comes from within or in interaction, the resulting behaviors are the same.
9. Sigelman and Tuch 1997. The question reads, "Do you think that most white Americans hold the following perceptions of black Americans? The perception that blacks (multiple answers): (1) Are more likely to commit violent crimes; (2) Are less intelligent than whites; (3) Would rather live off welfare than work; and (4) Are lazy."
10. Torres and Charles 2004.
11. Torres and Charles 2004.
12. Wout, Murphy, and Steele 2010.
13. Sigelman and Tuch 1997; Torres and Charles 2004. For example, Sigelman and Tuch (1997) found that 59 percent of whites agreed that blacks prefer to live off welfare, while 75 percent of blacks perceived that most whites believe blacks prefer to live off welfare. Torres and Charles found that black students' beliefs about whites' stereotypes about blacks were similar to whites' beliefs about whites' stereotypes about blacks.
14. Quillian 2006.
15. Wilson 1973.
16. Aries, too, finds that white students arrive at an elite college, Amherst, anxious about discussing race (Aries 2008).
17. For a discussion of how meaning and emotion are constructed through interaction, see Collins 2004.
18. Voyer 2011.
19. Pérez 2013. Strategies that comedians use to put themselves on the right side of the hurtline include making self-deprecating jokes; avoiding overt ridicule; talking about their own group; and expressing empathy for the group. Using racial jokes under these guidelines could propel a comedian's career; using them on the wrong side of the hurtline, however, could end a career. Michael Richards, an actor and

comedian famous for his role as Cosmo Kramer on the television show *Seinfeld*, retired from stand-up comedy soon after an incident in which he was criticized for clearly crossing the hurtline. Richards repeatedly berated a group of black hecklers with racist remarks, including "He's a N—!" (Farhi 2006).

20. Given the moral expectation that students speak up when they hear racial jokes, perhaps US respondents simply gave me the socially desirable response. After all, they knew the interview was for a study on diversity in higher education, and in their social world individuals want to be seen as intervening when racially offensive behaviors and words arise. Since I did not directly observe students' experiences with racial jokes in their high school or college experiences, I cannot know their *actual* behaviors in these situations. However, important meaning can be culled from the interview responses. That is, we learn not what students are *actually* doing, but *how they talk about* racial jokes; for discussions of this issue, see Khan and Jerolmack 2013; Lamont and Swidler 2014.

21. Anderson 2011, 253.

22. Tyson 2011.

23. Torres and Charles (2004) similarly find that white students on the University of Pennsylvania campus believe black students do not want to socialize with them, while black students frequently explain racial separation as rooted in white students' lack of interest, and even hostility, toward black students.

24. Wilson 1995.

25. Indeed, the highest-profile controversies over multiculturalism during the 1980s and 1990s took place on elite campuses (Bryson 2005). Although political correctness debates continue today (Binder and Wood 2013), they peaked during the 1980s and 1990s, when many high-profile campus controversies made it to the evening news and national newspapers (Bryson 2005; Wilson 1995), with conservative pundit Dinesh D'Souza frequently appearing as the voice of the right (D'Souza 1991).

26. Brown University lists one goal for students in the Ethnic Studies concentration as becoming "fluent in critical theories about race and ethnicity" (Brown University Department of American Studies 2015).

27. The concept of institutional racism suggests that whites hold white privilege, which threatens their self-image; whites respond by thinking of race as interpersonal rather than institutional (Lowery, Knowles, and Unzueta 2007; Unzueta and Lowery 2008).

28. Remember that this phenomenon might be unique to elite college campuses, perhaps a best-case scenario for settings in which racial bias is disdained and not tolerated. This may not hold in the broader US society, where whites may feel less concern about seeming prejudiced, and are less willing to accept diversity more broadly. For a review of racial attitudes in the United States, see Bobo et al. 2012; Hunt 2007; Quillian 2006.

29. Stets and Carter 2012.

30. Burke 1991; Stets and Carter 2012.

31. Collins 2004; Goff, Steele, and Davies 2008.

32. McClelland and Linnander 2006; Pettigrew and Tropp 2006. In particular, having

a randomly assigned freshman roommate of a different race in college has a positive impact on interracial interaction in subsequent years (Espenshade and Radford 2009; Sidanius et al. 2008).

33. Espenshade and Radford (2009) find, for example, that just 15 percent of whites at selective colleges have a close friendship with a black or Latino peer on campus. See also Massey 2003; Sidanius et al. 2008.

34. Beasley 2011.

35. McClelland and Linnander 2006.

36. McClelland and Linnander 2006.

37. The article said that Harvard "need not offer a course on African civilizations if there is none worthy of study" (Mironova 2010). The author also claimed that the topic of ethnic studies already gets more attention than it deserves.

38. The student described the leaflet as "President Obama and a cross on fire." I was unable to obtain an image of the leaflet, but the designer of it described it as "Obama's popular 'hope' poster enveloped by fire" and defended it as unrelated to lynching (Dellagrotta 2009). Other students disagreed (Curtis 2009).

39. Renowned professor of African and African American Studies Henry Louis Gates Jr. was arrested outside his Cambridge home in 2009 by Cambridge police officers who believed he was breaking in (Goodnough 2009).

40. Bernstein 2007.

41. Bonilla-Silva 2003.

42. While lay understandings of the term white supremacy suggest belief in virulent racism like that perpetrated by the Ku Klux Klan, scholars like Bonilla-Silva use the term to mean "social relations and practices that reinforce white privilege" (Bonilla-Silva 2003, 9); see also Bonilla-Silva 2001; Gillborn 2005.

43. Feagin and O'Brien 2003; Gallagher 2003; Hunt 2007.

44. Bonilla-Silva 2003, 71.

45. Lowery, Knowles, and Unzueta 2007; Unzueta and Lowery 2008.

46. Frankenberg 1993; McDermott and Samson 2005.

Chapter Six

1. Among university graduates, in response to the statement "Some people say that it is better for the country if different racial and ethnic groups maintain their distinct customs and traditions. Other say that it is better if those groups adapt and blend into the larger society. Which of these views comes closest to your view?" those who supported maintaining customs declined from 35 percent to 22 percent between 1995 and 2003, and those supporting adaptation and blending increased from 48 percent to 54 percent (British Social Attitudes Survey). Since 2002, Britons increasingly feel that ethnic minorities need to "demonstrate a real commitment to [Britain] before they can be considered British" (Ipsos MORI 2006). Britons also perceive ill effects related to racial diversity: they believe that racial prejudice has recently increased in the country, and they increasingly cite immigration/race as the most important issue facing Britain (25 percent in 2006; Ipsos MORI 2006).

2. Banting and Kymlicka 2006.
3. Ahmed 2012; Pilkington 2011.
4. Teles 1998.
5. Lipset 1975; Ramirez 2006.
6. Gitlin 1995, 126.
7. Ages sixteen to twenty-four (Higher Education Statistics Agency 2009, 2010; Office for National Statistics 2013).
8. Office for National Statistics 2013; Higher Education Statistics Agency 2009/2010. Percentages do not add up to 100 percent because others are classified as Other, Mixed, or Unknown.
9. Peach 2009.
10. Recall that in Britain "Asian" means South Asian; it does not include East or Southeast Asians.
11. Oxford University Student Union 2015b.
12. Oxford Univeresity Student Union 2015a.
13. Recall that I use second-generation to mean the immigrant second generation — that is, UK-born children of immigrants. I include students with one or both parents born outside the European Union in this category.
14. Over 80 percent of white students in the United States (thirty-eight of forty-six) had attended a diversity-related event, and nearly all students of color had done so (twenty-eight of thirty).
15. Junior Common Room, both a room in the college and the student-led organization that deals with residential life for undergraduates at Oxford's colleges.
16. A majority of Singaporeans are ethnically Chinese, which may explain Robert's confused description of Steven.
17. Around the time of this research, 14 percent of Oxford undergraduates came from secondary schools outside Britain (8.5 percent from outside the European Union), and close to 10 percent of Harvard and Brown students came from high schools outside the United States (Brown University Office of Institutional Research 2012; Harvard University Office of Institutional Research 2013; Oxford University Academic Administration Division 2015). Since that time international student enrollment has risen at all three universities.
18. Carter 2005; Warikoo 2011.
19. Allport 1954; Pettigrew and Tropp 2006.
20. Other evidence suggests that some students on Oxford's campus hold a power analysis perspective, even if none of those we interviewed did. For example, students participating in the "I, Too, Am Oxford" campaign may be more critical of the university than the attitudes I encountered in the in-depth interviews. Still, this group is a small minority of students at Oxford, highlighted by their absence from the cross-section of students interviewed for this project.
21. Swidler 1986.
22. Although the United Kingdom Race Relations Act of 1976 prohibits "positive discrimination," it allows for "positive action" in Britain. On the surface this suggests that any kind of preference for racial minorities is not allowed in admissions. However, the United States Civil Rights Act similarly prohibits racial discrimination,

yet certain forms of affirmative action for racial minorities in higher education admissions have been implemented, then challenged in court, and in some cases have been allowed under particular legal interpretations. For multiple social, cultural, and political reasons beyond the legal question, racial considerations in university admissions (as well as in hiring) have not been implemented in Britain, but it is possible that such considerations *could* withstand legal challenges (Teles 2001). Indeed, some British scholars have called for affirmative action in higher education admissions; for example, see O. Khan 2010; Reay 2015.

23. Analia's feelings that Oxford may not be for her match the perspectives of working-class students interviewed for Reay and her colleagues' study at another elite British university (Reay, Crozier, and Clayton 2009).

24. Lamont and da Silva 2009.

25. Three second-generation students were eligible for free school meals sometime during secondary school.

26. Boliver 2013; Parel and Boliver 2014; Shiner and Noden 2014.

27. Boliver 2013. In contrast, working-class students and state school graduates are *less* likely to apply to elite universities, holding grades constant. This may explain some, but not all, of the underrepresentation of Afro-Caribbeans, Pakistanis, and Bangladeshis, given their lower socioeconomic status. See also Parel and Boliver 2014; Shiner and Noden 2014.

28. "I Too Am Oxford" 2014.

29. In an interview with me (July 2011) Oxford's director of admissions suggested that Oxford admissions are increasingly centralized. For example, colleges are more likely to swap applications today than in the past, aided by the central admissions office. In addition, "Widening Access" schemes at selective British universities may pressure departments to accept more nontraditional candidates.

30. Ramirez 2006.

31. Meyer et al. 2007; Frank and Gabler 2006; Ramirez 2006.

32. Faust 2012.

33. Allouch and Buisson-Fenet 2009.

34. Allouch 2015.

35. For a review, see Quillian 2006.

36. Karabel 2005.

37. Alon 2009; Hoxby 2009; Soares 1999.

Chapter Seven

1. "I Too Am Oxford" 2014.

2. Kahn 2014.

3. Kuumba Singers of Harvard College 2015.

4. Kahn 2014.

5. Nyambi 2014.

6. Faust 2014.

7. "We Are All Oxford" 2014.

8. Datoo 2014.

9. DiMaggio 1997, 273.
10. Shepherd 2008a, 2008b.
11. I could not corroborate this report. Just after these interviews were completed, a Campus Conservatives group event was held in which student speakers were asked to share the most offensive joke they had ever told; one student used the N-word, and another shared a joke about lynching (Bates 2009).
12. Taylor 2007. Griffin has stepped down since then.
13. See Brooke 2006.
14. Some popular media writers have termed this "hipster racism" or "ironic racism." For example, see West 2012.
15. Nina Eliasoph (1999) makes this point in her discussion of a country-western dance group's use of racial jokes. Eliasoph suggests that to understand why members "go along" with offensive talk, we must understand what the talk of race *does* in the group—in this case it signals irreverence and a lack of seriousness; criticizing that talk as "racist" would then contravene the group's outward identity as only playful: "Objecting to such talk would have required reference to a more solid ground of meaning than participants were willing to impose on the situation; it would have required 'getting on a high horse,' as members put it" (Eliasoph 1999, 488). Hence members of the group went along with racist jokes in the "frontstage," even while "backstage" many expressed distaste for them.
16. Powell and Paton 1988.
17. Pérez 2013.
18. Eliasoph 1999.

Conclusion

1. Schildkraut 2011; Johnson 2006.
2. Jackman and Muha 1984.
3. See also Jackman 1994.
4. Schuman, Steeh, and Bobo 1997.
5. Citrin et al. 2001; Bell and Hartmann 2007.
6. Bobo and Kluegel 1993; Quillian 2006; Schuman, Steeh, and Bobo 1997.
7. Grodsky 2007.
8. Espenshade and Radford 2009; Hoxby and Avery 2012.
9. Shiner and Noden 2014.
10. Boliver 2013; Noden, Shiner, and Modood 2014; Parel and Boliver 2014.
11. UK Department for Education 2011; University of Oxford 2011b.
12. Boliver 2013.
13. Alon 2009; Reardon, Baker, and Klasik 2012; Soares 1999.
14. Reardon, Baker, and Klasik 2012.
15. Reardon, Baker, and Klasik 2012.
16. Espeland and Sauder 2016.
17. Reardon, Baker, and Klasik 2012.
18. Rivera 2015; Binder 2014.
19. Keep 2010.

20. Crace 2013.
21. Sutton Trust 2010.
22. Brint 2015.
23. S. Khan 2010; see also Hayes 2012.
24. Gaztambide-Fernandez 2009; S. Khan 2010.
25. Stevens 2007; Most high-achieving high school students will get into at least one selective college (Hull 2010; Carey 2014).
26. Rivera 2011.
27. Lemann 1999.
28. Samson 2013.
29. Knowles and Lowery 2011.
30. See, for example, Kymlicka 2007.
31. Johnston and Baumann 2007; Peterson and Kern 1996. See also S. Khan 2010.
32. Voyer 2011.
33. Much debate on the definition of "cosmopolitan" exists among scholars. On one extreme, Nussbaum and Cohen (1996) describe cosmopolitanism as more universalist in its commitments to people around the world rather than from a particular nation. More commonly, scholars describe cosmopolitanism as in between multiculturalism and universalism, or the "new cosmopolitanism," as David Hollinger (2001) calls it. For examples of new cosmopolitanism, see Appiah 2006; Hartmann and Gerteis 2005. Others point out that cosmopolitanism has elite connotations, and further that "ordinary cosmopolitanism" exists in some places as well (Lamont and Aksartova 2002; Anderson 2011; Warikoo 2004).
34. See also Gallagher 2003; Feagin and O'Brien 2003; Moore and Bell 2011.
35. Berrey 2015, 8.
36. Duru-Bellat and Tenret 2012.
37. Tocqueville 1994; see also McNamee and Miller 2004.
38. Weber 1930.
39. Duru-Bellat and Tenret 2012.
40. Johnson 2006.
41. Lamont 1992.
42. For examples of this "hard" multiculturalism, see Taylor 1994; Kymlicka 2007.
43. Sen 2000.
44. For a similar argument, see Guinier 2015; Mettler 2014.
45. Ramirez 2006, 135.
46. Faust 2009.
47. Faust 2009.
48. Bowen and Levin 2003; Espenshade, Chung, and Walling 2004; Hurwitz 2011; Kahlenberg 2010; Massey and Mooney 2007; Stevens 2007.
49. O'Connor and Schwab 2009.
50. O'Connor and Schwab 2009.
51. Allouch and Buisson-Fenet 2009. Many on the left in fact criticized Blair's Third Way for simply reproducing the neoliberalism of his Conservative Party predecessors, under the guise of a more inclusive party. For a discussion of these issues, see Giddens 2013; Jacques 1998.

52. In the United States, the lack of class diversity at elite colleges has gotten greater attention in the recent past. For example, see Bowen et al. 2005; Kahlenberg 2014.

53. Bourdieu 1984; Bourdieu and Passeron 1977.

54. Boliver 2013, 2016; Noden, Shiner, and Modood 2014; Parel and Boliver 2014.

55. Admissions tutors do participate in a training session, but it does not seem to include attention to bias (Mountford Zimdars 2016).

56. Katznelson 2005.

57. Alexander 2010.

58. Respondents were asked to rate on a Likert scale (1–7): "Some people say that it is better for America if different racial and ethnic groups maintain their distinct cultures. Others say that it is better if groups change so that they blend into the larger society as in the idea of a melting pot. . . . What comes closest to the way you feel?"

59. Regents of the University of California v. Bakke 438 US 265 (1978); Grutter v. Bollinger 539 U.S. 306 (2003); Hopwood v. Texas 78 F.3d 932 (1996).

60. For example, see Katznelson 2005; Rothstein 2014; Kennedy 2013; Cashin 2015; Guinier 2015.

61. Lipson 2007. See Canon and Bradley 1999 for a discussion of judicial implementation theory.

62. Lipson 2007.

63. Skrentny 2013.

64. Aries 2012.

65. Gurin and Nagda 2006.

66. Gurin, Nagda, and Zúñiga 2013, 3. For examples of this intergroup work in extracurricular activities, see Park 2013; Deckman 2013.

67. Program on Intergroup Relations 2014.

68. Gurin, Nagda, and Zúñiga 2013.

69. Park 2013.

70. Deckman 2013.

71. According to a study of teams of social workers by Erica Foldy and Tamara Buckley (2014), another successful model for addressing racial and ethnic differences among participants and their work with clients is workplaces that emphasize "color cognizance"—when teams recognize the salience of race and ethnicity—and an institutional and group culture that makes workers feel safe, including a learning orientation. See also Ely and Thomas 2001.

72. Grutter v. Bollinger 539 U.S. 306 (2003).

73. For example, recently some have suggested that *legal status* has come to deprive many Americans of their legal and human rights in the ways that being a racial minority did in the United States in the past (Waters and Kasinitz 2015).

74. Abdulkadiroğlu, Pathak, and Roth 2005.

75. Stone 2013.

76. Stone 2013, 577.

77. See Stone 2013; Schwartz 2005; Guinier 1997 for other arguments in favor of an admissions lottery.

78. For example, while in many states charter schools must enroll students by lottery,

charter schools are less likely than traditional public schools to enroll children with disabilities or those whose parents do not have the wherewithal to enroll in the lottery (Bulkley and Fisler 2003). Hence some have criticized the notion of choice for reproducing privilege under the guise of choice for all. For example, see Ball, Bowe, and Gewirtz 1996.

Appendix B

1. For example, see Bonilla-Silva 2003.
2. Khan and Jerolmack 2013.
3. Lamont and Swidler 2014.
4. See Lamont and Swidler 2014 for a similar argument.
5. Hansen and Kirkland (2011) employ a different kind of data to understand how students talk about diversity. They analyze the application essays of students applying to University of Michigan that were written in response to diversity-related prompts.
6. This included only students beyond the first semester. For a detailed discussion of how and when ethnicity matters, and the dangers of "groupism" in social analysis, see Brubaker 2004; Wimmer 2013.
7. While all interviews on each campus were completed in one calendar year, I conceal the precise year to further protect respondents' identities.
8. Goff, Steele, and Davies 2008; Richeson and Shelton 2007.
9. Hammersley and Atkinson 1995.
10. See appendix C for interview questions.
11. For example, see Armstrong and Hamilton 2013; Binder and Wood 2013; Jack 2014; Stevens 2007.
12. See S. Khan 2010 and Duneier 1999 for a similar argument. I protected respondents' identities in this research by not naming the particular houses or dorms from which we recruited students for interviews. In addition, when their details of parents' birthplace, field of study, and gender may have made students recognizable to others I changed one detail. Finally, I mask the precise years of the data collection.

REFERENCES

Abdulkadiroğlu, Atila, Parag A. Pathak, and Alvin E. Roth. 2005. "The New York City High School Match." *American Economic Review* 95 (2): 364–67.

Ahmed, Sara. 2012. *On Being Included: Racism and Diversity in Institutional Life.* Durham, NC: Duke University Press.

Alba, Richard D., and Victor Nee. 2003. *Remaking the American Mainstream: Assimilation and Contemporary Immigration.* Cambridge, MA: Harvard University Press.

Alexander, Michelle. 2010. *The New Jim Crow: Mass Incarceration in the Age of Colorblindness.* New York: New Press.

Allouch, Annabelle. 2015. "From Selection to Recruitment: Widening Participation, Access, and Outreach Work at Two Elite Universities." Prepared for Harvard Graduate School of Education Culture, Institutions, and Society Research Colloquium. Cambridge, MA.

Allouch, Annabelle, and Hélène Buisson-Fenet. 2009. "The Minor Roads to Excellence: Positive Action, Outreach Policies and the New Positioning of Elite High Schools in France and England." *International Studies in Sociology of Education* 19 (3–4): 229–44.

Allport, Gordon W. 1954. *The Nature of Prejudice.* Cambridge, MA: Addison-Wesley.

Almandrez, Mary Grace. 2013. *Third World Center Self-Study Report 2012–2013.* Accessed April 19, 2015. http://www.brown.edu/campus-life/support /students-of-color/sites/brown.edu.campus-life.support.students-of-color /files/uploads/TWCselfstudypublic.pdf.

Alon, Sigal. 2009. "The Evolution of Class Inequality in Higher Education: Competition, Exclusion, and Adaptation." *American Sociological Review* 74 (5): 731–55.

Anderson, Elijah. 2011. *The Cosmopolitan Canopy: Race and Civility in Everyday Life.* New York: W. W. Norton.

Antonio, Anthony L. 2001. "The Role of Interracial Interaction in the Devel-

opment of Leadership Skills and Cultural Knowledge and Understanding."
Research in Higher Education 42 (5): 593–617.

Appiah, Kwame. 2006. *Cosmopolitanism: Ethics in a World of Strangers*. New
York: W. W. Norton.

———. 1996. "Race, Culture, Identity: Misunderstood Connections." In *Color
Conscious: The Political Morality of Race*, edited by Kwame Anthony Appiah
and Amy Gutmann, 30–104. Princeton, NJ: Princeton University Press.

Aries, Elizabeth. 2008. *Race and Class Matters at an Elite College*. Philadelphia:
Temple University Press.

Aries, Elizabeth, with Richard Berman. 2012. *Speaking of Race and Class: The
Student Experience at an Elite College*. Philadelphia: Temple University
Press.

Armstrong, Elizabeth A., Laura T. Hamilton, and Brian Sweeney. 2006. "Sexual
Assault on Campus: A Multilevel, Integrative Approach to Party Rape." *Social
Problems* 53 (4): 483–99.

Armstrong, Elizabeth A., and Laura T. Hamilton. 2013. *Paying for the Party: How
College Maintains Inequality*. Cambridge, MA: Harvard University Press.

Arthur, John, and Amy Shapiro. 1995. *Campus Wars: Multiculturalism and the
Politics of Difference*. Boulder, CO: Westview Press.

Ball, Stephen J., Richard Bowe, and Sharon Gewirtz. 1996. "School Choice,
Social Class and Distinction: The Realization of Social Advantage in Education." *Journal of Education Policy* 11 (1): 89–112.

Baltzell, E. Digby. 1958. *Philadelphia Gentlemen: The Making of a National Upper
Class*. Glencoe, IL: Free Press.

———. 1964. *The Protestant Establishment: Aristocracy and Caste in America*.
New York: Random House.

Banerji, Shilpa. 2005. "Diversity Officers—Coming to a Campus Near You?"
Diverse: Issues in Higher Education 22 (20): 38–40.

Banks, James A. 1991. "Multicultural Education for Freedom's Sake." *Educational
Leadership* 49 (4): 32–36.

Banting, Keith G. and Will Kymlicka, eds. 2006. *Multiculturalism and the Welfare
State: Recognition and Redistribution in Contemporary Democracies*. New York:
Oxford University Press.

Bates, Daniel. 2009. "Race Shame Outrage as Oxford Student Tories Clap and
Cheer at N-Word Jokes during Meeting." Accessed July 15, 2014. http://www
.dailymail.co.uk/news/article-1192212/Race-shame-outrage-Oxford-student
-Tories-clap-cheer-N-word-jokes-meeting.html.

BBC News. 2011. "State Multiculturalism Has Failed, Says David Cameron."
Accessed April 2, 2015. http://www.bbc.com/news/uk-politics-12371994.

BearSync. 2015. "Browse for Organizations." Accessed August 18, 2015. http://
studentactivitiesoffice89668.0rgsync.com/BearSyncPublicSearch.

Beasley, Maya A. 2011. *Opting Out: Losing the Potential of America's Young Black
Elite*. Chicago: University of Chicago Press.

Bell, Daniel. 1973. *The Coming of Post-industrial Society: A Venture in Social Fore-
casting*. New York: Basic Books.

Bell, Derrick A. 1973. *Race, Racism, and American Law*. Law School Casebook Series. Boston: Little, Brown.

———. 1979. "*Brown v. Board of Education* and the Interest-Convergence Dilemma." *Harvard Law Review* 93:518–33.

Bell, Joyce M., and Douglas Hartmann. 2007. "Diversity in Everyday Discourse: The Cultural Ambiguities and Consequences of 'Happy Talk.'" *American Sociological Review* 72 (6): 895–914.

Bender, Thomas. 1997. "Politics, Intellect, and the American University, 1945–1995. *Daedalus* 126 (1): 1.

Benford, Robert D., and David A. Snow. 2000. "Framing Processes and Social Movements: An Overview and Assessment." *Annual Review of Sociology* 26 (1): 611–39.

Bernstein, Ben. 2007. "Police under Fire."Accessed July 15, 2014. http://www.browndailyherald.com/2007/02/14/police-under-fire.

Berrey, Ellen. 2011. "Why Diversity Became Orthodox in Higher Education, and How It Changed the Meaning of Race on Campus." *Critical Sociology* 37 (5): 573–96.

———. 2015. *The Enigma of Diversity: The Language of Race and the Limits of Racial Justice*. Chicago: University of Chicago Press.

Binder, Amy. 1993. "Constructing Racial Rhetoric: Media Depictions of Harm in Heavy Metal and Rap Music." *American Sociological Review* 58 (6): 753–67.

———. 2014. "Why Are Harvard Grads Still Flocking to Wall Street?" Accessed October 4, 2015. http://www.washingtonmonthly.com/magazine/september october_2014/features/why_are_harvard_grads_still_fl051758.php?page=all#.

Binder, Amy, and Kate Wood. 2013. *Becoming Right: How Campuses Shape Young Conservatives*. Princeton, NJ: Princeton University Press.

Blake, John. 2013. "Why Conservatives Call MLK Their Hero." Accessed April 14, 2015. http://www.cnn.com/2013/01/19/us/mlk-conservative.

Bloom, Allan David. 1987. *The Closing of the American Mind: How Higher Education Has Failed Democracy and Impoverished the Souls of Today's Students*. New York: Simon and Schuster.

Bobo, Lawrence. 1983. "Whites' Opposition to Busing: Symbolic Racism or Realistic Group Conflict?" *Journal of Personality and Social Psychology* 45 (6): 1196–1210.

———. 1999. "Prejudice as Group Position: Microfoundations of a Sociological Approach to Racism and Race Relations." *Journal of Social Issues* 55 (3): 445–72.

———. 2001. "Racial Attitudes and Relations at the Close of the Twentieth Century." In *America Becoming: Racial Trends and Their Consequences*, edited by Neil Smelser, William J. Wilson, and Faith Mitchell, 264–301. Washington, DC: National Academy Press.

Bobo, Lawrence., and Camille Z. Charles. 2009. "Race in the American Mind: From the Moynihan Report to the Obama Candidacy." *Annals of the American Academy of Political and Social Science* 621 (1): 243–59.

Bobo, Lawrence, Camille Z. Charles, Maria Krysan, and Alicia D. Simmons. 2012. "The Real Record on Racial Attitudes." In *Social Trends in American Life: Findings from the General Social Survey since 1972*, edited by Peter Marsden, 38–83. Princeton, NJ: Princeton University Press.

Bobo, Lawrence, and Cybelle Fox. 2003. "Race, Racism, and Discrimination: Bridging Problems, Methods, and Theory in Social Psychological Research." *Social Psychology Quarterly* 66 (4): 319–32.

Bobo, Lawrence, and James R. Kluegel. 1993. "Opposition to Race-Targeting: Self-Interest, Stratification Ideology, or Racial Attitudes?" *American Sociological Review* 58 (4): 443–64.

Bobo, Lawrence, James R. Kluegel, and Ryan A. Smith. 1997. "Laissez-Faire Racism: The Crystallization of a Kinder, Gentler Anti-Black Ideology." In *Racial Attitudes in the 1990s: Continuity and Change*, edited by Steven A. Tuch and Jack K. Martin. Westport, CT: Praeger.

Boliver, Vikki. 2013. "How Fair Is Access to More Prestigious UK Universities?" *British Journal of Sociology* 64 (2): 344–64.

———. 2016. "Exploring Ethnic Inequalities in Admission to Russell Group Universities." *Sociology* 50 (2): 247–66.

Bonilla-Silva, Eduardo. 2001. *White Supremacy and Racism in the Post–Civil Rights Era*. Boulder, CO: Lynne Rienner.

———. 2003. *Racism without Racists: Color-Blind Racism and the Persistence of Racial Inequality in the United States*. Lanham, MD: Rowman and Littlefield.

———. 2012. "The Invisible Weight of Whiteness: The Racial Grammar of Everyday Life in Contemporary America." *Ethnic and Racial Studies* 35 (2): 173–94.

Boren, Mark Edelman. 2001. *Student Resistance: A History of the Unruly Subject*. New York: Routledge.

Bourdieu, Pierre. 1984. *Distinction: A Social Critique of the Judgement of Taste*. Cambridge, MA: Harvard University Press.

Bourdieu, Pierre. 1996. *The State Nobility: Elite Schools in the Field of Power*. Stanford, CA: Stanford University Press.

Bourdieu, Pierre, and Jean-Claude Passeron. 1977. *Reproduction in Education, Society and Culture*. Translated by Richard Nice. Sage Studies in Social and Educational Change, vol. 5. London: Sage Publications.

Bowen, William G., and Derek Curtis Bok. 1998. *The Shape of the River: Long-Term Consequences of Considering Race in College and University Admissions*. Princeton, NJ: Princeton University Press.

Bowen, William G., Martin A. Kurzweil, Eugene M. Tobin, and Susanne C. Pichler. 2005. *Equity and Excellence in American Higher Education*. Thomas Jefferson Foundation Distinguished Lecture Series. Charlottesville: University of Virginia Press.

Bowen, William G., and Sarah A. Levin. 2003. *Reclaiming the Game: College Sports and Educational Values*. Princeton, NJ: Princeton University Press.

Bowles, Samuel, and Herbert Gintis. 1976. *Schooling in Capitalist America: Educational Reform and the Contradictions of Economic Life*. New York: Basic Books.

Brint, Steven. 2007. "Can Public Research Universities Compete?" In *Future of the American Public Research University*, edited by Robert L. Geiger, Carol L. Colbeck, Roger L. Williams, and Christian K. Anderson, 91–118. Rotterdam: Sense.

———. 2015. "Merit Square-Off: The Fight Over College Admissions." *Los Angeles Review of Books*, September 15.

Brooke, Chris. 2006. "Baa, Baa Rainbow Sheep." Accessed July 15, 2014. http://www.dailymail.co.uk/news/article-379114/Baa-baa-rainbow-sheep.html.

Brown Center for Students of Color. 2015. "Mission Statement." Accessed October 12, 2015. http://www.brown.edu/campus-life/support/students-of-color/about.

Brown University. 2015a. "Fund for the Education of the Children of Providence." Accessed August 18, 2015. http://www.brown.edu/initiatives/fund-for-children.

———. 2015b. "Public Art: Martin Puryear, Slavery Memorial, 2014." Accessed August 18, 2015. http://www.brown.edu/about/public-art/martin-puryear-slavery-memorial.

———. 2015c. "Undergraduate Admission." Accessed August 24, 2015. http://www.brown.edu/admission/undergraduate/apply.

———. 2015d. "Undergraduate Concentrations at Brown." Accessed October 12, 2015. http://www.brown.edu/academics/college/concentrations/#.

———. 2015e. "Undergraduate Student Orientation." Accessed October 16, 2015. http://www.brown.edu/academics/college/orientation.

Brown University Black Student Union. 2011. "Organization Home." Accessed October 6, 2011. http://mygroups.brown.edu/organization/organizationofunitedafricanpeoples.

Brown University Center for the Study of Slavery and Justice. 2015. "Home." Accessed August 18, 2015. http://www.brown.edu/initiatives/slavery-and-justice.

Brown University Department of American Studies. 2015. "Courses of Study: Student Goals (Ethnic Studies)." Accessed April 22, 2015. http://www.brown.edu/academics/american-studies/courses-study-student-goals.

Brown University News Service. 2001. "Brown Announces New Department of Africana Studies." Accessed October 12, 2015. http://www.brown.edu/Administration/News_Bureau/2000–01/00–155.html.

Brown University Office of College Admission. 2012. "Brown by the Numbers." Accessed May 6, 2015. http://www.brown.edu/admission/undergraduate/sites/brown.edu.admission.undergraduate/files/uploads/BrownByNumbers.pdf.

———. 2014. "Undergraduate Admission: Frequently Asked Questions." Accessed July 1, 2014. http://www.brown.edu/admission/undergraduate/apply-brown/frequently-asked-questions.

Brown University Office of Institutional Diversity. 2015. "Liza Cariago-Lo, Vice President for Academic Development, Diversity and Inclusion." Accessed April 19, 2015. http://www.brown.edu/about/administration/institutional

-diversity/liza-cariaga-lo-associate-provost-academic-development-and
-diversity-brown-university.

Brown University Office of Institutional Research. 2010. "Fall Enrollment 2010-
Brown University." Accessed October 6, 2011. http://www.brown.edu
/Administration/Institutional_Research/documents/Enrollment2010.pdf.

———. 2012. "Fall Census Enrollment." Accessed June 20, 2013. http://brown
.edu/about/administration/institutional-research/sites/brown.edu.about
.administration.institutional-research/files/uploads/Enrollment2012.pdf.

———. 2013. "Degrees and Completions." Accessed December 12, 2013. http://
www.brown.edu/about/administration/institutional-research/factbook
/degrees-and-completions.

———. 2015. "Academic Pursuits." Accessed March 13, 2015. http://www.brown
.edu/about/administration/institutional-research/factbook/enrollment.

Brown University Office of Residential Life. 2011. "Program Housing." Accessed
October 6, 2011. http://reslife.brown.edu/current_students/program_housing
.html.

Brown University Steering Committee on Slavery and Justice. 2011. "Slavery
and Justice Update." Accessed October 6, 2011. http://brown.edu/Research
/Slavery_Justice/report/update.html.

Brown University Third World Center. 2010. "Third World Center: 30 Years of
Unity through Diversity." Accessed October 6, 2011. http://www.brown.edu
/Student_Services/TWC/docs/TWCFactSheet.pdf.

———. 2011. "Third World Transition Program." Accessed October 6, 2011.
http://www.brown.edu/Student_Services/TWC/TWTP/index.html.

———. 2012. "What Is TWTP?" Accessed June 7, 2012. http://www.brown.edu
/Student_Services/TWC/TWTP/what-is-twtp.html.

Brown University–Tougaloo College Partnership. 2011. "About Us." Accessed
October 6, 2011. http://www.brown.edu/Administration/Brown_Tougaloo
/about.

Brown University TWC Strategic Planning Committee. 2014. "The Third World
Center Strategic Plan: 2014–2019." Accessed March 13, 2015. http://brown
.edu/campus-life/support/students-of-color/sites/brown.edu.campus-life
.support.students-of-color/files/uploads/TWCstrategicplan.releaseSept2014
_1.pdf.

Brubaker, Rogers. 2004. "Ethnicity without Groups." In *Ethnicity without Groups*,
7–27. Cambridge, MA: Harvard University.

Bruni, Frank. 2015. *Where You Go Is Not Who You'll Be: An Antidote to the College
Admissions Mania*. New York: Grand Central.

Bryson, Bethany P. 2005. *Making Multiculturalism: Boundaries and Meaning in
U.S. English Departments*. Stanford, CA: Stanford University Press.

Bulkley, Katrina, and Jennifer Fisler. 2003. "A Decade of Charter Schools: From
Theory to Practice." *Educational Policy* 17 (3): 317–42.

Burke, Penny J., and Jackie McManus. 2011. "Art for a Few: Exclusions and Mis-
recognitions in Higher Education Admissions Practices." *Discourse: Studies in
the Cultural Politics of Education* 32 (5): 699–712.

Burke, Peter J. 1991. "Identity Processes and Social Stress." *American Sociological Review* 56 (6): 836–49.

Bush, George W. 2010. *Decision Points*. New York: Crown.

Calhoun, Craig. 2008. "Cosmopolitanism and Nationalism." *Nations and Nationalism* 14 (3): 427–48.

Campbell, Jim. 2011. "Brown-Tougaloo Exchange." Accessed October 6, 2011. http://www.stg.brown.edu/projects/FreedomNow/campbell.html.

Canon, Bradley C., and Charles A. Johnson. 1999. *Judicial Policies: Implementation and Impact*, 2nd ed. Washington, DC: CQ Press.

Caplan, Lionel. 2001. *Children of Colonialism: Anglo-Indians in a Postcolonial World*. London: Bloomsbury Academic.

Carey, Kevin. 2014. "For Accomplished Students, Reaching a Good College Isn't as Hard as It Seems." Accessed October 6, 2015. http://www.nytimes.com /2014/11/30/upshot/for-accomplished-students-reaching-a-top-college-isnt -actually-that-hard.html?rref=upshot&abt=0002&abg=1&_r=0.

Carnevale, Anthony P., and Jeff Strohl. 2013. "Separate and Unequal: How Higher Education Reform Reinforces the Intergenerational Reproduction of White Racial Privilege." Georgetown Public Policy Institute. Accessed April 2, 2015. https://cew.georgetown.edu/wp-content/uploads/2014/11/SeparateUnequal .FR_.pdf.

Carson, John. 2003. "The Culture of Intelligence." In *The Cambridge History of Science*, edited by Theodore M. Porter and Dorothy Ross. Cambridge: Cambridge University Press.

Carter, Prudence. 2005. *Keepin' It Real: School Success Beyond Black and White, Transgressing Boundaries*. New York: Oxford University Press.

Cashin, Sheryll. 2015. *Place, Not Race: A New Vision of Opportunity in America*. Boston: Beacon Press.

Chen, Shu-Ling. 2000. "Debates over Third World Centers at Princeton, Brown and Harvard: Minority Student Activism and Institutional Responses in the 1960s and 1970s." Harvard University EdD diss., Harvard University.

Citrin, Jack, David O. Sears, Christopher Muste, and Cara Wong. 2001. "Multiculturalism in American Public Opinion." *British Journal of Political Science* 31 (2): 247.

Coates, Ta-Nehisi. 2014. "The Case for Reparations." *Atlantic*. Accessed July 8, 2014. http://www.theatlantic.com/features/archive/2014/05/the-case-for -reparations/361631.

Collins, Randall. 2004. *Interaction Ritual Chains*. Princeton Studies in Cultural Sociology. Princeton, NJ: Princeton University Press.

Consortium of Higher Education Lesbian Gay Bisexual Transgender Resource Professionals. 2015. Accessed October 10, 2015. http://www.lgbtcampus.org.

Cornell, Stephen E., and Douglas Hartmann. 1998. *Ethnicity and Race: Making Identities in a Changing World*. Sociology for a New Century. Thousand Oaks, CA: Pine Forge Press.

Crace, John. 2013. "Is PPE a Passport to Power — or the Ultimate Blagger's

Degree?" Accessed May 5, 2015. http://www.theguardian.com/education
/2013/sep/23/ppe-passport-power-degree-oxford.

Curtis, Meredith. 2009. "To the Editor: Brown Republicans' Tableslips in Poor
Taste." Accessed July 15, 2014. http://www.browndailyherald.com/2009/09
/23/letter-to-the-editor-brown-republicans-tableslips-in-poor-taste.

Dale, Stacy Berg, and Alan B. Krueger. 2002. "Estimating the Payoff to Attending a More Selective College: An Application of Selection on Observables and
Unobservables." *Quarterly Journal of Economics* 117 (4): 1491–1527.

———. 2011. "Estimating the Return to College Selectivity over the Career Using
Administrative Earnings Data." Accessed April 3, 2015. http://www.nber.org
/papers/w17159.pdf.

Datoo, Siraj. 2014. "Student Campaign Insists 'Oxford Is an Inclusive Place' Following Diversity Row." Accessed October 4, 2015. http://www.buzzfeed
.com/sirajdatoo/heres-everything-you-need-to-know-about-the-b-bffl#
.ksA10YR68.

Deckman, Sherry L. 2013. "Come as You Are: Negotiating Diversity and Authen-
ticity in One Black Student Organization." EdD diss., Harvard University.

De Groot, Gerard. 1998. *Student Protest: The Sixties and After*. New York: Addison
Wesley Longman.

Delbanco, Andrew. 2012. *College: What It Was, Is, and Should Be*. Princeton, NJ:
Princeton University Press.

Dellagrotta, Keith. 2009. "In Defense of Brown Republicans' Tableslips."
Accessed July 15, 2014. http://www.browndailyherald.com/2009/10/02/keith
-dellagrotta-10-in-defense-of-brown-republicans-tableslips.

Demerath, Peter. 2009. *Producing Success: The Culture of Personal Advancement
in an American High School*. Chicago: University of Chicago Press.

Deresiewicz, William. 2014. *Excellent Sheep: The Miseducation of the American
Elite and the Way to a Meaningful Life*. New York: Free Press.

Diamond, John B., Antonia Randolph, and James P. Spillane. 2004. "Teachers'
Expectations and Sense of Responsibility for Student Learning: The Importance of Race, Class, and Organizational Habitus." *Anthropology and Education Quarterly* 35 (1): 75–98.

DiMaggio, Paul J. 1997. "Culture and Cognition." *Annual Review of Sociology*
23:263–87.

DiMaggio, Paul J., and Walter W. Powell. 1983. "The Iron Cage Revisited: Institutional Isomorphism and Collective Rationality in Organizational Fields."
American Sociological Review 48 (2): 147–60.

Dobbin, Frank. 2009. *Inventing Equal Opportunity*. Princeton, NJ: Princeton University Press.

Donnelly, Erin. 2013. "Controversial Bake Sale at UCLA Prompts Protest."
Accessed July 31, 2015. http://dailybruin.com/2013/10/25/controversial-bake
-sale-at-ucla-prompts-protest.

Douthat, Ross G. 2005. *Privilege: Harvard and the Education of the Ruling Class*.
New York: Hyperion.

D'Souza, Dinesh. 1991. *Illiberal Education: The Politics of Race and Sex on Campus.* New York: Free Press.

Duneier, Mitchell. 1999. *Sidewalk.* New York: Farrar, Straus and Giroux.

Duru-Bellat, Marie, and Elise Tenret. 2012. "Who's for Meritocracy? Individual and Contextual Variations in the Faith." *Comparative Education Review* 56 (2): 223–47.

Dye, Thomas R. 2014. *Who's Running America? The Obama Reign.* Boulder, CO: Paradigm.

Eliasoph, Nina. 1999. "'Everyday Racism' in a Culture of Political Avoidance: Civil Society, Speech, and Taboo." *Social Problems* 46 (4): 479–502.

Ellis, Hannah. 2008. "Anne's Flag Tension Escalates." Accessed July 15, 2014. http://www.cherwell.org/news/2008/05/01/anne-s-flag-tension-escalates.

Ely, Robin J., and David Thomas. 2001. "Cultural Diversity at Work: The Effects of Diversity Perspectives on Work Group Processes and Outcomes." *Administrative Science Quarterly* 46 (2): 229–73.

Emerson, Michael O., Karen J. Chai, and George Yancey. 2001. "Does Race Matter in Residential Segregation? Exploring the Preferences of White Americans." *American Sociological Review* 66 (6): 922–35.

Espeland, Wendy N., and Michael Sauder. 2016. *Engines of Anxiety: Academic Rankings, Reputation, and Accountability.* New York: Russell Sage Foundation.

Espenshade, Thomas J., Chang Y. Chung, and Joan L. Walling. 2004. "Admission Preferences for Minority Students, Athletes, and Legacies at Elite Universities." *Social Science Quarterly* 85 (5): 1422–46.

Espenshade, Thomas J., and Alexandria W. Radford. 2009. *No Longer Separate, Not Yet Equal: Race and Class in Elite College Admission and Campus Life.* Princeton, NJ: Princeton University Press.

Farhi, Paul. 2006. "'Seinfeld' Comic Richards Apologizes for Racial Rant." *Washington Post.* Accessed July 15, 2014. http://www.washingtonpost.com/wp-dyn/content/article/2006/11/21/AR2006112100242.html.

Farkas, George. 2003. "Racial Disparities and Discrimination in Education: What Do We Know, How Do We Know It, and What Do We Need to Know?" *Teachers College Record* 105 (6): 1119–46.

Faust, Drew. 2009. "The University's Crisis of Purpose." *New York Times.* Accessed October 16, 2015. http://www.nytimes.com/2009/09/06/books/review/Faust-t.html.

———. 2012. "Toward a Global Strategy for Harvard." *Harvard Magazine.* Accessed September 27, 2012. http://harvardmagazine.com/2012/09/toward-a-global-strategy-for-harvard.

———. 2014. "To Sit at the Welcome Table." *Harvard Magazine.* Accessed October 4, 2015. http://harvardmagazine.com/2014/07/to-sit-at-the-welcome-table.

Feagin, Joe R. 2006. *Systemic Racism: A Theory of Oppression.* New York: Routledge.

Feagin, Joe R., and Eileen O'Brien. 2003. *White Men on Race: Power, Privilege, and the Shaping of Cultural Consciousness*. Boston: Beacon Press.

Federal Interagency Forum on Child and Family Statistics. 2015. *America's Children: Key National Indicators of Well-Being*. Table POP3. Washington, DC: US Government Printing Office. Accessed July 14, 2015. http://www.childstats .gov/pdf/ac2015/ac_15.pdf.

Ferree, Myra M., and David A. Merrill. 2000. "Hot Movements, Cold Cognition: Thinking about Social Movements in Gendered Frames." *Contemporary Sociology* 29 (3): 454–62.

Fiske, Susan T., and Patricia W. Linville. 1980. "What Does the Schema Concept Buy Us?" *Personality and Social Psychology Bulletin* 6 (4): 543–57.

Fitzsimmons, William R. 2009a. "Guidance Office: Answers from Harvard's Dean, Part 1." *New York Times*. Accessed May 6, 2015. http://thechoice.blogs .nytimes.com/2009/09/10/harvarddean-part1.

———. 2009b. "Guidance Office: Answers from Harvard's Dean, Part 5." *New York Times*. Accessed May 6, 2015. http://thechoice.blogs.nytimes.com/2009 /09/16/harvarddean-part5.

Flexner, Abraham. 1930. *Univerities, American, English, German*. New York: Oxford University Press.

Foldy, Erica, and Tamara R. Buckley. 2014. *The Color Bind: Talking (and Not Talking) about Race at Work*. New York: Russell Sage Foundation.

Foner, Nancy. 2005. *In a New Land: A Comparative View of Immigration*. New York: New York University Press.

Ford, Robert. 2008. "Is Racial Prejudice Declining in Britain?" *British Journal of Sociology* 59 (4): 609–36.

Fortgang, Tal. 2014. "Why I'll Never Apologize for My White Male Privilege." *Time*. Accessed July 7, 2014. http://time.com/85933/why-ill-never-apologize -for-my-white-male-privilege.

Frank, David John, and Jay Gabler. 2006. *Reconstructing the University: Worldwide Shifts in Academia in the 20th Century*. Stanford, CA: Stanford University Press.

Frankenberg, Ruth. 1993. *White Women, Race Matters: The Social Construction of Whiteness*. Minneapolis: University of Minnesota Press.

Freeman, Linton C., A. Kimball Romney, and Sue C. Freeman. 1987. "Cognitive Structure and Informant Accuracy." *American Anthropologist* 89 (2): 310–25.

Gaddis, S. Michael. 2014. "Discrimination in the Credential Society: An Audit Study of Race and College Selectivity in the Labor Market." *Social Forces* 93 (4): 1451–79.

Gallagher, Charles A. 2003. "Color-Blind Privilege: The Social and Political Functions of Erasing the Color Line in Post Race America." *Race, Gender and Class* 10 (4): 22–37.

Gaztambide-Fernandez, Rubén A. 2009. *The Best of the Best: Becoming Elite at an American Boarding School*. Cambridge, MA: Harvard University Press.

———. 2013. "Why the Arts Don't Do Anything: Toward a New Vision for Cultural Production in Education." *Harvard Educational Review* 83 (1): 211–36.

Geiger, Roger L. 2002. "The Competition for High-Ability Students: Universities in a Key Marketplace." In *The Future of the City of Intellect: The Changing American University*, edited by Steven Brint, 82–106. Stanford, CA: Stanford University Press.

Giddens, Anthony. 2013. *The Third Way and Its Critics*. London: Oxford University Press.

Gillborn, David. 2005. "Education Policy as an Act of White Supremacy: Whiteness, Critical Race Theory and Education Reform." *Journal of Education Policy* 20 (4): 485.

Gilroy, Paul. 2005. *Postcolonial Melancholia*. New York: Columbia University Press.

Gitlin, Todd. 1995. *The Twilight of Common Dreams: Why America Is Wracked by Culture Wars*. New York: Metropolitan Books.

Goff, Phillip Atiba, Claude M. Steele, and Paul G. Davies. 2008. "The Space between Us: Stereotype Threat and Distance in Interracial Contexts." *Journal of Personality and Social Psychology* 94 (1): 91–107.

Goffman, Erving. 1959. *The Presentation of Self in Everyday Life*. Garden City, NY: Doubleday.

———. 1974. *Frame Analysis: An Essay on the Organization of Experience*. Cambridge, MA: Harvard University Press.

Golden, Daniel. 2007. *The Price of Admission: How America's Ruling Class Buys Its Way into Elite Colleges—and Who Gets Left Outside the Gates*. New York: Three Rivers Press.

Goldman, Seth K. 2012. "Effects of the 2008 Obama Presidential Campaign on White Racial Prejudice." *Public Opinion Quarterly* 76 (4): 663–87.

Goodhart, David. 2004. "Too Diverse?" *Prospect* 95:30–37.

Goodnough, Abby. 2009. "Harvard Professor Jailed; Officer Is Accused of Bias." *New York Times*, A13.

Gordon, Larry. 2014a. "Acceptance Rates at Elite U.S. Colleges Decline." *Los Angeles Times*. Accesssed August 26, 2015. http://www.latimes.com/nation /la-me-college-admits-20140421-story.html.

———. 2014b. "UCLA and USC Investigate Racist, Sexist Fliers Sent to Campuses." *Los Angeles Times*. Accessed February 16, 2014. http://www.latimes .com/local/lanow/la-me-ln-racist-fliers-20140210-story.html.

Green, Denise O'Neil. 2004. "Justice and Diversity: Michigan's Response to Gratz, Grutter, and the Affirmative Action Debate." *Urban Education* 39 (4): 374–93.

Greenwald, Anthony G., Laurie A. Rudman, Brian A. Nosek, Mahzarin R. Banaji, Shelly D. Farnham, and Deborah S. Mellott. 2002. "A Unified Theory of Implicit Attitudes, Stereotypes, Self-Esteem, and Self-Concept." *Psychological Review* 109 (1): 3.

Grodsky, Eric. 2007. "Compensatory Sponsorship in Higher Education." *American Journal of Sociology* 112 (6): 1662–1712.

Grodsky, Eric, and Demetra Kalogrides. 2008. "The Declining Significance of

Race in College Admissions Decisions." *American Journal of Education* 115: 1–33.

Guinier, Lani. 1997. "The Real Bias in Higher Education." *New York Times*, June 24, A19.

———. 2015. *The Tyranny of the Meritocracy: Democratizing Higher Education in America*. Boston: Beacon Press.

Guren, Adam M. 2005. "Freshman Roommates, Meet Your Makers." *Harvard Crimson*, August 12, 2005.

Gurin, Patricia, Eric L. Dey, Sylvia Hurtado, and Gerald Gurin. 2002. "Diversity and Higher Education: Theory and Impact on Educational Outcomes." *Harvard Educational Review* 72 (3): 330.

Gurin, Patricia, and Biren A. Nagda. 2006. "Getting to the What, How, and Why of Diversity on Campus." *Educational Researcher* 35 (1): 20–24.

Gurin, Patricia, Biren A. Nagda, and Ximena Zúñiga. 2013. *Dialogue across Difference: Practice, Theory and Research on Intergroup Dialogue*. New York: Russell Sage Foundation.

Hammersley, Martyn, and Paul Atkinson. 1995. *Ethnography: Principles in Practice*. 2nd ed. New York: Routledge.

Harris, Martin. 2011. "How to Produce an Access Agreement for 2012–13. Office for Fair Access (OFFA)." Accessed October 7, 2015. http://www.offa.org .uk/wp-content/uploads/2011/03/2011-01-OFFA-How-to-produce-access -agreement-2012-13.pdf.

Hartmann, Douglas, and Joseph Gerteis. 2005. "Dealing with Diversity: Mapping Multiculturalism in Sociological Terms." *Sociological Theory* 23 (2): 218–40.

Harvard College. 2014. "Frequently Asked Questions: Applying to Harvard." Accessed July 31, 2014. https://college.harvard.edu/frequently-asked -questions.

Harvard College Admissions and Financial Aid. 2015. "First Generation Students." Accessed May 6, 2015. https://college.harvard.edu/admissions/hear -our-students/first-generation-students.

Harvard College Freshman Dean's Office. 2014. "Community Conversations." Accessed June 12, 2014. http://fdo.fas.harvard.edu/pages/community -conversations.

Harvard College Handbook for Students. 2014. "Fields of Concentration: African and African American Studies." Accessed March 13, 2015. http://handbook .fas.harvard.edu/icb/icb.do?keyword=k104674&pageid=icb.page673349& pageContentId=icb.pagecontent1470367&state=maximize&view=view.do& viewParam_name=African%20and%20African%20American%20Studies.

Harvard College Office of Admissions. 2009. "The Upperclass House System." Accessed June 6, 2012. http://admissions.college.harvard.edu/about/living /house_system.html.

———. 2011. "A Brief Profile of the Admitted Class of 2015." Accessed September 9, 2011. http://admissions.college.harvard.edu/apply/statistics.html.

Harvard College Office of Student Life. 2015. "Student Organization List." Accessed August 18, 2015. http://osl.fas.harvard.edu/student-organizations.

Harvard First-Year Urban Program. 2014. "About Our Program." Accessed July 11, 2014. http://www.hcs.harvard.edu/~fup.

Harvard Foundation for Intercultural and Race Relations. 2013. "SAC Update Fall 2013." Accessed August 18, 2015. http://harvardfoundation.fas.harvard.edu /blog/sac-update-fall-2013.

———. 2015a. "About." Accessed October 14, 2015. http://harvardfoundation.fas .harvard.edu/about.

———. 2015b. "Cultural Rhythms." Accessed April 20, 2015. http://harvard foundation.fas.harvard.edu/galleries/cultural-rhythms.

———. 2015c. "Race Relations Advising." Accessed October 14, 2015. http:// harvardfoundation.fas.harvard.edu/race-relations-advising.

Harvard University Department of African and African American Studies. 2015a. "AAAS Congratulates the Class of 2015!" Accessed August 18, 2015. http://aaas .fas.harvard.edu/news/aaas-congratulates-class-2015.

———. 2015b. "About: Other Key Moments." Accessed October 12, 2015. http:// aaas.fas.harvard.edu/other-key-moments.

Harvard University Office of Institutional Research. 2009. "Degree Student Enrollment." Accessed June 21, 2010. http://www.provost.harvard.edu /institutional_research/Provost_-_FB2009_10_Sec02_Enrollments.pdf.

———. 2013. "Historical Fact Books." Accessed December 12, 2013. http://oir .harvard.edu/historical-fact-books.

Harvard University Office of the Executive Vice President. 2015. "Lisa Coleman: Chief Diversity Officer and Special Assistant to the President." Accessed April 19, 2015. http://evp.harvard.edu/people/lisa-coleman.

Hayes, Christopher. 2012. *Twilight of the Elites: America after Meritocracy*. New York: Crown.

Heath, Anthony F., and James Tilley. 2005. "British National Identity and Attitudes toward Immigration." *International Journal on Multicultural Societies* 7:199–32.

Herrnstein, Richard J., and Charles A. Murray. 1994. *The Bell Curve: Intelligence and Class Structure in American Life*. New York: Free Press.

Higher Education Statistics Agency. 2009/2010. "Student Record."

Hill, Catherine, Christianne Corbett, and Andresse St. Rose. 2010. "Why So Few? Women in Science, Technology, Engineering, and Mathematics." Accessed August 19, 2014. http://www.aauw.org/files/2013/02/Why-So-Few-Women -in-Science-Technology-Engineering-and-Mathematics.pdf.

Hitlin, Steven, and Stephen Vaisey. 2013. "The New Sociology of Morality." *Annual Review of Sociology* 39 (1): 51–68.

Ho, Karen Zouwen. 2009. *Liquidated: An Ethnography of Wall Street*. Durham, NC: Duke University Press.

Hochschild, Jennifer L. 1996. Facing Up to the American Dream: Race, Class, and the Soul of the Nation. Princeton, NJ: Princeton University Press.

Hochschild, Jennifer L., Vesla M. Weaver, and Traci R. Burch. 2012. *Creating a New Racial Order: How Immigration, Multiracialism, Genomics, and the Young Can Remake Race in America*. Princeton, NJ: Princeton University Press.

Hoekstra, Mark. 2009. "The Effect of Attending the Flagship State University on Earnings: A Discontinuity-Based Approach." *Review of Economics and Statistics* 91 (4): 717–24.

Holland, Dorothy C., and Margaret A. Eisenhart. 1990. *Educated in Romance: Women, Achievement, and College Culture.* Chicago: University of Chicago Press.

Hollinger, David A. 1995. *Postethnic America: Beyond Multiculturalism.* New York: Basic Books.

———. 2001. "Not Universalists, Not Pluralists: The New Cosmopolitans Find Their Own Way." *Constellations: An International Journal of Critical and Democratic Theory* 8 (2): 236.

Hoxby, Caroline M. 2009. "The Changing Selectivity of American Colleges." *Journal of Economic Perspectives* 23 (4): 95–118.

Hoxby, Caroline M., and Christopher Avery. 2012. "The Missing 'One-Offs': The Hidden Supply of High-Achieving, Low Income Students." NBER Working Paper 18586.

Hoxby, Caroline M., and Sarah Turner. 2014. "Expanding College Opportunities for High-Achieving, Low Income Students." Discussion Paper 12–014. Accessed October 14, 2015. https://siepr.stanford.edu/?q=/system/files/shared/pubs/papers/12-014paper.pdf.

Huffington Post. 2011. "Alexandra Wallace, UCLA Student, Films Racist Rant." Accessed February 16, 2014. http://www.huffingtonpost.com/2011/03/14/alexandra-wallace-racist-video_n_835505.html.

———. 2012. "Harvard Voice's Racist, Anti-Asian Satire Piece Draws Ire of Harvard Community, Proves Being Witty Is Hard." Accessed February 16, 2014. http://www.huffingtonpost.com/2012/10/15/harvard-voices-racist-anti-asian-satire-draws-ire-harvard-community_n_1968631.html.

Hughey, Matthew W. 2009. "The (Dis)similarities of White Racial Identities: The Conceptual Framework of 'Hegemonic Whiteness.'" *Ethnic and Racial Studies* 33 (8): 1289–1309.

Hull, Jim. 2010. "Chasing the College Acceptance Letter: Is It Harder to Get into College? At a Glance." Accessed October 6, 2015. http://www.centerforpubliceducation.org/Main-Menu/Staffingstudents/Chasing-the-college-acceptance-letter-Is-it-harder-to-get-into-college-At-a-glance.

Hunt, Matthew O. 2007. "African American, Hispanic, and White Beliefs about Black/White Inequality, 1977–2004." *American Sociological Review* 72 (3): 390–415.

Huntington, Samuel P. 2004. *Who Are We? The Challenges to America's National Identity.* New York: Simon and Schuster.

Hurtado, Sylvia. 2005. "The Next Generation of Diversity and Intergroup Relations Research." *Journal of Social Issues* 61 (3): 595–610.

Hurwitz, Michael. 2011. "The Impact of Legacy Status on Undergraduate Admissions at Elite Colleges and Universities." *Economics of Education Review* 30 (3): 480–92.

"I Too Am Oxford." 2014. Accessed July 1, 2014. www.itooamoxford.tumblr.com.

Ipsos MORI. 2006. *Race Relations 2006*. London: Ipsos MORI.

Jack, Anthony A. 2014. "Culture Shock Revisited: The Social and Cultural Contingencies to Class Marginality." *Sociological Forum* 29 (2): 453–75.

Jackman, Mary R. 1994. *The Velvet Glove: Paternalism and Conflict in Gender, Class, and Race Relations*. Berkeley: University of California Press.

Jackman, Mary R., and Michael J. Muha. 1984. "Education and Intergroup Attitudes: Moral Enlightenment, Superficial Democratic Commitment, or Ideological Refinement?" *American Sociological Review* 49 (6): 751–69.

Jacques, Martin, ed. 1998. *Marxism Today*. November/December, special issue, "Wrong."

Jencks, Christopher. 1972. *Inequality: A Reassessment of the Effect of Family and Schooling in America*. New York: Basic Books.

Jennings, M. Kent, and Laura Stoker. 2008. "Another and Longer Look at the Impact of Higher Education on Political Involvement and Attitudes." Presented at Midwest Political Science Association Conference, Chicago.

Johnson, Heather B. 2006. *The American Dream and the Power of Wealth: Choosing Schools and Inheriting Inequality in the Land of Opportunity*. New York: Routledge.

Johnston, Josée, and Shyon Baumann. 2007. "Democracy versus Distinction: A Study of Omnivorousness in Gourmet Food Writing." *American Journal of Sociology* 113 (1): 165–204.

Kahlenberg, Richard D. 2010. *Affirmative Action for the Rich: Legacy Preferences in College Admissions*. New York: Century Foundation Press.

———. 2012. "Affirmative Action Based on Income." *Washington Post*. Accessed April 3, 2015. http://www.washingtonpost.com/opinions/affirmative-action -based-on-income/2012/11/08/a519f67e-17e9-11e2-9855-71f2b202721b_story .html.

———. 2014. *The Future of Affirmative Action: New Paths to Higher Education Diversity after Fisher v. University of Texas*. Indianapolis, IN: Lumina Foundation for Education and Century Foundation.

Kahn, Joseph P. 2014. "'I, Too, Am Harvard' Campaign Highlights Black Students' Frustrations." *Boston Globe*. Accessed October 4, 2015. http://www .bostonglobe.com/lifestyle/style/2014/03/06/the-too-harvard-photo -campaign-and-stage-event-highlights-black-students-frustrations-with -racial-stereotypes-campus/dY57mxCTTzOrHBoCbfd0sJ/story.html.

Kalev, Alexandra, Frank Dobbin, and Erin Kelly. 2006. "Best Practices or Best Guesses? Assessing the Efficacy of Corporate Affirmative Action and Diversity Policies." *American Sociological Review* 71 (4): 589–617.

Kandiyoti, Deniz. 1988. "Bargaining with Patriarchy." *Gender and Society* 2 (3): 274–90.

Karabel, Jerome. 2005. *The Chosen: The Hidden History of Admission and Exclusion at Harvard, Yale, and Princeton*. Boston: Houghton Mifflin.

Karabel, Jerome, and A. H. Halsey. 1977. *Power and Ideology in Education*. New York: Oxford University Press.

Karen, David. 1990. "Toward a Political-Organizational Model of Gatekeeping: The Case of Elite Colleges." *Sociology of Education* 63 (4): 227–40.

Kasinitz, Philip, John H. Mollenkopf, Mary C. Waters, and Jennifer Holdaway. 2008. *Inheriting the City: The Children of Immigrants Come of Age*. Cambridge, MA: Harvard University Press.

Katznelson, Ira. 1973. *Black Men, White Cities; Race, Politics, and Migration in the United States, 1900–30, and Britain, 1948–68*. London: Published for the Institute of Race Relations by Oxford University Press.

———. 2005. *When Affirmative Action Was White: An Untold History of Racial Inequality in Twentieth-Century America*. New York: W. W. Norton.

Kaushal, Neeraj, Katherine Magnuson, and Jane Waldfogel. 2011. "How Is Family Income Related to Investments in Children's Learning?" In *Whither Opportunity? Rising Inequality, Schools, and Children's Life Chances*, edited by Greg J. Duncan and Richard J. Murnane, 187–206. New York: Russell Sage Foundation.

Keep, Matthew. 2010. "Characteristics of the New House of Commons." Accessed May 5, 2015. http://www.parliament.uk/documents/commons/lib/research/key_issues/Key-Issues-Characteristics-of-the-new-House-of-Commons.pdf.

Kelsall, R. Keith. 1955. *Higher Civil Servants in Britain, from 1870 to the Present Day*. London: Routledge and Paul.

Kennedy, Randall. 2013. "In Praise of Affirmative Action." *Salon*. Accessed April 3, 2015. http://www.salon.com/2013/09/03/randall_kennedy_in_praise_of_affirmative_action.

Kerr, Clark. 2001. *The Uses of the University*. 5th ed. Cambridge, MA: Harvard University Press.

Kett, Joseph F. 2013. *Merit: The History of a Founding Ideal from the American Revolution to the Twenty-First Century*. Ithaca, NY: Cornell University Press.

Khan, Omar. 2010. "Self-Respect and Respecting Others: The Consequences of Affirmative Action in Selective Universities." In *Widening Participation and Race Equality*, edited by Debbie Weekes-Bernard, 37–41. London: Runnymede.

Khan, Shamus R. 2010. *Privilege: The Making of an Adolescent Elite at St. Paul's School*. Princeton Studies in Cultural Sociology. Princeton, NJ: Princeton University Press.

Khan, Shamus, and Colin Jerolmack. 2013. "Saying Meritocracy and Doing Privilege." *Sociological Quarterly* 54 (1): 9–19.

Kinder, Donald R., and Lynn M. Sanders. 1996. *Divided by Color: Racial Politics and Democratic Ideals, American Politics and Political Economy*. Chicago: University of Chicago Press.

Kinder, Donald R., and David O. Sears. 1981. "Prejudice and Politics: Symbolic Racism versus Racial Threats to the Good Life." *Journal of Personality and Social Psychology* 40 (3): 414–31.

King, Martin Luther, Jr. 1964. *Why We Can't Wait*. New York: Harper and Row.

Kirkland, Anna, and Ben B. Hansen. 2011. "'How Do I Bring Diversity?' Race and Class in the College Admissions Essay." *Law and Society Review* 45 (1): 103–38.

Kluegel, James R., and Eliot R. Smith. 1983. "Affirmative Action Attitudes: Effects of Self-Interest, Racial Affect, and Stratification Beliefs on Whites' Views." *Social Forces* 61 (3): 797–824.

Knowles, Eric D., and Brian S. Lowery. 2011. "Meritocracy, Self-Concerns, and Whites' Denial of Racial Inequity." *Self and Identity* 11 (2): 202–22.

Knowles, Eric D., Brian S. Lowery, Caitlin M. Hogan, and Rosalind M. Chow. 2009. "On the Malleability of Ideology: Motivated Construals of Color Blindness." *Journal of Personality and Social Psychology* 96 (4): 857–69.

Kopicki, Allison. 2014. "Answers on Affirmative Action Depend on How You Pose the Question." *New York Times.* Accessed April 3, 2015. http://www.nytimes .com/2014/04/23/upshot/answers-on-affirmative-action-depend-on-how -you-pose-the-question.html?wpisrc=nl_wonk&_r=0&abt=0002&abg=0.

Kumar, Gautam S. 2010. "To Randomize or Not to Randomize?" *Crimson.* Accessed October 16, 2015. http://www.thecrimson.com/article/2010 /5/27/house-students-system-housing/?page=3.

Kuumba Singers of Harvard College. 2015. "The Kuumba Singers of Harvard College." Accessed October 4, 2015. http://kuumbasingers.org.

Kymlicka, Will. 2007. *Multicultural Odysseys: Navigating the New International Politics of Diversity.* New York: Oxford University Press.

———. 2013. "Neoliberal Multiculturalism?" In *Social Resilience in the Neoliberal Era*, edited by Peter A. Hall and Michèle Lamont, 99–125. New York: Cambridge University Press.

Laar, Colette Van, Shana Levin, Stacey Sinclair, and Jim Sidanius. 2005. "The Effect of University Roommate Contact on Ethnic Attitudes and Behavior." *Journal of Experimental Social Psychology* 41 (4): 329–45.

Lacy, Karyn R. 2007. *Blue-Chip Black: Race, Class, and Status in the New Black Middle Class.* Berkeley: University of California Press.

Lakoff, George. 2004. *Don't Think of an Elephant! Know Your Values and Frame the Debate: The Essential Guide for Progressives.* White River Junction, VT: Chelsea Green.

Lammy, David. 2010. "The Oxbridge Whitewash." *Guardian.* Accessed May 23, 2011. http://www.guardian.co.uk/commentisfree/2010/dec/06/the-oxbridge -whitewash-black-students.

Lamont, Michèle. 1992. *Money, Morals, and Manners: The Culture of the French and American Upper-Middle Class.* Morality and Society. Chicago: University of Chicago Press.

———. 2000. *The Dignity of Working Men: Morality and the Boundaries of Race, Class, and Immigration.* New York: Russell Sage Foundation; Cambridge, MA: Harvard University Press.

———. 2009. *How Professors Think: Inside the Curious World of Academic Judgment.* Cambridge, MA: Harvard University Press.

Lamont, Michèle, and Sada Aksartova. 2002. "Ordinary Cosmopolitanisms." *Theory, Culture and Society* 19 (4): 1–25.

Lamont, Michèle, and Graziella Moraes da Silva. 2009. "Complementary Rather

Than Contradictory: Diversity and Excellence in Peer Review and Admissions in American Higher Education." *Twenty-First Century Society* 4 (1): 1–15.

Lamont, Michèle, and Ann Swidler. 2014. "Methodological Pluralism and the Possibilities and Limits of Interviewing." *Qualitative Sociology* 37 (2): 153–71.

Lanney, Jillian. 2014. "Students Question Use of Legacy Admission." *Brown Daily Herald*. Accessed April 25, 2015. http://www.browndailyherald.com/2014/04 /14/students-question-use-of-legacy-admission.

Lareau, Annette. 2011. *Unequal Childhoods: Class, Race, and Family Life*. Berkeley: University of California Press.

Lawrence, George H., and Thomas D. Kane. 1995. "Military Service and Racial Attitudes of White Veterans." *Armed Forces and Society* 22 (2): 235–55.

Lawrence-Lightfoot, Sara. 1997. *The Art and Science of Portraiture*. Edited by Jessica Hoffmann Davis. San Francisco, CA: Jossey-Bass.

Lemann, Nicholas. 1999. *The Big Test: The Secret History of the American Meritocracy*. New York: Farrar, Straus, and Giroux.

Lewis, Amanda E. 2003. *Race in the Schoolyard: Negotiating the Color Line in Classrooms and Communities*. New Brunswick, NJ: Rutgers University Press.

———. 2004. "'What Group?' Studying Whites and Whiteness in the Era of 'Color-Blindness.'" *Sociological Theory* 22 (4): 623–46.

Lewis, Amanda E., Mark Chesler, and Tyrone A. Forman. 2000. "The Impact of 'Colorblind' Ideologies on Students of Color: Intergroup Relations at a Predominantly White University." *Journal of Negro Education* 69 (1/2): 74–91.

Lieberman, Robert C. 2005. *Shaping Race Policy: The United States in Comparative Perspective*. Princeton Studies in American Politics. Princeton, NJ: Princeton University Press.

Lipset, Seymour M. 1975. *Education and Politics at Harvard: Two Essays Prepared for the Carnegie Commission on Higher Education*. Edited by David Riesman and Carnegie Commission on Higher Education. New York: McGraw-Hill.

Lipset, Seymour M., and Reinhard Bendix. 1992. *Social Mobility in Industrial Society*. New Brunswick, NJ: Transaction.

Lipson, Daniel N. 2007. "Embracing Diversity: The Institutionalization of Affirmative Action as Diversity Management at UC-Berkeley, UT-Austin, and UW-Madison." *Law and Social Inquiry* 32 (4): 985–1026.

Little, Alan, and John Westergaard. 1964. "The Trend of Class Differentials in Educational Opportunity in England and Wales." *British Journal of Sociology* 15 (4): 301–6.

Long, Mark C. 2008. "College Quality and Early Adult Outcomes." *Economics of Education Review* 27 (5): 588–602.

Louie, Vivian S. 2004. *Compelled to Excel: Immigration, Education, and Opportunity among Chinese Americans*. Stanford, CA: Stanford University Press.

Lowery, Brian S., Eric D. Knowles, and Miguel M. Unzueta. 2007. "Framing Inequity Safely: Whites' Motivated Perceptions of Racial Privilege." *Personality and Social Psychology Bulletin* 33 (9): 1237–50.

Lowery, Brian S., Miguel M. Unzueta, Eric D. Knowles, and Phillip A. Goff. 2006.

"Concern for the In-Group and Opposition to Affirmative Action." *Journal of Personality and Social Psychology* 90 (6): 961–74.

Lucas, Samuel Roundfield. 1999. *Tracking Inequality: Stratification and Mobility in American High Schools.* Sociology of Education. New York: Teachers College Press.

Mariani, Mack D., and Gordon J. Hewitt. 2008. "Indoctrination U? Faculty Ideology and Changes in Student Political Orientation." *PS: Political Science and Politics* 41 (4): 773–83.

Massey, Douglas S. 2003. *The Source of the River: The Social Origins of Freshmen at America's Selective Colleges and Universities.* Princeton, NJ: Princeton University Press.

Massey, Douglas S., and Margarita Mooney. 2007. "The Effects of America's Three Affirmative Action Programs on Academic Performance." *Social Problems* 54 (1): 99–117.

Massey, Douglas S., Margarita Mooney, Camille Z. Charles, and Kimberly C. Torres. 2007. "Black Immigrants and Black Natives Attending Selective Colleges and Universities in the United States." *American Journal of Education* 113 (2): 243.

McAdam, Doug. 1988. *Freedom Summer.* New York: Oxford University Press.

McClelland, Katherine, and Erika Linnander. 2006. "The Role of Contact and Information in Racial Attitude Change among White College Students." *Sociological Inquiry* 76 (1): 81–115.

McDermott, Monica, and Frank L. Samson. 2005. "White Racial and Ethnic Identity in the United States." *Annual Review of Sociology* 31 (1): 245–61.

McLaren, Lauren, and Mark Johnson. 2005. "Understanding the Rising Tide of Anti-immigrant Sentiment." In *British Social Attitudes: The 21st Report,* edited by Alison Park, Katarina Thomson, John Curtice, Catherine Bromley, and Miranda Phillips. London: Sage.

McLaurin-Chesson, Karen, and Myra Pong. 2004. "Third World History at Brown." Accessed October 6, 2011. http://www.brown.edu/Student_Services/TWC/history.html.

McNamee, Stephen J., and Robert K. Miller. 2004. *The Meritocracy Myth.* Lanham, MD: Rowman and Littlefield.

Meer, Nasar, and Tariq Modood. 2009. "The Multicultural State We're In: Muslims, 'Multiculture' and the 'Civic Re-balancing' of British Multiculturalism." *Political Studies* 57 (3): 473–97.

Mettler, Suzanne. 2014. *Degrees of Inequality: How the Politics of Higher Education Sabotaged the American Dream.* New York: Basic Books.

Meyer, John W., Francisco O. Ramirez, David J. Frank, and Evan Schofer. 2007. "Higher Education as an Institution." In *Sociology of Higher Education: Contributions and Their Contexts,* edited by Patricia J. Gumport, 187–221. Baltimore: Johns Hopkins University Press.

Milem, Jeffrey F., Mitchell J. Chang, and Anthony L. Antonio. 2005. "Making Diversity Work on Campus: A Research-Based Perspective." Accessed December 7, 2012. http://siher.stanford.edu/AntonioMilemChang_makingdiversity-work.pdf.

Mironova, Yelena S. 2010. "What an Education Means." *Crimson.* Accessed April 22, 2015. http://www.thecrimson.com/article/2010/9/24/one-such-harvard-educated.

Modood, Tariq. 2005. *Multicultural Politics: Racism, Ethnicity, and Muslims in Britain.* Minneapolis: University of Minnesota Press.

Moore, Wendy L., and Joyce M. Bell. 2011. "Maneuvers of Whiteness: 'Diversity' as a Mechanism of Retrenchment in the Affirmative Action Discourse." *Critical Sociology* 37 (5): 597–613.

Morning, Ann J. 2011. *The Nature of Race: How Scientists Think and Teach about Human Difference.* Berkeley: University of California Press.

Mountford Zimdars, Anna. 2016. *Meritocracy and the University: Selective Admission in England and the USA.* London: Bloomsbury.

Newcomb, Theodore M. 1943. *Personality and Social Change: Attitude Formation in a Student Community.* New York: Dryden Press.

Nickens, Margaret. 2014. "With Recent Growth, Harambee House Poised for New Era." *Brown Daily Herald*, February 5.

Noden, Philip, Michael Shiner, and Tariq Modood. 2014. "University Offer Rates for Candidates from Different Ethnic Categories." *Oxford Review of Education* 40 (3): 349–69.

Norton, Michael I., and Samuel R. Sommers. 2011. "Whites See Racism as a Zero-Sum Game That They Are Now Losing." *Perspectives on Psychological Science* 6 (3): 215–18.

Nussbaum, Martha C., and Joshua Cohen. 1996. *For Love of Country: Debating the Limits of Patriotism.* Boston: Beacon Press.

Nyambi, Mandi. 2014. "I, Too, Am Harvard." Accessed October 4, 2015. https://college.harvard.edu/admissions/hear-our-students/student-blogs/i-too-am-harvard.

O'Connor, Sandra Day, and Stewart J. Schwab. 2009. "Affirmative Action in Higher Education over the Next Twenty-Five Years: A Need for Study and Action." In *The Next Twenty-Five Years: Affirmative Action in Higher Education in the United States and South Africa*, edited by David L. Featherman, Martin Hall, and Marvin Krislov, 58–73. Ann Arbor: University of Michigan Press.

Office for Fair Access. 2015. "Quick Facts." Accessed September 29, 2015. https://www.offa.org.uk/press/quick-facts.

Office for National Statistics. 2013. "Highest Level of Qualification by Ethnic Group by Age." Accessed August 1, 2014. http://www.ons.gov.uk/ons/tax onomy/search/index.html?pageSize=50&sortBy=none&sortDirection=none &newquery=ethnicity&nscl=Children%2C+Education+and+Skills.

Oliver, Melvin L., and Thomas M. Shapiro. 1995. *Black Wealth/White Wealth: A New Perspective on Racial Inequality.* New York: Routledge.

Orfield, Gary, Erica D. Frankenberg, and Chungmei Lee. 2003. "The Resurgence of School Segregation." *Educational Leadership* 60 (4): 16.

Orfield, Gary, John Kucsera, and Genevieve Siegel-Hawley. 2012. "E Pluribus . . . Separation: Deepening Double Segregation for More Students." The Civil Rights Project, University of California Los Angeles. Accessed June 25, 2013. http://civilrightsproject.ucla.edu/research/k-12-education/integration -and-diversity/mlk-national/e-pluribus . . . separation-deepening-double -segregation-for-more-students/orfield_epluribus_revised_omplete_2012 .pdf.

Oxford University Academic Administration Division. 2015. "Full Details of Domicile (by Year)." Accessed April 23, 2015. http://public.tableau.com/views /Studentstatistics-UniversityofOxford_2/NationalityDomicile?%3AshowViz Home=no#1.

Oxford University Student Union. 2015a. "Oxford University African and Caribbean Society." Accessed September 16, 2015. http://ousu.org/organisation /6751.

———. 2015b. "Oxford University Majlis Asian Society." Accessed September 16, 2015. http://ousu.org/organisation/7095.

Page-Gould, Elizabeth, Rodolfo Mendoza-Denton, and Linda R. Tropp. 2008. "With a Little Help from My Cross-Group Friend: Reducing Anxiety in Intergroup Contexts through Cross-Group Friendship." *Journal of Personality and Social Psychology* 95 (5): 1080–94.

Pager, Devah, and Hana Shepherd. 2008. "The Sociology of Discrimination: Racial Discrimination in Employment, Housing, Credit, and Consumer Markets." *Annual Review of Sociology* 34 (1): 181–209.

Parel, Kurien, and Vikki Boliver. 2014. "Ethnicity Trumps School Background as a Predictor of Admission to Elite UK Universities." In *Economics of Higher Education*, May 9.

Park, Julie J. 2013. *When Diversity Drops: Race, Religion, and Affirmative Action in Higher Education*. New York: Rutgers University Press.

Pattillo-McCoy, Mary E. 1999. *Black Picket Fences: Privilege and Peril among the Black Middle Class*. Chicago: University of Chicago Press.

Peach, Ceri. 2009. "Slippery Segregation: Discovering or Manufacturing Ghettos?" *Journal of Ethnic and Migration Studies* 35 (9): 1381–95.

Pedersen, Jesper S., and Frank Dobbin. 2006. "In Search of Identity and Legitimation: Bridging Organizational Culture and Neoinstitutionalism." *American Behavioral Scientist* 49 (7): 897–907.

Pérez, Raúl. 2013. "Learning to Make Racism Funny in the 'Color-Blind' Era: Stand-Up Comedy Students, Performance Strategies, and the (Re)production of Racist Jokes in Public." *Discourse and Society* 24 (4): 478–503.

Peterson, Richard, and Roger Kern. 1996. "Changing Highbrow Taste: From Snob to Omnivore." *American Sociological Review* 61 (5): 900–917.

Peterson, Richard, and Albert Simkus. 1992. "How Musical Tastes Mark Occupational Status Groups." In *Cultivating Differences: Symbolic Boundaries and the Making of Inequality*, edited by Michèle Lamont and Marcel Fournier, 152-86. Chicago: University of Chicago Press.

Pettigrew, Thomas F., and Linda R. Tropp. 2006. "A Meta-analytic Test of Inter-group Contact Theory." *Journal of Personality and Social Psychology* 90 (5): 751–83.

Pew Research Center. 2009. "Majority Continues to Support Civil Unions." Accessed March 23, 2015. http://www.pewforum.org/2009/10/09/majority-continues-to-support-civil-unions.

———. 2014. "Millenials in Adulthood: Detached from Institutions, Networked with Friends." Accessed August 23, 2014. http://www.pewsocialtrends.org/files/2014/03/2014-03-07_generations-report-version-for-web.pdf.

Pew Research Center for the People and the Press. 2005. "Beyond Red vs. Blue." Accessed July 2, 2014. http://www.people-press.org/2005/05/10/beyond-red-vs-blue.

Phillips Brooks House. 2015. "Identity Discussions, Workshops, and Trainings: Community Conversations." Accessed April 19, 2015. http://publicservice.fas.harvard.edu/identity-discussions-workshops-and-trainings.

Pilkington, Andrew. 2011. *Institutional Racism in the Academy: A Case Study.* Stoke-on-Trent, UK: Trentham Books.

Pollock, Mica. 2004. *Colormute: Race Talk Dilemmas in an American School.* Princeton, NJ: Princeton University Press.

Powell, Chris, and George E. C. Paton. 1988. *Humour in Society: Resistance and Control.* New York: St. Martin's Press.

Program on Intergroup Relations. 2014. "About the Program on Intergroup Relations." Accessed September 5, 2014. http://igr.umich.edu/about.

Quillian, Lincoln. 2006. "New Approaches to Understanding Racial Prejudice and Discrimination." *Annual Review of Sociology* 32 (1): 299–328.

Radford, Alexandria W. 2013. *Top Student, Top School? How Social Class Shapes Where Valedictorians Go to College.* Chicago: University of Chicago Press.

Ramakrishnan, S. Karthick, and Taeku Lee. 2012. "The Policy Priorities and Issue Preferences of Asian Americans and Pacific Islanders." National Asian American Survey. Accessed April 30, 2014. http://www.naasurvey.com/resources/Home/NAAS12-sep25-issues.pdf.

Ramirez, Francisco O. 2006. "Growing Commonalities and Persistent Differences in Higher Education: Universities between Global Models and National Legacies." In *The New Institutionalism in Education*, edited by Heinz-Dieter and Brian R. Meyer, 123–41. Albany: State University of New York Press.

Reardon, Sean F., Rachel Baker, and Daniel Klasik. 2012. "Race, Income, and Enrollment Patterns in Highly Selective Colleges, 1982–2004." Accessed April 30, 2015. https://cepa.stanford.edu/sites/default/files/race%20income%20%26%20selective%20college%20enrollment%20august%203%202012.pdf.

Reay, Diane. 2015. "Time to Change: Bringing Oxbridge into the 21st Century." In *Aiming Higher: Race, Inequality and Diversity in the Academy*, edited by Claire Alexander and Jason Arday, 19-20. London: Runnymede.

Reay, Diane, Gill Crozier, and John Clayton. 2009. "'Strangers in Paradise'? Working-Class Students in Elite Universities." *Sociology* 43 (6): 1103–21.

Reuben, Julie A. 2001. "Merit, Mission, and Minority Students: A History of Debates over Special Admissions Programs." In *A Faithful Mirror: Reflections on the College Board and Education in America*, edited by Michael C. Johanek, 195–243. New York: College Board.

Richeson, Jennifer A., and J. Nicole Shelton. 2007. "Negotiating Interracial Interactions: Costs, Consequences, and Possibilities." *Current Directions in Psychological Science* 16 (6): 316–20.

Rivera, Lauren A. 2011. "Ivies, Extracurriculars, and Exclusion: Elite Employers' Use of Educational Credentials." *Research in Social Stratification and Mobility* 29 (1): 71–90.

———. 2015. *Pedigree: How Elite Students Get Elite Jobs*. Princeton, NJ: Princeton University Press.

Rojas, Fabio. 2007. *From Black Power to Black Studies: How a Radical Social Movement Became an Academic Discipline*. Baltimore: Johns Hopkins University Press.

Roth, Wendy D. 2012. *Race Migrations: Latinos and the Cultural Transformation of Race*. Stanford, CA: Stanford University Press.

Rothstein, Richard. 2014. "The Colorblind Bind: Focusing College-Student Recruitment on Poor Neighborhoods Can Overlook Middle-Class African Americans Entitled to Affirmative Action." *American Prospect* 25 (4): 70–75.

Samson, Frank L. 2013. "Multiple Group Threat and Malleable White Attitudes Towards Academic Merit." *Du Bois Review: Social Science Research on Race* 10 (1): 233–60.

Sander, Richard H. 2004. "A Systemic Analysis of Affirmative Action in American Law Schools." *Stanford Law Review* 57 (2): 367–483.

Sauder, Michael. 2006. "Third Parties and Status Position: How the Characteristics of Status Systems Matter." *Theory and Society* 35 (3): 299–21.

Savage, Mike, David Wright, and Modesto Gayo-Cal. 2010. "Cosmopolitan Nationalism and the Cultural Reach of the White British." *Nations and Nationalism* 16 (4): 598–615.

Schildkraut, Deborah J. 2011. *Americanism in the Twenty-First Century: Public Opinion in the Age of Immigration*. New York: Cambridge University Press.

Schonfeld, Zack. 2014. "Why Did Time.Com Republish a Princeton Freshman's Screed about White Privilege?" *Newsweek*. Accessed July 7, 2014. http://www.newsweek.com/why-did-timecom-republish-princeton-freshmans-screed-about-white-privilege-250100.

Schuman, Howard, and Jacqueline Scott. 1989. "Generations and Collective Memories." *American Sociological Review* 54 (3): 359–81.

Schuman, Howard, Charlotte Steeh, and Lawrence Bobo. 1997. *Racial Attitudes in America: Trends and Interpretations*. Cambridge, MA: Harvard University Press.

Schwartz, Barry. 2005. "Top Colleges Should Select Randomly from a Pool of 'Good Enough.'" *Chronicle of Higher Education* 51 (25): B20–B25.

Sears, David O. 1993. "Symbolic Politics: A Socio-psychological Theory." In

Explorations in Political Psychology, edited by Shanto Iyengar and William J. McGuire, 113–49. Durham, NC: Duke University Press.

Sears, David O., and P. J. Henry. 2003. "The Origins of Symbolic Racism." *Journal of Personality and Social Psychology* 85 (2): 259–75.

Sen, Amartya. 2000. "Merit and Justice." In *Meritocracy and Economic Inequality*, edited by Kenneth Arrow, Samuel Bowles, and Steven Durlauf, 5–16. Princeton, NJ: Princeton University Press.

Sharkey, Patrick. 2013. *Stuck in Place: Urban Neighborhoods and the End of Progress toward Racial Equality*. Chicago: University of Chicago Press.

———. 2014. "Spatial Segmentation and the Black Middle Class." *American Journal of Sociology* 119 (4): 903.

Shepherd, Jessica. 2008a. "Oxford Rugby Team Get Diversity Lessons." *Guardian*. Accessed July 15, 2014. http://www.theguardian.com/education/2008 /dec/12/oxford-rugby-racism-diversity-lessons.

———. 2008b. "Oxford Students in 'Bring a Fit Jew' Party Row." *Guardian*. Accessed July 15, 2014. http://www.theguardian.com/education/2008/nov /14/oxford-students-bring-a-jew-party.

Shiner, Michael, and Philip Noden. 2014. "'Why Are You Applying There?' 'Race,' Class and the Construction of Higher Education 'Choice' in the United Kingdom." *British Journal of Sociology of Education* 36 (8): 1–22.

Shook, Natalie J., and Russell H. Fazio. 2008. "Interracial Roommate Relationships: An Experimental Field Test of the Contact Hypothesis." *Psychological Science* 19 (7): 717–23.

Sidanius, Jim, Shana Levin, Colette van Laar, and David O. Sears. 2008. *The Diversity Challenge: Social Identity and Intergroup Relations on the College Campus*. New York: Russell Sage Foundation.

Sigelman, Lee, and Steven A. Tuch. 1997. "Metastereotypes: Blacks' Perceptions of Whites' Stereotypes of Blacks." *Public Opinion Quarterly* 61 (1): 87–101.

Skiba, Russell J., Robert S. Michael, Abra C. Nardo, and Reece L. Peterson. 2002. "The Color of Discipline: Sources of Racial and Gender Disproportionality in School Punishment." *Urban Review* 34 (4): 317–42.

Skrentny, John David. 2002. *The Minority Rights Revolution*. Cambridge, MA: Belknap Press of Harvard University Press.

———. 2013. *After Civil Rights: Racial Realism in the New American Workplace*. Princeton, NJ: Princeton University Press.

Sleeter, Christine E., and Peter McLaren. 1995. *Multicultural Education, Critical Pedagogy, and the Politics of Difference*. Albany: State University of New York Press.

Small, Mario L. 2004. *Villa Victoria: The Transformation of Social Capital in a Boston Barrio*. Chicago: University of Chicago Press.

Small, Mario L., David J. Harding, and Michèle Lamont. 2010. "Reconsidering Culture and Poverty." *Annals of the American Academy of Political and Social Science* 629 (1): 6–27.

Smith, Robert C. 2006. *Mexican New York: Transnational Lives of New Immigrants*. Berkeley: University of California Press.

Smith, Sandra S., and Mignon Moore. 2000. "Intraracial Diversity and Relations among African-Americans: Closeness among Black Students at a Predominantly White University." *American Journal of Sociology* 106 (1): 1–39.

Sniderman, Paul M., and Edward G. Carmines. 1996. "Beyond Race: Social Justice as a Race Neutral Ideal." *American Journal of Political Science* 40 (1): 33.

———. 1997. *Reaching Beyond Race*. Cambridge, MA: Harvard University Press.

Soares, Joseph A. 1999. *The Decline of Privilege: The Modernization of Oxford University*. Stanford, CA: Stanford University Press.

Sowell, Thomas. 2004. *Affirmative Action around the World: An Empirical Study*. New Haven, CT: Yale University Press.

Staiger, Annegret. 2004. "Whiteness as Giftedness: Racial Formation at an Urban High School." *Social Problems* 51 (2): 161–81.

Stearns, Elizabeth, Claudia Buchmann, and Kara Bonneau. 2009. "Interracial Friendships in the Transition to College: Do Birds of a Feather Flock Together Once They Leave the Nest?" *Sociology of Education* 82 (2): 173–95.

Steele, Claude M., and Joshua Aronson. 1995. "Stereotype Threat and the Intellectual Test Performance of African Americans." *Journal of Personality and Social Psychology* 69 (5): 797–811.

Steele, Shelby. 1990. *The Content of Our Character: A New Vision of Race in America*. New York: St. Martin's Press.

Steinberg, Jacques. 2002. *The Gatekeepers: Inside the Admissions Process of a Premier College*. New York: Viking.

Stets, Jan E., and Michael J. Carter. 2012. "A Theory of the Self for the Sociology of Morality." *American Sociological Review* 77 (1): 120–40.

Stevens, Mitchell L. 2007. *Creating a Class: College Admissions and the Education of Elites*. Cambridge, MA: Harvard University Press.

Stevens, Mitchell L., Elizabeth A. Armstrong, and Richard Arum. 2008. "Sieve, Incubator, Temple, Hub: Empirical and Theoretical Advances in the Sociology of Higher Education." *Annual Review of Sociology* 34 (1): 127–51.

Stevens, Mitchell L., and Josipa Roksa. 2011. "The Diversity Imperative in Elite Admissions." In *Diversity in American Higher Education: Toward a More Comprehensive Approach*, edited by Lisa M. Stulberg and Sharon L. Weinberg, 63–73. New York: Routledge.

Stone, Peter. 2013. "Access to Higher Education by the Luck of the Draw." *Comparative Education Review* 57 (3): 577–99.

Stuber, Jenny M. 2011. *Inside the College Gates: How Class and Culture Matter in Higher Education*. Lanham, MD: Lexington Books.

Stulberg, Lisa M., and Anthony S. Chen. 2014. "The Origins of Race-Conscious Affirmative Action in Undergraduate Admissions: A Comparative Analysis of Institutional Change in Higher Education." *Sociology of Education* 87 (1): 36–52.

Sutton Trust. 2010. "The Educational Backgrounds of Members of Parliament in 2010." Accessed October 19, 2015. http://www.suttontrust.com/wp-content/uploads/2010/05/1MPs_educational_backgrounds_2010_A.pdf.

Swidler, Ann. 1986. "Culture in Action: Symbols and Strategies." *American Socio-logical Review* 51 (2): 273–86.

Taylor, Charles. 1994. "The Politics of Recognition." In *Multiculturalism: Examining the Politics of Recognition*, edited by Amy Gutmann, 25–73. Princeton, NJ: Princeton University Press.

Taylor, Matthew. 2007. "BNP Leader and Holocaust Denier Invited to Oxford Union." *Guardian*. Accessed July 15, 2014. http://www.theguardian.com/uk /2007/oct/12/race.students.

Teles, Steven M. 1998. "Why Is There No Affirmative Action in Britain?" *American Behavioral Scientist* 41 (7): 1004.

———. 2001. "Positive Action or Affirmative Action? The Persistence of Britain's Antidiscrimination Regime." In *Color Lines: Affirmative Action, Immigration, and Civil Rights Options for America*, edited by John D. Skrentny, 241–69. Chicago: University of Chicago Press.

Telles, Edward E. 2004. *Race in Another America: The Significance of Skin Color in Brazil*. Princeton, NJ: Princeton University Press.

Tocqueville, Alexis de. 1994. *Democracy in America*. New York: Knopf.

Torres, Kimberly C., and Camille Z. Charles. 2004. "Metastereotypes and the Black-White Divide: A Qualitative View of Race on an Elite College Campus." *Du Bois Review: Social Science Research on Race* 1 (1): 115–49.

Tyson, Karolyn. 2011. *Integration Interrupted: Tracking, Black Students, and Acting White after "Brown."* New York: Oxford University Press.

Underwood, Alice M. 2010. "'Sustained Dialogue' Urges Conversation." *Crimson*. Accessed October 16, 2015. http://www.thecrimson.com/article/2010/11/10 /dialogue-harvard-sustained-people.

UK Department for Education. 2011. "Schools, Pupils and Their Characteristics." Accessed May 24, 2012. http://www.education.gov.uk/researchandstatistics /statistics/statistics-by-topic/schoolpupilcharacteristics/a00196810/schools -pupils-and-their-characteristics-january-2.

———. 2014. "Statistical First Release: GCSE and Equivalent Attainment by Pupil Characteristics in England, 2012/13 (Sfr 05/2014)." Accessed April 9, 2015. https://www.gov.uk/government/uploads/system/uploads/attachment _data/file/280689/SFR05_2014_Text_FINAL.pdf.

UK Social Mobility and Child Poverty Commission. 2014. "Elitist Britain?" Accessed April 3, 2015. https://www.gov.uk/government/uploads/system /uploads/attachment_data/file/347915/Elitist_Britain_-_Final.pdf.

US Census Bureau. 2012. *Statistical Abstract of the United States*. Table 11: "Resident Population by Race, Hispanic Origin, and Single Years of Age: 2009." Accessed August 1, 2014. https://www.census.gov/compendia/statab/cats /population/estimates_and_projections_by_age_sex_raceethnicity.html.

US Department of Education, National Center for Education Statistics. 2009: Total Fall Enrollment in Degree-Granting Institutions, by Level of Enrollment, Sex, Attendance Status, and Type and Control of Institution: 2008." Accessed April 4, 2015. http://nces.ed.gov/programs/digest/d09/tables/dt09 _194.asp.

U.S. News and World Report. 2011a. "Best Colleges 2012: Brown University." Accessed October 13, 2011. http://colleges.usnews.rankingsandreviews.com /best-colleges/brown-university-3401.

———. 2011b. "Best Colleges 2012: Harvard University." Accessed October 13, 2011. http://colleges.usnews.rankingsandreviews.com/best-colleges/harvard -university-2155.

University Administration and Services. 2015. "Equality and Diversity Annual Reports." University of Oxford. Accessed September 29, 2015. https://www .admin.ox.ac.uk/eop/equalityreporting/annualreports.

University of Oxford. 2011a. "At Your Interview, 17 March 2011." Accessed September 9, 2011. http://www.ox.ac.uk/admissions/undergraduate_courses /how_to_apply/interviews/interview_videos.html.

———. 2011b. "Undergraduate Admissions Statistics: School Type." Accessed May 30, 2011. http://www.ox.ac.uk/about_the_university/facts_and_figures /undergraduate_admissions_statistics/school_type.html.

———. 2014. "A Guide to Oxford for American Students." Accessed July 31, 2014. http://www.ox.ac.uk/sites/files/oxford/field/field_document/A%20guide %20to%20oxford%20for%20America%20students.pdf.

———. 2015a. "Student Numbers." Accessed October 15, 2015. http://www.ox.ac .uk/about/facts-and-figures/student-numbers.

———. 2015b. "Application Statistics." Accessed May 6, 2015. http://public .tableau.com/views/UoO_UG_Admissons2/AcceptanceRate?%3Ashow VizHome=no#2.

———. 2015c. "Contextual Data." Accessed September 30, 2015. http://www.ox .ac.uk/admissions/undergraduate/applying-to-oxford/decisions/contextual -data.

University of Oxford and Office for Fair Access. 2011. "Access Agreeement between the University of Oxford and the Office for Fair Access." Accessed September 29, 2015. https://www.offa.org.uk/agreements/OXUN%20Access %20Agreement%202011-12%20app%2011.2.11%20.pdf.

———. 2012. "Access Agreement." Accessed September 29, 2015. https://www .offa.org.uk/agreements/University%200f%200xford%20AA%20with%20 ITT_0156a.pdf.

———. 2015. "University of Oxford Agreement with the Office for Fair Access 2015–16." Accessed May 4, 2015. http://www.offa.org.uk/agreements /University%200f%200xford.pdf.

Unz, Ron. 2012. "The Myth of American Meritocracy." *American Conservative,* December, 14–45.

Unzueta, Miguel M., and Brian S. Lowery. 2008. "Defining Racism Safely: The Role of Self-Image Maintenance on White Americans' Conceptions of Racism." *Journal of Experimental Social Psychology* 44 (6): 1491–97.

Vasagar, Jeevan. 2011. "Oxford University and David Cameron Clash over Black Student Numbers." *Guardian.* Accessed May 23, 2011. http://www.guardian .co.uk/education/2011/apr/11/oxford-cameron-black-students?INTCMP= SRCH.

Voyer, Andrea. 2011. "Disciplined to Diversity: Learning the Language of Multi-culturalism." *Ethnic and Racial Studies* 34 (11): 1874–93.

Waite, Roger. 2008. "Black Mischief." *Crimson.* Accessed October 16, 2015. http://www.thecrimson.com/article/2008/10/13/black-mischief-in-more-genteel-days.

Walton, Gregory M., and Geoffrey L. Cohen. 2007. "A Question of Belonging: Race, Social Fit, and Achievement." *Journal of Personality and Social Psychology* 92 (1): 82–96.

Warikoo, Natasha. 2004. "Cosmopolitan Ethnicity: Second Generation Indo-Caribbean Identities." In *Becoming New Yorkers: Ethnographies of a New Second Generation*, edited by Philip Kasinitz, John H. Mollenkopf, and Mary C. Waters, 361-92. New York: Russell Sage Foundation.

———. 2011. *Balancing Acts: Youth Culture in the Global City.* Berkeley: University of California Press.

Waters, Mary C., and Philip Kasinitz. 2015. "The War on Crime and the War on Immigrants: Racial and Legal Exclusion in 21st Century United States." In *Fear, Anxiety and National Identity: Immigration and Belonging in North America and Europe*, edited by Nancy Foner and Patrick Simon. New York: Russell Sage Foundation.

"We Are All Oxford." 2014. Accessed October 4, 2015. www.wealloxford.tumblr.com.

Weber, Max. 1930. *The Protestant Ethic and the Spirit of Capitalism.* New York: Scribner.

Weis, Lois, Kristin Cipollone, and Heather Jenkins. 2014. *Class Warfare: Class, Race, and College Admissions in Top-Tier Secondary Schools.* Chicago: University of Chicago Press.

West, Lindy. 2012. "A Complete Guide to 'Hipster Racism.'" *Jezebel.* Accessed April 23, 2015. http://jezebel.com/5905291/a-complete-guide-to-hipster-racism.

Wilson, James Q., and Richard J. Herrnstein. 1985. *Crime and Human Nature.* New York: Simon and Schuster.

Wilson, John K. 1995. *The Myth of Political Correctness: The Conservative Attack on Higher Education.* Durham, NC: Duke University Press.

Wilson, William J. 1973. *Power, Racism, and Privilege: Race Relations in Theoretical and Sociohistorical Perspectives.* New York: Macmillan.

Wimmer, Andreas. 2013. *Ethnic Boundary Making: Institutions, Power, Networks.* Oxford Studies in Culture and Politics. New York: Oxford University Press.

Woo, Deborah. 2000. *Glass Ceilings and Asian Americans: The New Face of Workplace Barriers.* Critical Perspectives on Asian Pacific Americans. Walnut Creek, CA: AltaMira Press.

Worland, Justin. 2011. "Legacy Admit Rate at 30 Percent." *Crimson.* Accessed July 3, 2014. http://www.thecrimson.com/article/2011/5/11/admissions-fitzsimmons-legacy-legacies.

Wout, Daryl A., Mary C. Murphy, and Claude M. Steele. 2010. "When Your

Friends Matter: The Effect of White Students' Racial Friendship Networks on Meta-perceptions and Perceived Identity Contingencies." *Journal of Experimental Social Psychology* 46 (6): 1035–41.

Yosso, Tara J., Laurence Parker, Daniel G. Solarzano, and Marvin Lynn. 2004. "From Jim Crow to Affirmative Action and Back Again: A Critical Race Discussion of Racialized Rationales and Access to Higher Education." *Review of Research in Education* 28:1–25.

Young, Michael D. 1958. *The Rise of the Meritocracy, 1870–2033: An Essay on Education and Equality.* London. Thames and Hudson.

Zhen, Zeng, and Yu Xie. 2004. "Asian-Americans' Earnings Disadvantage Reexamined: The Role of Place of Education." *American Journal of Sociology* 109 (5): 1075–1108.

Zimdars, Anna. 2010. "Fairness and Undergraduate Admission: A Qualitative Exploration of Admissions Choices at the University of Oxford." *Oxford Review of Education* 36 (3): 207–323.

Zimdars, Anna, Alice Sullivan, and Anthony Heath. 2009. "Elite Higher Education Admissions in the Arts and Sciences: Is Cultural Capital the Key?" Sociology 43 (4): 648–66.

Zuberi, Tukufu, and Eduardo Bonilla-Silva. 2008. *White Logic, White Methods: Racism and Methodology.* Lanham, MD: Rowman and Littlefield.

Zúñiga, Ximena, Biren A. Nagda, and Todd D. Sevig. 2002. "Intergroup Dialogues: An Educational Model for Cultivating Engagement across Differences." *Equity and Excellence in Education* 35 (1): 7–17.

INDEX

activism. *See* student activism

admissions: acceptance rates for applicants of same achievement level and, 20, 29, 149, 156, 183, 193; admissions interviews and, 27–29, 154, 156, 158–60, 193, 225n110, 244n55; alumni donations and, 234–35n14; aptitude or potential and, 154, 158–59; athletics and, 234n13; bias in, 149, 193, 244n55; blank slate approach to, 150, 157; calibrated evaluations of merit and, 90–92, 96–98, 109, 152–54, 156, 158–59, 192; changing process at Oxford and, 241n29; collective merit and, 92–101, 107–10, 122, 132, 234n11; decision makers in the United States versus Oxford and, 30; declining acceptance rates and, 181; discrimination in, 14–15; factors considered in, 20–21, 24–27, 150, 154–56, 225n110; incentives to apply and, 222n33; increasing inequality in, 183; as increasingly competitive, 161; institutional isomorphism and, 96; legacy admission and, 17, 55, 94–95, 109, 191, 192, 234–35nn14–15; lotteries for, 200–202, 244–45n78; more qualified applicants than seats and, 201–2; need-blind, 88; as nonmerito-cratic, 88, 154–56; published acceptance rates and, 200; quota systems and, 31; recruiting and, 16–17, 157; reproduction of elitism and, 89, 94, 234–35n14; students' agreement with admissions policies and, 108–9, 148–151, 158–61, 181–82, 184–85, 189, 240n20; students' decision to apply and, 222n33; students' self-grooming for, 159–60. *See also* affirmative action

affirmative action: academic and social supports and, 192; admissions officers' support for, 18, 222n35; "affirmative action bake sales" and, 5; alternative means of achieving diversity and, 221–22n21; Asian Americans and, 31, 225n120; author's peers' perspectives on, 3; calibrated evaluations of merit and, 91–92, 97, 192, 195; class-based, 12, 17, 57, 192; collective merit and, 96–101, 103; color-blindness frame and, 44, 227n15; comparative racial advantage and, 57; conservatives and, 234n7; culture of poverty frame and, 58; culture wars and, 21; deservingness of campus peers and, 157–58; diversity as rationale for, 12, 16, 54, 61; di-

terrorism, 128–29, 139

Third World Center (Brown): biracial students and, 233n36; budget of, 68, 232n20; criticisms of, 72–74, 81, 229n37; debates over, 135; historical roots of oppression and, 84; institutional supports for ethnic identity and, 146; mission of, 68; name change of, 68, 232n19; political correctness and, 130–31; power analysis frame and, 37, 66, 72, 75–76, 107; as response to student pressure, 68; shifting of dominant narratives of race and, 195; space allocation for, 74, 233n35; White People Talking workshop at, 52; whites' difficulty connecting with, 75, 81; whites' participation and, 197

Third World Transition Program (Brown): Asian Americans and, 187; community building and, 72; content of, 67–68; criticisms of, 72–73, 74–75, 103; debates over, 135; demographics of participants in, 67; diversity and elitism and, 56; historical roots of oppression and, 84; as life-changing, 71–72, 125; name of, 216; perspectives of minority versus white students on, 212; power analysis frame and, 37, 54, 66, 72, 75–76, 107, 146; student empowerment in, 70; as student-run, 67; students' hesitance about author's research and, 69–70; whites' participation and, 197

Thomas, Clarence, 227n15

Thomas, David, 233–34n56

Tocqueville, Alexis de, 18, 188

Torres, Kimberly, 116, 237n13, 238n23

Tougaloo College, 67

Truman, Harry, and Truman administration, 18

Tuch, Steven, 237n9, 237n13

Tufts University, 231n8

tuition and financial aid: linked to access in Britain, 19, 223n48; need-blind admissions and, 88; percent of students applying for and receiving, 26, 224–25n98

Tumblr campaigns, 163

United Kingdom. *See* Great Britain

United States: attendance at diversity-related events in, 142, 240n13; belief in individualism and, 18; fluid definition of merit in, 26; Gilded Age growth of aristocracy in, 225n112; land grant universities and, 29; meritocracy in national identity of, 7, 18, 22; nature of multiculturalism in, 140; one-drop rule in, 45; race frames in, versus Britain, 147–48, 159; race identity foregrounded in, 18; role of elite universities in, 29–30; use of *American* and, 39

university education. *See* college and university education

University of California, 225n122

University of London, 39

US Supreme Court: affirmative action as permissible and, 16; challenges to affirmative action and, 221–22n21; diversity as rationale for affirmative action and, 43, 44, 54, 96, 98, 196; judicial implementation theory and, 196; rulings of versus state bans on affirmative action, 221–22n21. *See also specific cases*

Vaisey, Stephen, 237n8

Vargas, Jose Antonio, 195

voting behavior, 88

Voyer, Andrea, 231n4

Weber, Max, 188

West, Kanye, 114–15

White People (documentary), 195

white privilege: accusations of racism